# Cinematic Uses
# of the Past

# Cinematic Uses of the Past

Marcia Landy

University of Minnesota Press

Minneapolis / London

A different version of Chapter 1 appeared as "History, Folklore, and Common Sense: Sembène's Films and Discourses of Postcoloniality" in *Postcolonial Discourse and Changing Cultural Contexts: Theory and Criticism,* edited by Gita Rajan and Radhika Mohanram (Westport, Conn.: Greenwood Press, 1995). Copyright 1995 by Greenwood Publishing Group, Inc., Westport, Connecticut. Reprinted by permission. A version of Chapter 2 appeared as "Which Way Is America?: Americanism and the Italian Western" in *boundary 2,* vol. 23, no. 1 (Spring 1996): 35–61. Copyright 1996 by Duke University Press. Reprinted by permission.

Published by the University of Minnesota Press
111 Third Avenue South, Suite 290, Minneapolis, MN 55401–2520
Printed in the United States of America on acid-free paper

Library of Congress Cataloging-in-Publication Data

Landy, Marcia, 1931–
    Cinematic uses of the past / Marcia Landy.
        p.    cm.
    Includes bibliographical references and index.
    ISBN 0-8166-2824-6 (hardcover)
    ISBN 0-8166-2825-4 (pbk.)
    1. Historical films—History and criticism.   2. Motion pictures and history.   I. Title.
    PN1995.9.H5L36   1997
    791.43'658—dc20                                        96-22176

# Contents

# Illustrations

# Acknowledgments

In discussing gift giving, Jacques Derrida writes in *Given Time*: "The problem of the gift has to do with its nature that is *excessive in advance, a priori exaggerated*. A donating experience that would not be delivered over, *a priori*, to some immoderation, in other words, a moderate, measured gift would not be a gift." In acknowledging the gift of time expended by others on my manuscript, I am aware of the excesses of the debts incurred. I am particularly indebted to Lucy Fischer, my friend and colleague of many years, for commenting copiously and constructively on an early version of the work. Similarly, I am grateful to Michael Hays for his criticism. Others who have read and commented on sections of the manuscript include Dana Polan, Amy Villarejo, and Sabine Hake. Alison Cuddy assisted me in the preparation of the final version of the work, and I am grateful to her for her analysis of its style and content. I am also deeply appreciative of the bibliographic assistance of Dana Crudup and of Kathy Delfosse's conscientious and careful copyediting. Without the financial support I received from the University of Pittsburgh Office of Research, it would have been difficult to complete the project. Most of all, I want to express my indebtedness to Stanley Shostak. He has been the person most involved in my scholarly life and has given abundantly of his time in reading and discussing with me the various versions of this work.

# Introduction

Social and cultural transformations rooted in economic catastrophes, wars, revolution, counterrevolution, colonization, and decolonization have marked this century and are part of the history of cinema and cinematic uses of the past. My book explores the nature of cinema's investments in the past. I engage these questions: What is popular history? How can it be recognized? What differing cultural investments can be accounted for by it? I discuss British, Hollywood, Italian, and African films, as either genre or antigenre, in order to highlight the multivalent and striated characteristics of popular history. The ways these films use history are embedded in what Antonio Gramsci described as "popular philosophy" in his discussion of "common sense." In their reanimation of the past, these films speak in a language that appeals to the broadest possible audiences, thus leaving themselves open to the criticism of at least simplifying and even of falsifying history. The language of these films feeds on the multivalent nature of everyday life and touches on prevailing conceptions of nation, gender, sexuality, and ethnicity.

Although popular philosophy in its use of history may appear to have a unified ideological position in its attempts to draw on differing constituencies in the culture and in its address to other cultures, it often betrays its eclectic terms of construction and hence its investments. In its commonsensical orientation, popular history, as opposed to official history, unwittingly exposes an inevitable disjunction between, on the one hand, the expectations that the text arouses and, on the other, the contingent nature of audience expectation and knowledge. Historical representations may often seem to reiterate dominant cultural ideas and values, but a closer scrutiny reveals that popular history represented through the cinema is a pastiche of conceptions about the world: a fusion of current and practical strategies of survival couched in clichéd, proverbial language characteristic of commonsensical approaches to knowledge. However, glaring signs of the limitations of these formulaic articulations are apparent. Cinema's

1

prodigious tendency to absorb images and sounds from other arts, such as painting, photography, music, literature, and architecture, also betrays the eclecticism and polyglossia of commonsensical approaches to experience. In this book I use the Gramscian conception of common sense to identify how popular representation relies on strategies—particularly affective strategies—to presume that there is a shared experience.

## Rethinking History and Memory

The preoccupation with history and memory, closely tied to issues of identity based on nationality, gender, race, and sexual orientation, is one of the major indications of a "fin de millennium" cultural and economic crisis that often comes disguised within the notion of "an end to history." But as Jacques Derrida has cautioned, we may not be witnessing an end to history so much as an end to revered and traditional notions of historicity. History has become a battleground of competing positions. In writings on postmodernism, the past appears as a Disneyland, as tourist attraction, spectacle, and nostalgia.[1] In neoliberalism as in fascism, familiar events and images from the past are invoked as rallying points, as forces for cohesion and consensus in the interests of national solidarity.[2] Memory has also been invoked by postcolonial theorists and filmmakers in the interests of subaltern groups and as a critical weapon against reductive forms of identity politics.[3] Though it is possible to identify different interests at work in contemporary conflicts over the nature and role of historicizing, what is clear is the loss of a confident and commonly shared notion of history as orderly, purposive, and uniformly progressive.

In the current reevaluation of history, the work of Antonio Gramsci has assumed prominence, both as a tool for understanding the political conflicts that animated the 1960s and more recently as a way of rethinking changing relations between state and civil society and of rethinking the role of culture in producing consensus and hegemony. Gramsci is posthumously one of the leading theoreticians of the social and cultural scene of the 1960s; his writings are also important for understanding the social critiques in the European cinema of the 1960s (especially Italian cinema) that directly or indirectly address questions of history. Gramsci's ideas continue to have an impact on the growing body of critical work on popular and mass culture. Parallel to current work in poststructuralist theory, Gramsci's writings challenge mono-lithic notions of ideology, offering instead more nuanced and multiva-lent critical tools for understanding appropriations of the past. In this context, his interrogations of representation are a critique of conserv-ative, liberal, and monolithic Marxist forms of historiography. His writings on Italian history are exemplary for their recognition of the need to differentiate interests and investments in the past. In particu-lar, his concept of "passive revolution," which he applied to the Risorgimento as well as to fascism, resonates for those who seek to challenge notions of history as universal, progressive, and teleologi-cal.[4] His conception of historical failure as the appearance of change in the face of repetition, similar to Karl Marx's conception of history in *The Eighteenth Brumaire of Louis Napoleon,* can be described by the motto of Giuseppe di Lampedusa's novel *The Leopard* (*Il gatto-pardo*): "All must change, so that all can remain the same."

In his probing of the Risorgimento, which he regarded as a failed revolution and a prolegomenon to fascism, Gramsci analyzed how es-tablished ruling groups reconsolidated their power in the name of na-tional unification and populism, thwarting change through consensus and coercion by the elimination or absorption of more radical groups. His analysis of the Risorgimento, intimately tied to his analysis of Ital-ian fascism, is exemplary for the ways it differentiates historical in-vestments at a moment when there appears to be consensus. Instead of a totalizing notion of the Risorgimento and of fascism, Gramsci insists on the need to identify the various strata that either succumb, main-tain ascendancy, or come into prominence. It is this analysis that ani-mates, for example, the two Luchino Visconti films specifically set in the Risorgimento: *Senso* (1954) and *The Leopard* (*Il gattopardo,* 1963). Gramsci's analyses of the social and cultural history of the Risorgimento provide a grid to challenge the monolithic nature of tra-ditional and academic forms of historicizing that elide the importance of the everyday, of the subjective, and of the nature and power of com-mon sense.

Gramsci extracts those elements from the past that are conducive to an understanding of failure and perhaps of future success. The Risorg-imento is instructive for him in identifying residual elements of the past in the present and for the light this residue sheds on the relation-ship of historical knowledge to the uses and abuses of power. Gram-sci's insistence on the importance of common sense as folklore can be linked to Friedrich Nietzsche's critique of historical excess as an over-valuation of past experience to the detriment of the present.

Common sense as folklore is Gramsci's instrument for examining the persistence of the past and its rejuvenation of new forms. In contrast to a conception of folklore as primitive, pre-historical, and hence antihistorical, he describes it in more dynamic terms: Folklore is "tied to the culture of the dominant class, and in its own way, [folklore] has drawn from it the motifs which have then become inserted into combinations with the previous traditions."[5] Furthermore, he proposes that

> Folklore should . . . be studied as a "conception of the world and life" implicit to a large extent in determinate (in time and space) strata of society and in opposition (also for the most part implicit, mechanical, and objective) to "official" conceptions of the world (or in a broader sense, the conceptions of the cultured parts of historically determinate societies) that have succeeded one another in the historical process (hence the strict relationship between folklore and "common sense," which is philosophical folklore).[6]

Common sense as folklore serves tradition; it serves "as 'philosophy,' as a specific mode of thought with a certain content of beliefs and opinions, and as an attitude of amiable indulgence, though at the same time contemptuous, toward anything abstruse and ingenious."[7] Folklore is the stratified residue of all the "conceptions of the world and of life that have succeeded one another in history."[8] In folklore, therefore, one finds the strata, the "conditions of past life," though not in any systematic, critical, or analytic form. Thus Gramsci acknowledges the multiform and fragmentary nature of historicizing and the importance of identifying and acknowledging the different and contradictory strands that constitute the ways that the past is embedded in common sense—not necessarily good sense. Although common sense is not, according to Gramsci, false, neither is it true: "Common sense is an ambiguous, contradictory and multiform concept, and . . . to refer to common sense as a confirmation of truth is nonsense."[9]

In dissecting common sense, one must be attuned to the different strata of its historical forms and contents. For example, Gramsci's discussion of the changes overtaking Europe in the 1920s and 1930s in his notes on "Americanism and Fordism" is an instance of how he disarticulates different, specific, and uneven elements that characterize commonsensical thinking.[10] The heterogeneity of common sense relies on fragmented knowledge derived from past institutions—from religion, morality, earlier philosophy, social customs, literature, and popular wisdom.[11] In the process of detecting the elements of folklore that constitute common sense, he is sensitive to folklore's numerous and constantly shifting forms; its specific, immediate, and local manifestations; and its general uses of the past. That common sense is neither false nor true suggests that an exploration of the dependence of common sense on folklore must be wary of judgment. Critical elements are also present and accounted for in commonsensical thinking.

Though folklore bears a relationship to Roland Barthes's conception of myth, there are important differences between Gramscian folklore and Barthesian mythologies. Like Gramsci, Barthes resists the inherently static and biologistic quality of traditional uses of myth in attempting to account for the "'naturalness' with which newspapers, art, and common sense constantly dress up a reality which, even though it is the one we live in, is undoubtedly determined by history."[12] Barthes is particularly troubled by the confusion of "Nature and History." Similarly, Gramsci seeks to identify folklore as a form of language and as historically specific. He shares with Barthes the sense that folklore distorts but does not render totally invisible the concepts to which it alludes.

The major differences between Barthes's work on myth and Gramsci's on common sense and folklore, and the differences that animate my study, are that the Gramscian conception of common sense as folklore is less structured, more attentive to the different and contradictory strands that constitute uses of the past, and less monolithic and binary than Barthesian ideological analysis. Gramsci facilitates an understanding of historicizing as multivalent, dissecting the ways contradictory positions are made to appear harmonious. In his discussions of common sense, he stresses its fragmentary nature, especially the ways in which it projects undigested, noncoordinated elements from the past onto the present. Scattered throughout his writings are a number of suggestions about popular forms (e.g., funeral oratory, legalisms, hagiography, melodrama, opera, and prophetic literature) that provide clues to the strata of popular history that are embedded in cultural texts. His comments on "Americanism and Fordism" are highly suggestive for understanding the unevenness of cultural transmission in a global context.

Gramsci's discussion of intellectuals is inextricable from his conception of common sense as popular philosophy. He does not distinguish between intellectuals and nonintellectuals, and he writes:

> There is no human activity from which every form of intellectual participation can be excluded: *homo faber* cannot be separated from *homo sapiens*. Each man, finally, outside his professional activity, carries on some form of intellectual activity, that is, he is a "philosopher," an artist, a man of taste, he participates in a particular conception of the world, has a conscious line of moral conduct, and therefore contributes to sustain a conception of the world or to modify it, that is, to bring into being new modes of thought.[13]

Popular history and popular philosophy are therefore contradictory constructions, not mere ideology or escapism.

Common sense is the domain of both traditional and organic intellectuals—that is, those who are by profession identified with intellectual labor (e.g., ecclesiastics, lawyers, professors) and those who are to a greater or lesser degree imbued with a critical conception of the world. This conception of the world is closely connected to representations of the past and to conceptions of power. Considerations of value are inseparable from questions of representation, since lurking in reductive economic considerations are the broader questions of how value is constituted and of what role it plays in commodifying and circulating knowledge. In the discussion of the importance of melodrama to historical representation, I probe the affective component of common sense, interrogating it for its contribution to understanding the role that the division of labor and affective value play in the dissemination and maintenance of cultural knowledge.

Stuart Hall and other members of the Birmingham Centre for Contemporary Cultural Studies have studied and disseminated variations of Gramsci's ideas concerning hegemony.[14] Gramsci's emphasis on the importance of attending to culture—not as mere superstructure to the economic base but as a vital element in analyzing the nature of change as well as resistance to change—has been central to Hall's rethinking of economistic and narrowly political analyses of historical representation. Hall reminds his readers:

> Gramsci . . . came face to face with the revolutionary character of History itself. When a conjuncture unrolls, there is no "going back." History shifts gears. The terrain changes. You are in a new moment. . . . In addition (and this is one of the main reasons why his thought is so

pertinent to us today) he had to face the capacity of the right—specifically of European fascism—to hegemonise that defeat.[15]

At stake in Hall's use of Gramsci to rethink historicism is a challenge to intellectuals who cling to Marxism as a "theory of the obvious." So called by Gramsci earlier in the century, "Marxism as a theory of the obvious" specifically relies on a reductive notion of economics as the motor of history without taking into account an understanding of Marx's writing that also configures the role and nature of politics and of the constitution of the subject of history. For example, Hall asks, "[H]ow do we make sense of an ideology which is not coherent, which speaks in our ear with the voice of freewheeling, utilitarian, marketman and in the other ear with the voice of respectable, bourgeois, patriarchal man?"[16] How is it possible that common sense, with its emphasis on history as a major source in the creation and consolidation of identity, can seduce subordinated and dominated classes? According to Hall, the former vanguard of class struggle is recouped "as subordinate subjects into a historical project which 'hegemonises' what we used—erroneously—to think of as their 'necessary class interests.'"[17]

Hall's Gramscian orientation thus leads toward exploring how essentialist and biological notions of identity rely on the affectively unifying dimensions of common sense. The past can be affirmed as a reservoir of known, tried-and-true solutions to experience. Among the known and affective characteristics of history and memory is the expectation of misfortune: The world appears as threatening, and failure seems to be more likely than success. In his emphasis on attending to Gramscian common sense, Hall reminds us that common sense is not false consciousness. Nor is common sense a mere narrative. The past comes to us in terms of a different, less causally delineated, less obvious, and heavily affect-laden sense of the world.

Echoing the imperative concern with moving away from the obvious in relation to historicizing, Gilles Deleuze suggests that history is also "dreams and nightmares, ideas and visions, impetuses and actions of the subjects involved, while the givens of the situation merely contained causes and effects against which one could only struggle."[18] Deleuze's writings, especially in *Cinema 1* and *Cinema 2* on the movement and time image, are especially fruitful for looking beyond narrative analysis to understand how images function as "sheets of the past," as "crystals of time," reflecting and refracting images from past and present, questions of presence and absence. Like Gramsci's and Hall's writings on common sense, Deleuze's work enables a reading of history that helps to expose the fragmentary, tentative, and changing nature of memory.

Fredric Jameson too has been a major protagonist in keeping alive the necessity of thinking historically but of rethinking historicism. He asserts that "history is *not* a text, not a narrative, master or other-wise . . . [that] as an absent cause, it is inaccessible to us except in tex-tual form, and that our approach to it and to the Real itself necessarily passes through its prior textualization, its narrativization in the politi-cal unconscious."[19] His unrelenting struggle in the face of challenges to history is to identify how to apprehend history "through its effects, and never directly as some reified force."[20] For him the central theme in historicizing is the "collective struggle to wrest a realm of Freedom from a realm of Necessity," and the task becomes one of "restoring to the surface of the text the repressed and buried reality of this funda-mental history."[21] The concept of allegory becomes a means to an "opening up of the text to multiple meanings, to successive rewritings and overwritings, which are generated as so many levels and as so many supplementary interpretations."[22] The recognition of the many-layered nature of allegorizing not only reveals the presence of common sense but exposes the very operation of allegory itself.

In *The Geopolitical Aesthetic,* Jameson further argues for the im-portance of a "cultural politics, a politics of everyday life" in the face of "a reification and a commodification that have become so univer-salized as to seem well-nigh natural and organic entities and forms."[23] Given the advanced character of commodity production since the time Gramsci was writing, the task of deciphering relations between culture and politics is not only more urgent but also more complex. However, there are points of affinity between Jameson's emphasis on allegory and Gramsci's conception of common sense as fractured history and of folklore as a means of understanding the "politics of everyday life." Allegory and common sense are both polysemic. As a residue of previ-ous conceptions of the world, they constitute a modern folklore, a fu-sion of past and present modes for apprehending the world. In their narrativization, they offer clues to what Marx termed the fetishism of commodities, the ways in which commodities appear to take on a life of their own so as to seem natural and organic. The critical act of de-cipherment inheres in the multivalent character of the social text, which is not hermetically sealed but contains clues as to how value is constituted. However, in the case of Gramsci, common sense presupposes a different relation to cultural knowledge than Jameson's, one that assumes a greater, though fragmented and diffuse, degree of critical awareness on the part of audiences of mass and popular culture. Jameson appears to posit a newer, more structured and totalizing notion of culture, of its production and reception, and particularly of the effects of commodification. However, Jameson's work has paved the way for what Colin MacCabe has described as "cognitive mapping . . . a metaphor which needs to be unpacked into a series of concepts which would link the psychic and the social."[24]

Jameson's concern with a "geopolitical aesthetic" further reminds us of the importance of rethinking the hegemony of Western forms of history and the effects they have had in legitimizing imperialism and colonialism. Edward W. Said too has underlined the imperative of a "history of the imperial adventure rendered in cultural terms."[25] In particular, Said has stressed the importance of addressing a historiography that is "contrapuntal and often nomadic. . . . [P]artly because of empire, all cultures are involved in one another; none is single and pure, all are hybrid, heterogeneous, extraordinarily differentiated, and unmonolithic."[26] Said's contributions to rethinking historicizing, as well as those by other postcolonial critics, reveal a debt to Gramsci and to Frantz Fanon,[27] specifically in his emphasis on the importance of identifying the nature and characteristics of official historicizing, its holds and erasures, and its conflictual basis.

In the enterprise of rethinking history, the work of the Subaltern Studies Group is particularly concerned with theorizing change as well as resistances to change to allow for a different and more disseminative and refined sense of social power and domination. In general, the postcolonial enterprise parallels Gramsci's concern with history in that it seeks to reexamine the uses of history and memory, to rethink the complex nature of interactions between social classes, and in particular to rethink the character of subaltern life.[28] By broadening the base of historical representation, postcolonial critics reexamine the history of imperialism, colonialism, and neocolonialism. In this context, the critics bring to light new, forgotten or neglected documents that challenge both conservative and liberal accounts of the relationship between colonizer and colonized. Gayatri Chakravorty Spivak has commented that the work of the Subaltern Studies Group should more properly be aligned to a deconstructive approach. As she writes, "[t]he group . . . tracks failures in attempts to displace discursive fields."[29] Tracking failure entails a more critical approach to historical narratives that rely on traditional melodramatic scenarios of progress and universalism. But Spivak has cautioned that these attempts to track fields of power in history are problematic if sufficient attention is not paid to the critical positioning of the figure of woman "as a structural rather than marginal issue."[30]

Spivak, like Ousmane Sembène (both in Sembène's writings and in his films), is particularly concerned with generating adequate theories of cultural qua political representation, specifically in the enterprise of demythologizing questions of identity and subjectivity.[31] Like Gramsci's, their works are sensitive to the need to explore questions of power and history in such a way that critics' positions and investments in their objects of examination are apparent. The writings of Spivak and the films of Sembène address the multiple, connected, and over-determined aspects of economic and cultural life, specifically the immediate ways in which local customs, folklore, seemingly insignificant documents, rumor, and gossip are important to disarticulating the unified and "objective" narratives that are part of official historicizing. Official historicizing challenges the various narratives that constitute traditional humanistic and idealistic notions of global progressive history. Like Sembène, Spivak does not speak for or carelessly of the subaltern; she is always mindful too that there can be no adequate account of the history of colonization or of decolonization without a critical understanding of their role in capital and its value codings.

In discussing historical representation in film, I am mindful too of the importance of rethinking subject positions in some other form than traditional melodramatic conceptions of victim and aggressor that do not address their contradictory and complicated interconnections. Since consensus functions to equalize and neutralize relations between subaltern and ruling groups, I probe the importance of historical representation as the important ground on which such contradictory cultural interactions occur.

## Changing Forms of History in Film

In pre–World War II cinema, representations of history are often assumed to share a common style and rhetorical stance, as represented by such diverse films as *1860* (1933), *Scipione l'Africano* (1937), and *Fire over England* (1937). For example, Alexander Korda's *The Private Life of Henry VIII* (1933) and *Rembrandt* (1936) veer toward the elegiac, invoking a traditional motif of *ars moriendi,* the common fact of death and of dying well and purposively. These nationalistic, patriotic documents invoke great figures of the past as allegories for the present in the face of threats to national consolidation. However, a close examination of the historical films of this period destroys the sense of uniformity, revealing that the films have different aesthetic and ideological forms. In the case of Greta Garbo's *Queen Christina* (1933) and *Conquest* (1937), star vehicles that play with the elusive gendered and sexual identity of the star/diva, the monumental and patriotic orientation is subdued in favor of a more critical and psychological treatment of the interested uses of the past. A biopic like *The Scarlet Empress* (1934), which seems to be monumental and epic in its uses of imagery, sound, and editing, functions as an allegory but not as an allegory of national affirmation. In the films the past is invoked through the portrait of charismatic authority figures and through highly choreographed scenes of national unity, through stirring battle scenes, and through high-sounding oratory.

A film that was not successful commercially, *The Scarlet Empress,* in its obvious and aggressive critical treatment of its historical subject, exploits its relations to the past, its uses of the conventions of the biopic, and its treatment of the star to critically address the present. This film is further evidence of the presence of critical treatments of biography as popular history in the 1930s. The film reveals the potential of the biopic to address history. Its allusiveness and its stylistic manipulation of received folklore provide evidence of the film's resistance to nostalgia and its use of the past for present interests.

In the post–World War II era, representations of history are complicated by the experiences of war, fascism, and struggles over communism. In particular, the Italian neorealists were suspicious of the grand scale of the historical productions of the 1930s and early 1940s. In their predilection for everyday reality—"faithfulness to everyday life in the scenario"[32]—they strove to fulfill what Umberto Barbaro mandated: "If we in Italy wish to abandon once and for all our trashy histories . . . we must try the cinema of realism."[33] The emphasis on contemporary events—for example, on the immediate history of the Resistance and of the Liberation in such films as *Rome, Open City*

(1945) and *The Bicycle Thief* (1948)—was apparent not only in Italy in the years immediately after the war but also in other national cinemas in the West, in Japan, and in India and ultimately in the emerging nations of Africa and Latin America.

By the late 1950s in Italy, however, the popular historical film had made a comeback, though clothed in new garb: in comic, satiric, and even epic forms. The strong men from the silent cinema—Ulysses, Hercules, and Maciste—returned to the screen with a vengeance, as did Italian movies in the western genre. The adventure and action films, neglected by critics and historians of the cinema, were excoriated by reviewers for their egregious emphasis on violence, but little effort was expended in seeking to understand not only the restoration of popular action forms in cinema but the films' return to historical subjects. Critics did not examine the films for the serious concerns expressed by their resurrection of history, nor for the fact that they self-consciously dramatized a crisis in representation. The identification of cultural malaise was reserved for such auteurs as Michelangelo Antonioni, Bernardo Bertolucci, and Federico Fellini. Since the popular historical films made no pretense to realism or to the conventions of modernist complexity, they did not seem to warrant critical attention.[34] Such films flaunted the very qualities that had animated both neorealism and various expressions of the New Wave in filmmaking in Italy, France, and Britain. Though the gladiatorial epics and the spaghetti and sauerkraut westerns made no pretense of portraying contemporary life or of being overtly critical of contemporary social institutions, they offered the same challenge as did the Hollywood films of an earlier era, inviting the critic to examine the conditions of their historical emergence and their historical predilections. The films especially challenged the critic to rethink the parameters, forms, styles, and subject matter of historical representation.

A close examination of these films' texts also reveals a concern with preoccupations of the various New Wave forms of filmmaking as expressed in Italy by the films of Pier Paolo Pasolini, and Bertolucci and the early works of the Taviani brothers and in France by François Truffaut, Claude Chabrol, and Jean Luc Godard. The spaghetti westerns also reveal an affinity with such Latin American texts as Glauber Rocha's *Antonio das Mortes* (1969) and with African texts such as Sembène's *Emitai* (1976). In each film, the uses of the past include a parody of indigenous and western forms and the union of fantasy and realism. The style itself becomes a critique of cultural domination and an attempt to forge a more adequate language to address the crisis of cultural politics. The Italian westerns were complicated by their use of American and Italian actors and by being set in Spain rather than in the American West. Their heavy use of close-ups and of montage editing and their florid application of the Ennio Morricone scores offered another clue to their union of style and historical concerns. The films occupy a critical place in the history of cinema along with Pasolini's savage portraits of fascism. As allegories of the persistence of institutional practices derived from the past, especially the fascist past still alive in the present, the spaghetti westerns dissect the residual and violent aspects of religion, technology, sexual practices, and public cum private morality, probing official and public legitimation of statist power, magnifying self-interest and brutality.

The 1980s and 1990s have not seen an abatement of historical films. Rather, the uses of history have escalated and assumed a variety of forms. Heritage films, such as *Chariots of Fire* (1981), *Another Country* (1984), and *Maurice* (1987), have appeared on screen and on British Broadcasting Corporation (BBC) television, offering commonsensical versions of the imperial past.[35] Science fiction films, such as *Blade Runner* (1982), *They Live* (1988), and *Frankenstein Unbound* (1990) among others, have created their versions of the past by way of future scenarios.[36] The horror film has been resurrected in the 1980s and 1990s in such films as *The Lair of the White Worm* (1988), *Bram Stoker's Dracula* (1994), and *Interview with the Vampire* (1994). Similarly, Bertolucci has maintained his romance with history and ideology in such films as *The Last Emperor* (1987), as has Chen Kaige in *Farewell, My Concubine* (1994). However, the Holocaust has been one of the most widely used subjects for film and television in the last decades of the twentieth century, with such works as *Holocaust* (1979), *Heimat* (1984), *Shoah* (1985), and most recently the extremely popular *Schindler's List* (1993) provoking a range of responses from hostility to veneration and highlighting profound cultural conflicts that center on the uses and abuses of the past. The numerous revisitings of the past are most often characterized by scenarios involving antagonism between sexual and gendered identity in relation to national discourses.

## Critical Perspectives on the Uses of History in Film

Geoffrey Nowell-Smith has written that "[t]he history of the cinema is the history of the twentieth century. Cinema is embedded deep into what one might call the external histories of the century—those of economics and politics for example—but even more deeply into the history of modern subjectivity."[37] With the appearance of such works as Pierre Sorlin's *The Film in History: Restaging the Past*; Marc Ferro's *Cinema and History*; Anthony Aldgate's *Cinema and History: British Newsreels and the Spanish Civil War*; Jeffrey Richards's *The Age of the Dream Palace: Cinema and Society in Britain, 1930–1939*; Robert Burgoyne's *Bertolucci's 1900: A Narrative and Historical Analysis*; Michael Paul Rogin's *Ronald Reagan: The Movie and Other Episodes in Political Demonology*; George Custen's *Bio/Pics: How Hollywood Constructed Public History*; Robert Rosenstone's edited volume, *Revisioning History: Film and the Construction of a New Past*; and Peter Baxter's *Just Watch! Sternberg, Paramount, and America*, there has been a movement away from a reductive and negative assessment of the cinematic uses of history.[38] As part of the broader critical enterprise characteristic of current studies of representation, these writers challenge traditional attitudes that valorize empirical truth and objectivity as the only criteria for judging the veracity of historical representation.

The arguments waged in film and cultural studies around questions of realism have been geared to undermining a belief in universal criteria of judgment and knowledge. In the words of Bill Nichols, we need to be trained to "see signs where there appears to be only natural and obvious meaning."[39] A critical reading that exposes the discursive nature of representation does not deny that the uses of history may, wittingly or unwittingly, make capitalism, cultural imperialism, nationalism, biological determinism, or individual initiative seem to be natural. Rather, studies of representation, including this book, offer strategies for understanding the forms this naturalization assumes.

In addressing the question of monumental history as represented in the French silent cinema by Abel Gance's *Napoléon* (1927), Richard Abel's analysis challenges conventional readings of earlier historical films as polemic and as politically univalent and transparent. "What position can one take," asks Abel, "toward this rhapsodic celebration of a single powerful leader, a sort of Gallicized Hegelian ideal of the hero in history—anachronistic, chauvinistic, and perhaps even fascistic? For Gance, his hero must have seemed the Romantic artist in apotheosis—as he saw himself—a towering figure who made the real world, not an imaginary one, his province of action."[40] In Abel's examination of the film, he suggests that its reflexivity and experimental aesthetics override or at least conflict with the ostensible politics of the film, producing a form of monumental historicizing that is not unambiguously devoted to a reiteration of familiar historical conventions relating to national common sense. Rather, we have a treatment of the past connected to the Eisensteinian, modernist experimentation with historical images that is not easily interpreted.

Similarly Sue Harper, writing about the uses of history in that most unlikely set of films, the excessively stylized British Gainsborough melodramas, reminds us of the unfortunate and monolithic ways in which history is often regarded in the popular cinema. That the Gainsborough films were disparaged by critics as "escapist" reveals the complex nature of the uses of history in cinema and particularly in British films that have been disparaged as antihistorical. Harper provides not a traditional view of social history but a specific reading of the films' "historical pleasures," which entail an understanding of the uneven but necessary fusion of objective and subjective elements in cinematic presentations of the past. In the Gainsborough films, there is no overwhelming attempt to provide historical verisimilitude.

The Gainsborough films are not antiquarian in the Nietzschean sense of the term. Rather, they rely on selective uses of detail. An item of clothing, a brooch, a hairdo, a piece of furniture suffices to indicate that the films are set in "the historical past as a site of sensual pleasure."[41] The importance of Harper's work on the films resides in her insistence on the conjunction of history and melodrama as a means of conveying "a vision of 'history' as a country where only feelings reside, not socio-political conflicts."[42] Yet in the appeal to feminine audiences, the films entertain issues pertaining to "morality, and class, and gender power."[43] The trappings of the past serve as an occasion to expose the limitations of the present. Through Harper's analysis of the uses of history in the films, one can begin to appreciate the heterogeneous elements that inhere in historical representations and the designs of history on specific members of the audiences.

Patrice Petro's *Joyless Streets: Women and Melodramatic Representation in Weimar Germany* brings together a range of concerns that are central to the problem of historicizing, conjoining melodrama, history, mass culture, and spectatorship. Cautious in its approach to psychoanalysis, Petro's work is exemplary for the ways it addresses and challenges monolithic notions of spectatorship arising from binary conceptions of gender and sexuality. Her work insists on the importance of historicizing the position of women in Weimar society as "spectators, as subjects, as part of a national audience . . . in such a way that no aspect of that history can remain the same."[44]

World War II as represented both in the 1940s and in the present has been a major focus of historical investigation. The collection of essays edited by Geoff Hurd, *National Fictions: World War II in British Films and Television,* is exemplary for its insistence on the need to reconfigure popular memory. Drawing on a range of documents—early histories, pamphlets, personal accounts, films of the time, and contemporary reconstructions—the authors whose essays are collected here relate "these historical knowledges to the broader relationship of past to present, which generates popular interest in them today."[45] The Holocaust too has been a major impetus in rethinking the uses of history in the present. Critical works such as Anton Kaes's *From Hitler to Heimat: The Return of History as Film* and Eric L. Santner's *Stranded Objects: Mourning, Memory, and Film in Postwar Germany* probe the uses of history in the German cinema to examine connections and ruptures between the present and the past, situating their discussions in the context of current debates about the nature and efficacy of historical representation.[46] Similarly, the writers and filmmakers represented in the collection of essays *Questions of Third Cinema,* edited by Jim Pines and Paul Willemen,[47] are all engaged with questions concerning the nature of history and memory in relation to postcolonial cinemas.

## The Properties of Historical Films

As the lifeblood of commonsensical thinking, melodrama is an essential ingredient of consensus. However, consensus depends on interaction, needing more than mere passivity, and successful modes of representation use the past to incarnate a sense of common experience. Commonality cannot be located merely in the coercive dimensions of public power but must be traced in the public and private arenas of social life. Any tracking of consensus necessitates an interlocking understanding of familial, juridical, psychiatric, educational, religious, and natural and social scientific forms of the dissemination of knowledge. Institutional discourses are not neutral but are laden with affect deriving from investments in particular cultural and political positions. The commonsensical specialization of melodrama in affective experience entails encounters with medicine, the law, and religion and with conflicts over power, legitimacy, and identity.

Official or elite historical representations, especially monumental narratives of national formation, are saturated with melodrama. The melodramas take the form of threats to national continuity, inevitably involving scenarios of physical and spiritual struggle; of personal, familial, and group sacrifice; of patriotism; and of an intense and excessive concentration on belonging and exclusion. Such scenarios are justified in terms of biological determinism, especially in relation to questions of individual and group survival. The melodramatic qua operatic is fused with the romantic and elegiac sense of the *ars moriendi*.

In tracking the affective dimensions of historical representation, the work of Friedrich Nietzsche is illuminating. Nietzsche's extensive comments on the "excesses" of historicizing point to the affective investment in the past that is characteristic of melodrama and its reliance on commonsensical articulations. In prefacing his discussion of history in *Untimely Meditations*, Nietzsche comments that "I am here attempting to look afresh at something of which our time is rightly proud—its cultivation of history—as being injurious to it, a defect and deficiency in it, because I believe, indeed, that we are all suffering from a consuming fever of history and ought at least to recognize that we are suffering from it."[48] Using the metaphor of health and disease common to melodrama, Nietzsche suggests that the obsession with the past can function in melodramatic terms as a source of psychic suffering and as a cultural disease. Still pursuing the metaphor of health, he suggests that forgetting is as crucial to well-being as remembering: "*[T]he unhistorical and the historical are necessary in equal measure for the health of an individual, of a people and of a culture.*"[49] Thus although he acknowledges the hurtfulness of history, he also acknowledges the necessity of confronting the past.

Nietzsche locates the "excesses of history" in three specific modes of reconstructing the past: the monumental, the antiquarian, and the critical. In each of these, the excess of attachment seems to reside in the overveneration of great individuals from the past and the use of the past as an uncritical guide to the present. The melodramatic excess of monumentalism is best summed up by Nietzsche's comment:

> Monumental history is the masquerade costume in which [historians'] hatred of the great and powerful of their own age is disguised as satiated admiration for the great and powerful of past ages, and muffled in which they invert the real meaning of that mode of regarding history into its opposite. Whether they are aware of it or not, they act as though their motto were: let the dead bury the living.[50]

Nietzsche's use of the language of masquerade along with the language of power in relation to monumental historical representation challenges notions of "objective history" and its disinterestedness. His language of masquerade underscores the theatrical nature of monumentalism and its ties to melodrama.

Monumental history further resembles melodrama in its fascination with power, violence, and fanaticism. This form of history

> deceives by analogies; with seductive similarities it inspires the courageous to foolhardiness and the inspired to fanaticism; and when we think of this kind of history in the hands and heads of gifted egoists and visionary scoundrels then we see empires destroyed, princes murdered, wars and revolutions launched and the number of historical "effects in themselves," that is to say, effects without sufficient cause, again augmented.[51]

This statement captures the melodramatic, indeed operatic, qualities of monumental history and its reliance on metalepsis, that is, the explanation of causes by their effects. Above all, it is repetitive with its emphasis on emulation through analogy: "As long as the soul of historiography lies in the great *stimuli* that a man of power derives from it, as long as the past has to be described as worthy of imitation, as imitable and possible for a second time, it of course incurs the danger of becoming somewhat distorted, beautified, and coming close to free poetic invention."[52]

In the case of antiquarian history, the overvaluation of the past is signaled through a reverence for artifacts and information from the past so excessive that "it knows only how to *preserve* life, not how to engender it; it always undervalues that which is becoming because it has no instinct for divining it—as monumental history, for example, has. Thus it hinders any firm resolve to attempt something new, thus it paralyses the man of action who, as one who acts, will and must offend some piety or other."[53] The melodramatic nature of this form of history as excess is evident in Nietzsche's use of the image of paralysis. If monumentalism encourages the fascination with and emulation of "strange and unnatural" personalities, antiquarian history feeds on a frozen and fetishized attachment to past individuals as objects.

The third type of excess identified by Nietzsche arises from critical history, which, by contrast to antiquarianism, is iconoclastic in its "attempts to break up and dissolve a part of the past."[54] Here Nietzsche identifies a reverse melodramatic scenario. In contrast to the excesses generated by overveneration of the past, the excesses of critical history are relativism, a denial of the past and of others' actions, and the overvaluation of individual subjectivity and agency. The drama here is one of negativity stemming from a refusal to acknowledge that "since we are the outcome of earlier generations, we are also the outcome of their aberrations, passions, and errors and indeed of their crimes."[55] As a corrective to the monolithic nature of critical excess, with its negation of boundaries and limits, Nietzsche suggests that "the best we can do is to confront our inherited and hereditary nature with our knowledge of it . . . always a dangerous attempt because it is hard to know the limit to denial of the past."[56]

Nietzsche's taxonomy of historical excess can be made compatible with Antonio Gramsci's discussions of affective investment in common sense and folklore.[57] Melodrama and history feed on familiarity, ritualization, repetition, and overvaluation of the past to produce a déjà vu sense of "Yes, that is the way it was and is." Melodrama meets common sense in its valorization of the experiential, the obvious, and the familiar, and in its ambivalence toward the new and different, often communicating the matter of official history through its reliance on proverbs, prophecies, truisms, and the celebration of repetition. However, in its selective uses of the past, melodrama also reveals where it falls afoul of memory, an issue of preeminent concern in films that are critical of traditional history.

Aphorisms, truisms, oratory, and prophecy are images from the past that are embedded in proverbial statements; they are, however, not antiquarian but are aligned to modern knowledge—psychiatry, medicine, law, and science. This melange of information relies on the past not only to interpret and explain but also to create an aura of tested and sanctioned experience. Because the folklore of common sense resorts to collective experience, it appears to be dangerous to refute it. Yet folklore's contradictions are barely concealed in its reiterative, formulaic, and stylized forms of representation. Melodrama and its specialization in the confrontation and management of affect promises a way of managing the world, of coping with complexity and crisis. As common sense, melodrama strives, and may succeed in the short run, to unite the subject with history. Thus, Nietzsche's notion of historical excess, like Gramsci's description of common sense as folklore, underscores the role of subjectivity in historicizing and provides us with forms to understand melodramatic investment—all of which can be transposed to cinematic history.

In specific historical reenactments on film, one strategy in particular stands out as a major vehicle of history and memory: the flashback. Aware of the need to resist monolithic and multidimensional aspects of history on film, Maureen Turim writes:

> If flashbacks give us images of memory, the personal archives of the past, they also give us images of history, the shared and recorded past. In fact, flashbacks in film often merge the two levels of remembering the past, giving large-scale social and political history the subjective mode of a single, fictional individual's remembered experience. This process can be called the "subjective memory," which here has the double sense of the rendering of history as a subjective experience of a character in the fiction, and the formation of the Subject in history as the viewer of the film identifying with the fictional characters positioned in a fictive social reality.[58]

The crucial elements of this quotation involve the notion of a shared past as recorded through the medium of film, the dual relationship between film subject and spectator, and the centrality of and interplay between subjectivities. In examining the flashback in film, it is important to resist a static model that posits sameness of function. As Turim elaborates, "A close study of the variations in flashback is actually a means of questioning the conceptual foundations of history in relation to narrative and narrative in its relationship to history."[59] Her enterprise is an exercise not only in opening up the relation of flashbacks to social history and philosophy but in exposing how an "analysis of the films themselves is considered a project of multiple perspectives."[60]

The flashback serves to communicate information about the past—chronology, genealogy, motive, and the like—and this information can serve proleptically and teleologically to underscore determinism. Flashbacks, especially in biopics, often serve to create an organic sense of unfolding events and especially a sense of inevitability. This sense of inevitability can thus assist common sense by evoking "memories" of the familiar and recognizable landmarks of national, familial, and individual "experience." Flashbacks can enhance introspection; they can function as retrospection. As Deleuze reminds us, the flashback can consume the past through action images or it can serve as an instrument for reflection on the past. This distinction is not merely chronological—that is confined to the divide between pre– and post–World War II cinema—but it is a distinction that must be read in terms of conflicting historical predilections.

Concomitant with the reliance on flashback as a medium for representations of history and memory, cinematic uses of the past rely on specific and reiterative forms of narration. Subjects speak through indirect or direct address, iconography, gesture, narrative action, mise-en-scène, voice-over, dialogue, and music. In the uses of language, one can recognize the tendency toward aphorism, witty and pithy phrases, proverbial sayings, and nebulous profundities in the form of truisms and clichés. However, the conventions are hardly restricted to the dialogue; they are also evident in the familiar landscapes (often derived from painting and photographs), in the costuming, and in the diverse ways in which music is used both rhetorically (to create affective intensity) and operatically (to animate the melodrama), reinforcing or providing a counterpoint to individual and group conflicts.

Melodramatic representations of history in film are often, like opera, more dependent on gesture and music than on narrative. Like the gesture, music serves to complicate any easy readability of images of the past. As Peter Brooks has reminded us, one of the major characteristics of melodrama is its tendency toward muteness, its ability to remind us of the limits of the spoken word and hence of the constraints of official representations. Therefore any understanding of the melodramatic as a component of historical representation must contend with this muteness, which I identify with the ambiguities and silences of common sense, with its contradictory fusing of affective material onto familiar past events. In the monumental historical film, the melodramatic takes the form of the operatic, employing techniques common to grand opera or, in some instances, actually drawing on the scenarios and arias from opera.

The popular and sometimes populist perspectives of such earlier historical films as *The Birth of a Nation* (1915), *Napoléon, 1860, Fire over England,* and *Ivan the Terrible* (1942) and of such later films as *Chariots of Fire, Gandhi* (1982), and *Schindler's List* are evident in their intertextuality: their dependence on architecture; their use of familiar buildings and landmarks; their reliance on painting (especially portraiture), photographs, or theatrical performances; and their specific uses of voice-overs, titles, and oratorical delivery to affirm their sense of the past. By contrast, such films as *The Leopard* (1963), *Alexandria Why?* (1978), *Lili Marleen* (1980), *Another Country,* and *Le Camp de Thiaroye* (1989) draw on traditional images invoking national unity but for the purposes of questioning the basis and legitimacy of that unity and of challenging the commonsensical language of much historical representation.

As it is embodied in Hollywood, British, and European cinema, national folklore is heavily indebted to and in fact constituted by the phenomenon of stardom. Whereas past studies of stardom considered it antithetical to historical representation, another symptom of Hollywood's "dream factory," current critical studies have complicated the historical role attributed to the institution of stardom and the role it plays in understanding the uses of history in the cinema. As Christine Gledhill writes, the "study of stars becomes an issue in the social production and circulation of meaning, linking industry and text, film and society."[61] Analyses of stardom, exemplified by Richard Dyer's *Stars,* has made it evident that the star is a complex orchestration of national, sexual, and gendered values.[62] The star is crucial to the biopic, the costume drama, the historical film, and other instances of history in film, often offering a homology between the historical character and the star figure. In the Hollywood studio films of the 1930s, the exceptionality of the historical figures and of the stars who played them coincided, suggesting the presence of reflexivity concerning this type of representation. The star served as a carrier of social and economic value in the contemporary culture, thus conferring meaning on the figures and events selected from the past. Conversely and concomitantly, the name of the historical figure bestowed further value on the figure of the star, the institution of stardom, and the currency of biography and history as process.

The star, like the operatic diva, is the melodramatic figure par excellence, since part of his or her individual history as well as the history of the institution of stardom resides in extratextual knowledge circulating about the personal history and vicissitudes of the figure.

Folklore functions here as common sense in the ways that specific qualities of such figures tap deeply into cultural lore, conjoining star characteristics—physiognomy, hair color (e.g., blondeness), body parts, physical size, gestures, movement, voice timbre, sexual determinacy or indeterminacy—to issues of power and transgression. The folklore of the star (or diva) circulates through various forms of publicity: through reviews, tabloids, popular illustrated magazines, newspaper reports, gossip, and rumor; through identification with the roles the stars play and the allusions to the stars in other popular forms.[63] The star image *is* history, and in itself has much to teach about the uses of the past. Thus, aside from the star's role as a historical character in films, the notion of stardom (and of the diva) is in its own right a historical and cultural artifact and, more important, a carrier of historical knowledge concerning past and present.

While the earlier system of star production has been eclipsed, many contemporary historical films continue to rely on monumental historicizing, clothing their narratives in the common sense of the present. The films are geared to using actors whose personalities are submerged in the historical figures they play (consider, for example, Ben Kingsley in *Gandhi*). Moreover the figures selected as historical subjects are not necessarily the great; they are also enlisted from the tabloids, as was the case of Joanne Whalley's impersonation of Christine Keeler in *Scandal* (1989), or Miranda Richardson's recreation of Ruth Ellis in *Dance with a Stranger* (1985). The figures are very likely to be drawn from marginal or counterhegemonic groups and are vehicles for critical explorations of the past in relation to the present.

If there are any stable points of reference in such currents and countercurrents of historical representations in cinema, they are connected to conflicts posed in the 1960s involving the role of the state, questions of social power, and especially the need to reexamine the role of individual agency. National identity, like the issue of identity generally, continues to be problematic in the age of internationalism. National folklore is not always recognized as national or even as folklore; rather, it is more generally recognized as a powerful universal melodrama of individual and group survival. This melodrama relies on tensions between the private and the public spheres, specifically the contradictory position of femininity and heterosexuality in relation to the family and its role in economic and social production. The presence of folklore in the role of popular history can serve a number of different concerns: It can serve to protect existing national interest or to reenact national and regional conflicts or conflicts over ethnicity; it can serve as an elegy for irrecoverable national prestige and as a call to a reaffirmation of a group identity. Conversely, this folklore can also lead to the creation of scenarios that are critical of univalent narratives of national affirmation.

My book is by no means an exhaustive treatment of all of the possible permutations of historical representation; rather, its aim is to contribute to the current debate about the nature and importance of historical representation. In my identification of the multilayered and hybrid cultural strands that constitute popular history, my discussion relies heavily on the assumption of a complicity between melodrama and the uses of the past, especially as melodrama provides the familiar and formulaic scenarios, typology, images, gestures, and sounds that animate common sense as folklore. I explore the melodramatic in relation to the operatic as a strategy not only for linking cinema historically to the other arts but as a strategy for producing the sense of monumentality on which many historical films rely. I am interested in the traditional reliance of historical films on monumentality, but as the selection of films reveals, I am also interested in exploring films that appear to be critical of monumentalism.

The uses of history that I discuss are characterized by eclecticism and compromise. They embed a wide range of rhetorical devices, which are often masked by melodrama. Even where the films seem to be celebrating the familiar ideology of fascism (as in Alessandro Blasetti's *1860*), the films are not monolithic. Films that appear to be most invested in a particular political position must seduce their opposition; hence they incorporate counterpositions in the interests of dramatizing and enhancing the potential for consent. In their dependence on melodrama, the films portray the forces that undermine their desired sense of historical ends as viable but threatening, as plausible but also illegitimate. Historical events and characters are made to appear inevitable through the use of prolepsis or foreshadowing. Since the history that is represented is already known, there is no suspense. Instead, in the spirit of melodrama, the emphasis is on the affect accompanying the predicted outcome. Characteristic of commonsensical appeals, the texts are attuned to the need to incorporate different levels of meaning in an effort to appeal to a range of constituencies and of political positions.

In exploring the way that popular history comes to be represented in cinema, I address the past and present nature and uses of genre, the institution of stardom as an agent in historical representation, the importance of the operatic mode to collusion between history and melodrama, the importance of the elegiac to the discursive properties of melodrama and its designs on the past, and differences in the treatments of official history in relation to the role of memory. I use the term "official history," recognizing that in the context of common sense the term may be redundant. On the other hand, the term serves as a means of demarcating traditional historical discourses from those that seek to intervene in those discourses, drawing attention to elided or erased moments of the past. In general the films I have selected best orchestrate these issues, but my analyses should apply to a broader range of films than those I discuss.

Chapter 1, "Folklore, Memory, and Postcoloniality in Ousmane Sembène's Films," examines two films by Sembène, *Le Camp de Thiaroye* (1989) and *Guelwaar* (or *Gelwaar,* 1992), as essays on the nature of history and popular memory. The films' explorations of repetition in the context of the history of colonialism and neocolonialism are an interrogation of repetition and difference. As critiques of official history, Sembène's films reveal their familiarity with poststructuralist theory and an awareness of globality that explores connections between Europe, the United States, and Africa, probing the ways in which race and gender interact but are not isometric. In their interrogations of history, the films are aware of the pitfalls of originary thinking and of nostalgia for past forms of life that have now been rendered obsolete. In his critique of abuses of the past, Sembène is attentive particularly to memory's occlusion or erasure of events that are intrinsic to an understanding of the present.

*Le Camp de Thiaroye* takes an episode that has been forgotten: the French destruction of African men upon their return to Africa after having served the French colonial power in the European war. It is not the memorializing of the event in itself that is important. The recollection of past events becomes a pre-text and a prolegomena to plumbing the common sense, repetition, and melodrama that characterize the life of the subaltern in the interests of change. Relying on the work of earlier historical writers such as Frantz Fanon and Aimé Césaire, *Le Camp de Thiaroye* treats an earlier historical event but calls attention to the contemporary reenactment of past attitudes and behavior. By contrast, Sembène's *Guelwaar* rejects the formal properties of the generic historical film. Instead, the film takes an event in the present, an event based on an actual occurrence—the disappearance of a Christian corpse that is finally located in a Muslim cemetery—and focuses on the manifold ways in which the past is alive in the present. These films raise questions about themselves as cultural instruments and more generally about the historical (and possibly transformative) role of culture.

Chapter 2, "'Which Way Is West?': Americanism, History, and the Italian Western," explores the uses of history in a popular Italian film genre: the spaghetti western. With the exception of Christopher Frayling,[64] most critics who have written on the spaghetti western neglect the genre's immersion in contemporary cultural history. Instead, these critics stress the spaghetti western's indebtedness to Hollywood filmmaking and to the western genre. By relying on genre analysis, focusing on formal conventions and on the influence of the U.S. mythology of the frontier, they have missed the opportunity to address the Italian western's uses of history and its critique of Italian (and European) history and culture and, what is more important, to understand the cinematic and cultural meaning of what Gramsci termed "Americanism." The films are not mere derivatives of U.S. history and geography but are symptomatic of the complexity of cultural transmission in the age of globality.

Through a discussion of Sergio Leone's *Duck, You Sucker* (*Giù la testa*, 1971, distributed also as *A Fistful of Dynamite*), I explore the hybrid nature of the Italian western, seeking to retrieve the genre from approaches that attempt to trivialize or aestheticize it. By detaching it from the specificity of U.S. culture and history, I explore the grafting of history onto cultural phenomena, which are, in the process, transformed into something far different from the originary source. The chapter questions the prevalence of binary melodramatic thinking that characterizes discussions of historical representation—oppositions between the United States and Europe, between East and West—as well as chronological notions of influence.

Chapter 3, "The Operatic as History: Two Risorgimento Narratives," concentrates on two films—Blasetti's *1860* and Visconti's *The Leopard*—that are situated in the context of the Risorgimento. While the Blasetti film ostensibly dramatizes the Risorgimento as a prefiguration of fascism and the fascist hero, it is not simplistic propaganda but a text that draws on images from past and present—nineteenth-century painting, music, and operatic style—to present its allegory. In *1860* Blasetti exposes the eclectic nature of what Gramsci termed "passive revolution," a view of the Risorgimento as a "revolution without revolution," consolidating ruling groups rather than producing national unity.

*The Leopard* also draws on opera, literature, painting, architecture, and melodrama but as an ostensible challenge to official history; however, in contrast to *1860*, *The Leopard* draws on specific arias from opera as well as on an operatic style to produce a critical, antimonumental treatment of the same period. The collusion between the melodramatic and operatic in *The Leopard* is treated in self-conscious and parodic form, thus producing a double critique—of the common sense that circulates about the Risorgimento and of the forms of representation that have characterized it.

Chapter 4, "Sheets of the Past: Folklore, the Biopic, and *The Scarlet Empress*," discusses the Dietrich–von Sternberg film as an exemplary text to examine uses of the past in Hollywood cinema. I argue that conventional forms of measuring historical representation in cinema against formal and academic history occlude understanding of the complex nature of the commercial cinema's uses of the past. I connect the film's stylistic treatment, which is usually attributed to the eccentricities of its two auteurs—Marlene Dietrich and Josef von Sternberg—to a conjunction of studio history, autobiographical material relating to star and producer, questions of ethnicity in Hollywood and in the broader culture, and culturally circulating notions of gender and sexuality. A reading of the film in conjunction with a reading of the cultural climate of the 1930s through the lens of Hollywood reveals that rather than erasing history, the film's uses of history are characteristic of the common sense of popular modes of historicizing: fragmented and melodramatic. Using the biography of Catherine the Great as pre-text, the histories in the film orchestrate what can now be seen as a critical pastiche of contemporary U.S. culture of the 1930s. The film's excessive melodramatic treatment and its exaggerations critically parody monumental history, inviting an examination of clichéd and formulaic treatments of cinematic historicizing.

Chapter 5, "'You Remember Diana Dors, Don't You?': History, Femininity, and the Law in 1950s and 1980s British Cinema," focuses on the figure of Ruth Ellis, the last woman in England to be hanged for a crime. Through a series of concentric circles involving accounts of the Ruth Ellis case, the autobiographical writings of Diana Dors (a popular British film and television star of the 1950s), and a discussion of the two films *Yield to the Night* (1956) and *Dance with a Stranger*, I seek to complicate the relation of media to social history. The chapter stresses the *reciprocal* though uneven relations between production and reception, between stars and audiences, and between past and present. In the Ellis case, the memory of Ruth Ellis becomes the locus of historical discourses involving gender, sexuality, the body politic, stardom, popular culture, conceptions of the relation of the public to the private sphere, and especially of legality and discourses of nation.

*Yield to the Night* and *Dance with a Stranger* are exemplary of the striated nature of popular history. Embedded in both films is the cinematic history of the *Blonde Sinner* (the American title for the film) as the figure of sexual transgression, and I examine how melodrama reinforces the connection between femininity and criminality. The chapter explores connections between the emergence in the 1950s of unexceptional and marginal figures of transgressive sexuality as historical subjects and the evolution of tabloid culture. The melodramatic treatment, especially the emphasis on the self-fashioning of the blonde protagonists, calls attention to the ways in which media images circulate in the culture and are, through their evocation of star lore, the commonsensical repository of residual as well as emergent cultural values.

Chapter 6, "Historical Capital: Mourning, Melodrama, and Nazism," focuses on a current Hollywood historical film, *Schindler's List,* which recreates the Holocaust through its treatment of Oskar Schindler, the savior of eleven hundred Jews. As exemplified by such critical works as Anton Kaes's *From Hitler to Heimat,* Eric L. Santner's *Stranded Objects,* and Thomas Elsaesser's *New German Cinema,* discussions of that period are fraught with contentiousness over the status of history and memory at the present time and especially over the prevalence of psychoanalytic formulas for addressing past history.

To explore the long-standing relationship between memory, melodrama, and mourning, the chapter includes a discussion of films produced under National Socialism, probing connections between these earlier films and more recent television films such as *Holocaust* and *Heimat,* as well as the phenomenon of burgeoning Holocaust museums. *Schindler's List* shares with these texts a heavy dependence on established folklore in representations of Nazism and the Holocaust, on melodrama, and especially on an elegiac treatment of characters and events that valorizes the importance of "never forgetting," in psycho-analytic terms, as a precondition for change. Central to the discussion is the question of whether many representations of National Socialism and of the Holocaust do not reiterate the monolithic nature of "fascinating fascism" and its monumentalizing of the past. I conclude with a discussion of Rainer Werner Fassbinder's *Veronika Voss* (1982) as an alternative to the production of monumentalizing versions of the Nazi past.

This chapter orchestrates concerns addressed in the previous chapters—the efficacy of identifying common sense and folklore as a critical tool for assessing melodramatic representation in relation to history: the character of its affective investments in the past, its scenarios of oppression and of survival, and its involvement in narratives of loss and recovery. From a critical perspective, the chapter emphasizes that melodrama cannot be ignored in exposing the protean and multifarious ways that history circulates as capital, with affect as its currency in the hope of restitution. The chapter also examines the efficacy of an antimelodramatic form of representation that both acknowledges melodrama's seductiveness and also, in homeopathic fashion, invokes excess against itself to challenge monumentalism and antiquarianism. By introducing questions of failure in the form of elided or buried memories, antimelodrama disturbs the elegiac sense with its scenarios of mourning, its fascination with dying and with monuments, and its penchant for heroism and villainy, providing an opportunity to think more critically about the circulation of historical capital and its cultural and political effects.

# 1

## Folklore, Memory, and Postcoloniality in Ousmane Sembène's Films

In his discussion of national formations, Frantz Fanon writes:

> The artist who has decided to illustrate the truths of the nation turns
> paradoxically toward the past and away from actual events. What he ul-
> timately intends to embrace are in fact the castoffs of thought, its shells
> and corpses, a knowledge which has been stabilized once and for all.
> But the native intellectual who wishes to create an authentic work of art
> must realize that the truths of a nation are in the first place its realities.
> He must go on until he has found the seething pot out of which the
> learning of the future will emerge.[1]

Broadly sketched, Fanon's comments corroborate Gramsci's analysis of the nature and importance of intellectuals and of cultural transformation as a prerequisite of meaningful political change. Culture
can serve as a stabilizing or destabilizing force: The problem is to find
the means to distinguish between the cultural forms and political instruments of hegemony and those of counterhegemony. Fanon suggests
that an understanding of history is essential to understanding political
and cultural change: One must recognize the problematic nature of a
quest for origins and authenticity that antedate colonialism, the importance of language as fundamental to an identification and analysis
of the interactions between dominant and subaltern groups, the role of
folklore as a repository of knowledge of the past, and especially the
potential role of intellectuals in the dissemination of knowledge.

Viewed from the vantage point of postcolonial theory, an examination of the relationship between residual and emergent forms of
knowledge is a precondition for contesting the monolithic strategies of
official history. Official, elitist history erases the fundamental, though
contradictory, role of the people. As Ranajit Guha has written: "What
clearly is left out of this un-historical historiography is the *politics of
the people.*"[2] Guha's notion of "the people" is a specific, if problematic, reference to subaltern groups (in contrast to a conception of "the

people" as a homogenous entity) and entails a delicate examination of relations between dominant and subaltern groups, an examination that neither idealizes various subaltern groups nor positions them as unknowing melodramatic victims for whom the well-meaning cultural and political analysts speak. The knowledge of subaltern groups can be derived from cultural lore, but this lore requires a multivalent analysis derived from economic, political, and cultural archives. Culture has to be rethought—less in terms of narrow notions of base and superstructure and more in terms of more interactive and reciprocal relations between economic and cultural phenomena—so as to identify the economic dimensions of culture and the cultural dimensions of economy. Amilcar Cabral wrote: "Culture is simultaneously the fruit of a people's history and a determinant of history. . . . Ignorance of this fact may explain the failure of several attempts at foreign domination—as well as the failure of some international liberation movements."[3] Cabral, like Fanon and Gramsci, was concerned with the role of intellectuals. "Neocolonialism would indeed find no realization," writes Hussein Abdilahi' Bulhan, "without the presence of two necessary conditions: (1) the formation of an intelligentsia born amidst the oppressed but bound in a symbiotic class relation with the oppressor, and (2) the gradual peripheralization if not the total destruction of the indigenous culture as a world hegemony of Euro-American cultures is imposed."[4]

Through a discussion of the work of Ousmane Sembène, this chapter addresses the way he uses the past in his films to identify and understand the role of culture as a stabilizing or destabilizing force. History and memory are central to his artistic production: His novels and films encyclopedically probe relations between Africa and the West, the role of intellectuals as enhancing or retarding the process of social transformation, the nature of storytelling as a means of bringing past and present into conflict, the role of cinema as an instrument of memorializing, and the role of religion, formulated in commonsensical terms of survival, as both enabling and debilitating in the process of exploring notions of what constitutes "the people." Sembène's Marxism is neither doctrinaire nor reductive.[5] It is a hybrid Marxism suited to his understanding of African history and culture, to his own history as an organic intellectual, and to his theoretical and pragmatic understanding of international capital and global politics as they are expressed in Africa and in particular in Senegal. His knowledge of cinema on a global and historical scale, of U.S. and European cinema (as well as that of the former Soviet Union), is evident in the reflexive ways in which he uses the cinema not only as a narrative medium but also as a critical essay on and about cinema. The various stylistic and thematic strategies that he adopts in all of his films and writings indicate that he has assimilated the works of earlier critics of colonialism and neocolonialism, such as Fanon and Cabral, in grappling with the problematics of identity, race, language, and history.

## Sembène Ousmane: Explorations of Difference

Though acknowledged as a filmmaker, Sembène is also a writer of novels, novellas, and short stories. His most well-known literary work is *God's Bits of Wood*, though other literary works are known through their transformation into such films as *Le Docker noir* (1956), *La Noire de* (1966), *Mandabi* (1968), and *Xala* (1974), among others. His films, from his documentary *L'Empire Sonhrai* (1963) to his most recent film *Guelwaar* (with Thierno Faty Sow, 1992), offer a range of styles, themes, and points of view, but the continuity informing them has most of all to do with his notion that "[l]e cinéma est l'école du soir du peuple" [cinema is the night school of the people].[6] Sembène remains committed to the pedagogical value of film as an instrument for social change despite the economic and political difficulties he has experienced in bringing films to African audiences.[7] His films address primarily—though not exclusively—African audiences, and the pedagogy lies in their attempts to reach out effectively to both literate and nonliterate Senegalese viewers.[8] Increasingly, his "unpopular popular" cinema has gained recognition among African, European, and more recently North American intellectuals for its ability to orchestrate and make accessible a range of complex and antagonistic theoretical and political issues. However, in speaking about the political effects of film, Sembène has said: "We have no illusions. The problems of Senegalese cinema are bound up with a cultural policy still to be defined by Senegal. We also know that film problems cannot be resolved in ignorance of the other aspects of the social life of a country."[9]

"The remarkable consistency" of Sembène's work inheres in his "preoccupation with the struggles of the working poor and the unemployed; and also with the exploitation and oppression of a relentless capitalism that seriously threatens the social and cultural structures of society as well as the inner recesses of the mind."[10] Sembène's novels, short stories, and films are not limited to a dramatization and analysis of external social conditions; rather, like Fanon's work, they probe ways of understanding the psychology of postcoloniality and its relations to a history of colonialism.

Thanks to the work of Françoise Pfaff, the importance of the *griot,* the storyteller, the keeper of cultural memory, in Sembène's work has been commented upon. Pfaff has repeatedly underscored that Sembène is a *griot* for modern times, his works the repository of moral, ethical, and historical knowledge, and Teshome Gabriel has characterized African cinema as directly opposite to Hollywood cinema as well as to European cinema in its insistence on memory.[11] He emphasizes the importance of storytelling—not fiction or ethnography—to African cinema, though he minimizes the importance of hybridity of postcolonial forms of representation. Sembène's "quest for the truth of African morality tales"[12] brings past and present into a dialogue rather than producing a nostalgic reenactment of a past that can never be resurrected. In the storytelling that he brings to bear on contemporary issues of neocolonialism, social class, power, and modern capitalism, the contest between official history and memory resonates loudly. Mbye Cham, in his discussion of memory in Sembène's *Ceddo* (1976), reveals that Sembène's narrative is not inert historical reconstruction; instead it "recreates the structures of power and power relations in the nineteenth century."[13] What is remarkable about the film and paradigmatic of Sembène's mode of historicizing is the way he eschews the binary structures of melodrama. Rather than simply identifying the problem as French colonization, the film returns to an earlier time, to the time of the spread of Islam in Africa. In this fashion, it "counteracts the official Senegalese–Islamic version of the West as the sole source of Africa's cultural contamination and degradation with a new version which splits Islam's roots away from Islamic soil, casts Islam as heavily infused with Arab culture, and conflates it with Euro-Christianity."[14] What Cham reveals is the consistent refusal on the filmmaker's part to attribute righteousness to any particular group or to see power as emanating from a single source. Sembène's irreverence toward official history in his recourse to memory unseats idealistic notions of culture, social structures, and of progress. Speaking of his conception of the importance of popular memory, and of its importance to cinema specifically in relation to his film *Le Camp de Thiaroye,*

Sembène has said that the film is "the memory of history which we keep alive."[15]

Sembène's films are antagonistic to dominant discourses of subalternity and identity, challenging official history's strategies of universalizing, naturalizing, and hierarchizing. He neither valorizes theory over practice nor the reverse. He does not assume an originary and unassailable form of knowledge. In relation to the question of origins, his work appears to corroborate the following comments by Homi K. Bhabha:

> The enunciation of cultural difference problematises the division of past and present, tradition and modernity, at the level of cultural representation and its authoritative address. It is the problem of how, in signifying the present, something comes to be represented, relocated, and translated in the name of tradition, in the guise of pastness that is not necessarily a faithful sign of historical memory but a strategy of representing authority in terms of the artifice of the archaic.[16]

The past can only be retrieved imperfectly through the present and is only useful to the present. As this relates to the history of subalternity, there is no way to construct an authentic version of subaltern life as it "once was"; there are only strategies for critically constructing another version from the residual fragments in the present.

In the preoccupation with time and memory, this storytelling is "of the people to come." African cinema "is not, as the West would like, a cinema which dances, but a cinema which talks, a cinema of the speech-act. It is in this way that it avoids fiction and ethnology."[17] Linking Sembène's work to that of Glauber Rocha, Deleuze finds that these filmmakers are involved in neither mythology nor fiction but in storytelling that is a "production of collective utterance capable of raising misery to a strange positivity."[18] The postcolonial critique is aimed at narratives that are the products of the national form, with its historical obsessions, its representation of Manichaean struggle, its appeals to nature and destiny, and its problematic relation to questions involving geographic and cultural boundaries. The national and imperial narrative certainty of a subject—the people—is shared by the center and margins, but not isomorphically. For example, the national narrative was appropriated for emergent nations in the post–World War II world with a number of variations and effects. In *Xala* Sembène himself has satirized this narrative. His films have consistently been critical of the ways in which the African bourgeoisie has internalized and remains dependent on the culture of the French Enlightenment, a culture that is intimately connected to notions of universalism and racism.

The national narrative relies on common sense as articulated by Gramsci and involves a melange of discursive elements derived from tradition and official history. The national narrative has relied on monumental and antiquarian history, with their excessive veneration of the past—of great men, heroic deeds, and grand narratives. Narratives involving the past are never innocent; they are instrumental in enhancing or occluding interests in the present. The attachment to figures and events in the past is not in itself pernicious. What is excessive in hegemonic historiography is its uncritical investment in formulaic, sanctified versions of the past. Gayatri Spivak has been critical of historiographies by well-meaning Western intellectuals that reveal an ignorance of "the history of imperialism, in the epistemic violence that constituted/effaced a subject that was obliged to cathect (occupy in response to desire) the space of the Imperialist's self-consolidating Other."[19] Spivak's comments call attention to how recollection of the past is tied closely to the issue of the critic's sense of responsibility. This responsibility entails a recognition, first of all, that one cannot escape complicity with the objects of analysis and critique and, second, that the responsibility is "to the text, not the other way around."[20] Hence any exploration of the uses of history must be sensitive to the ways that interpretation can function to "disguise the mechanism of unrestricted capital investment."[21] Along with the knowledge of one's responsibility to recognize the history of imperialism and to be attentive to the epistemological violence that inheres in confrontations with otherness, a critical history requires the ability to recognize and differentiate various "sheets of the past," the memories that pass by and those that are retained, those that signal nostalgia and those that are illuminating about automatism and formulaic behavior.[22] A rethinking of history recognizes the presence and the pitfalls of commonsensical thinking: its resistance to complexity, its mistrust of intellectualism, its reverence for the past, its parochialism, its binarism (especially in relation to gender and sexuality), and its penchant for the common sense of experience in the form of melodrama.

As the repository of historical sediments from the distant past to the present, and perhaps as the "philosophy" of the masses, common sense is not unreflective or dysfunctional.[23] The modes of forgetting and of rewriting the past endemic to common sense have their pragmatic value for safeguarding conditions of survival in the present. The trouble with common sense is its fragmentary and uncritical nature, which militates against complexity and analysis. In order to provide a basis for understanding the past, common sense as popular philosophy, as the philosophy of the subaltern, requires critical intervention to be made applicable for the present. The point is not to read the mind of the subaltern or to "interpret" common sense but to examine its sedimented, coexisting layers of different experiences and forms of knowledge. The glue that holds these disparate and contradictory elements together is melodrama, with its penchant for affect, identity, catastrophe, and salvation.

*Xala* is a consummate dramatization of the folklore of common sense. Its invocation of history has many layers, not all of them negative and none of them exclusive. The film portrays long-standing antagonisms between rural and urban life, signifying the clash between tribal life and modernity, a clash that has economic and cultural implications for the people. Antagonisms are established through the relationship between the rural dispossessed, the beggars, and the urban bourgeoisie. The history of Senegal is allegorized in the portrayal of the three wives of El Hadji, the protagonist: Adja, the first, the devout, practicing traditional Muslim woman, is skilled in renunciation and acceptance. Oumi, the second, is a hybrid figure, a transitional image for the relationship between African tradition and modernity, devoted to consumer fetishes: wigs, costume jewelry, Western dress, fashion magazines, and money. N'Gone, the third, is herself a fetish, an ironic conflation of tribal fetishism and the fetishism of commodities under late capitalism, identified with automobiles, photographic images, and whiteness. The film's emphasis on the various manifestations of fetishism—economic, political, religious, and sexual—calls attention to "the 'supernatural' power of money, which creates and animates the movement of commodities, embodying its own imperishable value in the perishable bodies of commodities; or, on the other hand, as a 'natural' effect of the relation between commodities, which establishes an expression of their values and the proportions in which they can be exchanged by way of social institutions."[24] The fetishes are a clue to the coexistence of the "supernatural" with the "natural" and to the workings of allegory as a strategy for unlocking the mystery of value associated with the seemingly magical operation of the fetish. In ency-

clopedic fashion, the allegory connects gender and sexuality to familialism, familialism to social class, social class to nation, and all of these
to "the supernatural power of money."

The indigenous bourgeoisie treat "national liberation" as an opportunity to further their own economic and political interests at the expense of other, subaltern groups, thus perpetuating the conditions of
colonialism in new forms. The film explodes the folklore of a new nation in formation by dramatizing how the African bourgeoisie repeat,
with only a few differences, the old French colonial ruling class. As
Sembène probes the limits and possibilities of resistance, he dramatizes
how notions of "Africanity" are contaminated by residual colonialist
(and equally problematic) neocolonialist thinking involving questions
of nationalism, transnationalism, language, class, and race. His postcolonial critique is a dramatization and analysis of nationalism, specifically but not solely of French nationalism, but also of African assimilation and attempts to resist nationalism. In discussing national forms
and nationalism, Etienne Balibar describes how "bourgeois formations passed one another reciprocally in a 'process without a subject,'
by restructuring the state in the national form and by modifying the
status of all the other classes. This explains the simultaneous genesis of
nationalism and cosmopolitanism."[25] The narrative of nationalism is
an "already known," pregiven construction that is presented to its audiences with "the continuity of a subject."[26] France not only exported
its bureaucratic elites and its consumer commodities, it also exported
European culture to Africa—including European conceptions of ethnic, racial, and gendered identity—and European notions of what constitutes the "people," language, education, religion, and history.

In the opening of *Xala,* the new Senegalese power elite enacts a
mock ritual of exorcism by ejecting French statues, the symbols of
colonial rule, from the Chambre de Commerce. This episode serves as
the prelude to (and the enigma of) the film's narrative, which exposes
the terms of repetition and difference: an image of the expropriation
and exploitation of the people by new ruling groups who are a variation on the old. The film probes and ultimately explodes the reductive
assumption that independence merely involves the supplanting of the
old ruling class by indigenous groups. In seriocomic terms centering
on sexual impotence, *"xala,"* the film probes the subjective scars of
colonialism. The curse of the *xala* of El Hadji dramatizes the ways the
new rulers have internalized the culture of colonialism, rendering them

powerless despite their positions of authority. In such terms, Sembène reveals the combined force of cultural and economic hegemony, exposing the hypocrisy of Africanity through narrative agents like El Hadji, who delude themselves that they are now free to invent themselves according to an African past. The film confirms that there is no literal return to a world that has been systematically destroyed.

In its intricate and critical weaving of melodrama and antimelodrama to illustrate sameness and difference, *Xala* dramatizes antagonism between past and present. Melodrama—never abandoned—takes on a new valence, shifting from a preoccupation with effects to an examination of causes. The culture, for better or worse, is now a hybrid. On the one side, the film offers the image of Rama, El Hadji's educated daughter, who has a poster of Charlie Chaplin in her room but who respects the traditional rights of Adja as her mother and as El Hadji's first wife. On the other side, the film offers El Hadji himself and his second and third wives and their families, whose Africanity is a commodity like their clothing, television sets, and automobiles. Even the imam, who temporarily lifts the curse of El Hadji's *xala* on the condition that the check with which El Hadji pays him is sound (and who reinstates the *xala* when the check bounces), understands the rules of exchange value. The return of the *xala* to El Hadji is a further reminder that exchange cannot be reduced to monetary terms. In the portrait of El Hadji's quest for sexual potency, the film relentlessly connects international capitalism to sexuality, marriage, and kinship and to social and political power.

The exorcism performed by a group of beggars on El Hadji that ends the film—they spit on his naked body as they confront him with his sins against them—offers a complex instance of the ways in which Sembène uses folklore. The episode is a parable in the manner of the *griot* as described by Pfaff, a lesson in power and countervailing power. The film portrays the congregation of beggars as representative of a collective form of existence that is threatened by men like El Hadji; hence they chastise him. The scene is a stark instance of the uses of satiric invective whose purgative designs may be aimed not only at El Hadji but at the African audience. Specifically in relation to the question of the material effects of power, this scene is also a reminder of the body politics ever present in Sembène's films, which dramatize the effects of power on the literal bodies of both victim and oppressor. In relation to the question of memory, the film's climax is the moment in which the beggars jog El Hadji's (and the audience's) memory. One of the beggars, a relative, confronts him with the way in which El Hadji cheated him out of his land. Long after the scene fades to black, the sound of the beggars' expectorating continues. This allegory of history leaves the audience in the dark, contemplating El Hadji's humiliation and complicity, as part of the parable of the failure of "independence."

Recording and assessing the meaning of failure is of utmost importance to the role that memory plays in Sembène's work, and allegory functions as a means of probing the many levels and implications of that failure. Though critical readings of his work often attribute pessimism or optimism to the devastating critique that Sembène aims at contemporary politics, such assessments seem inadequate to the complex analysis he offers of failure, and they misrepresent his pedagogical and open-ended view of the role of history. The recognition of failure is a precondition for learning from the past, and Sembène explores the ways that short-term failure may in the long run be productive. Speaking to the question of failure in relation to the historiography of colonial India, Ranajit Guha writes: "It is the study of *this historic failure of the nation to come into its own*, a failure due to the inadequacy of the bourgeoisie as well as of the working class . . . *which constitutes the central problematic of the historiography of colonial India*."[27]

In Gayatri Spivak's terms, the tracking of failure serves "to displace discursive fields."[28] It enables a more analytic, less univalently melodramatic understanding of the past, undermining linear views of history, challenging discourses of progress, and bringing to the surface narratives of the defeated rather than of the victor, narratives that have been effaced or misrecognized by official history. For example, in his notes on the Risorgimento, Gramsci records Italy's failure to become unified, and this failure becomes the basis for an understanding of later developments in Italian history, namely, the rise of fascism.[29] On the subject of historicism or official history, Walter Benjamin has also asked with whom the adherents of historicism "actually empathize," and he answers: "with the victor [and] empathy with the victor invariably benefits the ruler."[30] *Xala* does not celebrate "the triumphal procession in which the present rulers step over those who are lying prostrate."[31] The film does not resign itself to this prostration, nor does *Le Camp de Thiaroye*.

The men of Ousmane Sembène's and Thierno Faty Sow's *Le Camp de Thiaroye*. Courtesy of New Yorker Films.

## *Le Camp de Thiaroye:* History, Memory, and Failure

*Le Camp de Thiaroye* is an essay in film that explores the importance of rethinking official history, the nature and effects of subalternity, the role of intellectuals, the character of African cinema, and the politics of culture. In this respect, the film is of a piece with the writings on postcoloniality of Homi K. Bhabha, Gayatri Chakravorty Spivak, Immanuel Wallerstein, and Etienne Balibar (including the work of the Subaltern Studies Group, especially in its Gramscian concerns with hegemony).[32]

Taking an incident from midcentury—the return of a group of Senegalese *tirailleurs* from active service and also from imprisonment in Europe by the Nazis, their treatment at the hands of their French colonial master, and their revolt against that master—the film brings the past to bear on the present. *Le Camp de Thiaroye* can be regarded as an excursus on the problematic and complex nature of the meaning and effects of global culture in the last decades of the twentieth century and as a telling expression and instance of the hybridity inherent in postcolonial forms of representation. The film invokes the discourse of European fascism in its analysis of African political struggle, linking

European fascism to colonialism. Dramatizing the impossibility of a return to the past, utilizing local stories, autobiography, and brief newsreel footage, and drawing on a range of characters from different parts of Africa and from France, the film explores and complicates notions of culture, identity, and race. The concern with African involvement in European wars in *Le Camp de Thiaroye* recalls an image from *La Noire de* in which Diouanna dances on the World War I monument and the images from *Emitai* of the burning of the village of Effok and the massacre of the men by the French. In *Le Camp de Thiaroye*, Sergeant Diatta is from Effok, and his uncle and aunt have come to exhort him to return home to the village now that he has returned from military service in Europe. That Sembène served in the French army during the war adds the element of autobiography that is also present in *La Noir de* and *Emitai*.[33]

In its preoccupation with language as culture, *Le Camp de Thiaroye* looks closely at the fusion of universalism and racism. Official history invokes an idea of *the* people, calling on notions of universalism that suppress difference in the name of commonality. As Immanuel Wallerstein has argued: "Universalism and racism may seem on the surface strange bedfellows, if not virtually antithetical doctrines—one open, the other closed; one equalizing, the other polarizing; one inviting rational discourse, the other incarnating prejudice. . . . Yet . . . we should look more closely at the ways in which they may have been compatible."[34] Embedded in the very structure and style of narration in *Le Camp de Thiaroye* is a cartography of racism and universalism.

The style of *Le Camp de Thiaroye* involves combining forms, including mixing indigenous and Western musical types. The languages employed are various: indigenous, European, and hybrid. The characters are European, African, and Europeanized Africans. The ideas of the past are derived from oral history, official colonialist discourse, mythic and literary allusions, cinema history, folklore, and common sense. The structuring of time in narrative is not linear or unitary but fragmentary and episodic. This history is based on the need to forget what is remembered and to remember what is forgotten. The past exists in the shape of ghosts, filled with secrets that are productive of disease and ritualized violence and peopled with mutes and invalids.[35] The melodramatic domestication of the world functions on the terrain of the family, of the politics of the body, and of the body politic. The monumental national narrative relies on a melodramatic scenario in which the forces of light and darkness collide to produce an image of the enlightened and just nation. The language of the nation-state is built upon discourses of the family, the prodigal son, the obedient daughter, and the wise father lawgiver. The face of the loyal subject is the mirror of this family bred from the "family of nations." Thus, secrecy, divisiveness—the splitting of the good and bad siblings—and the identification of originary events (also arising from the family) are part of this "folklore" that is fused with questions of loyalty, silence, and suffering. The emphasis that Nietzsche places not only on remembering but on forgetting is central to *Le Camp de Thiaroye*, in which history as repetition is destructive and in which the memory of failure in the present can intervene as a means of distinguishing between sameness and difference.

Official or hegemonic history is not often recognized as melodrama, nor is it recognized as folklore (in the Gramscian sense), despite the fact that it relies on both melodrama and folklore. The narrative of nation relies on affect generated from service, sacrifice, and loss. It cannot tolerate the admission of failure. In struggling with this narrative, Sembène's invoking of the past works with and against melodrama. Affect is not totally eliminated from narrative, but Sembène interrogates the conditions that produce victimization, pain, and suffering. This interrogation requires a critical sense of history, of the possible reasons for rehearsing the past, and a rethinking of naturalized commonsensical explanations of behavior. Thus his postcolonial critique is sensitive to melodramatic obsession with its refusal to admit cross-fertilization and sameness in difference. In his return to the past, Sembène probes the various ways in which the blurring of sameness and difference are obstacles to learning. Deleuze talks about the existence of cliché not as "failed recognition" but as familiarity, placed in close proximity to other forms of remembering. Folklore functions not as failed recognition but as problematic familiarity. Memory by contrast is fluid, enabling a disarticulation of pieces of the past, the sediments that constitute the sheets of the past. The cliché constitutes the past, frozen and available for constant recycling but also open to recognition. When the clichéd image or word is placed in proximity to the immediacy and fluidity of memory, there is the possibility of an awareness of time and of change. By invoking the reiterative slogan, prophecy, and platitude, Sembène exposes the familiar and commonsensical valorization of experience and the virtues of familiarity as propounded through cliché.[36] The hybridity of Sembène's style—his use of languages and his melange of characters—serve as a strategy to expose the seamless clichéd quality that is the mark of common sense. *Le Camp de Thiaroye* is directed toward undermining predictable and uncritical forms of thought, speech, and gesture. Thus Sembène juxtaposes African language and culture to Western (particularly French) language and culture, reminding his audiences that the narratives of colonialism and neocolonialism are not homogeneous. Homi K. Bhabha argues that hybridity is a position to be contended with in relation to a different, more complex, and possibly more efficacious conception of postcoloniality; he writes that "the transformational value of change lies in the re-articulation, or translation, of elements that are *neither the One* (unitary working class) *nor the Other* (the politics of gender) *but something else besides* which contests the terms and territories of both."[37] This "something else" is the "in-between" of hybridity. Such narratives do not rely on essentialism, on firm and immutable conceptions of a continental, national, ethnic, racial, or tribal identity. They do not present themselves in monumental, continuist, or linear terms, and they seek to engage with the uses and abuses of history.

Perhaps rather than regarding this hybrid form of cinema as necessarily oppositional (though it does often oppose), it is better to identify (as Sembène has done) the inevitable cross-fertilization, for better and for worse, of African culture by the colonial narrative and to recognize that renarrativization is not a matter of the substitution of one narrative for another but a matter of examining the status of narrative. Since the narratives of mass culture are, in Spivak's words, ferociously "nation-centered" and uncritical,[38] social and political analysis should address the ways in which national cultures and identities are constructed as a "problem of discursive production, an effect structure rather than a cause."[39] She reminds us to look to the various ways in which the international division of intellectual and manual labor, education, language, and forms of exchange value underpin and determine binary conceptions of nation, race, gender, and ethnicity—often occluding women's labor and sexuality—and she reminds us of the necessity to refuse reductive analyses, especially confusion between cause and effect in accounting for inequality. By analyzing and valorizing the hybrid elements of postcolonial discourse, it may be possible to escape the reiterative illogic and binarism of the prevailing ways that the relations between nationalism, colonialism, and neocolonialism are misrecognized.[40] This hybridity is manifested in the mixing and blurring of the boundaries of different generic modes and expressive forms: documentary, newsreel, tales, short stories, poetry, trance, dream, incantation, hallucinatory forms, parables, novels, autobiography, and biography.[41]

Sembène's uses of the past are not in the generic modes of adventure films, costume dramas, or biopics. Such forms are closest to the language of official historicizing, even when they seem to undermine that history. Conventional images in such films are constructed from the simulacra of "documentation"—books that open, maps, photographs, readings from letters, journals, "incomplete accounts," reports made after the event, even songs associated with the individual that are part of a national mythology[42]—and are associated with the clichés of film history. Sembène's form of remembering can be gleaned not so much from existing documents as from oral history and from current events, as is the case in his uses of newspaper articles. While he is aware of the conventions of historical films, he often uses them in ways that expose the striated nature of contemporary African culture, drawing on a collage of images from past and present that contribute to multiple layers of narrative and that are carriers of different histories. Historical differences are often communicated through the characters. Based on the events leading to the revolt of Senegalese *tirailleurs* against the French during World War II, *Le Camp de Thiaroye* combines fact and fiction to "keep alive the memory of history."[43] Unlike a monumental history, which situates a great hero at the center of the narrative, this film gives no character a heroic treatment in the conventional sense. No narrative of conversion and transformation alters the inexorability of the events. No savior appears who can avert the destruction. Pays, the one character who attempts to warn the others of impending danger, is incapable of speech and is unable to command respect and credibility. There is no standard of Africanity that offers redemption. The critique of Africanity has gone far beyond that of *Xala*. *Le Camp de Thiaroye* provides no common culture to which the men can adhere; instead it offers a plethora of differences that have to be recognized. As in *Emitai*, the gods are silent and have vanished. In terms of the complex, disjunctive, and reiterative style of *Le Camp de Thiaroye*, Sembène rejects a familiar and transparent form of representation that would simplify the film's problematics.

The film offers an examination and a critique—not a total rejection—of folklore. In its exploration of common sense, of the common sense of religion, for example, the film probes the contradictory nature of ritualized behaviors, the consolatory dimensions of national/cultural identity, the role of economics as the bottom line of revolutionary struggle, the lure of family and of "roots," the "saving" dimensions of culture and intellect, and the idea that a "man's word is his bond." The issues are exposed as strategies for survival and as reductive and self-destructive. From the vantage points of economics, social class, race, ethnicity, intellect, rural and urban conflict, generational struggle, and history, the film rejects traditional analyses, inviting a complex reading of individuals and events in light of its rethinking of the nature of history and memory. Sembène's story of the camp—what happened to the men on their return from fighting for the French in Europe and from the German prisoner-of-war camps—is not the familiar one. In its representation in European and Hollywood film, fascism has been most often associated with Europe and has taken place on European soil. Racism comes into play in Africa not as a phenomenon of violated personal identity, not as an individual phenomenon, and not as a familiar melodrama of villainy but as an antimelodrama of systemic exploitation. Racism is an institution inseparable from the international division of labor and from hierarchies of exchange value. Systemic violence is enacted upon people of color, who are treated as expendable.[44] Their labor has limited value to the colonizer, who is, in the final analysis, bent on destroying the workers after they have ceased being useful. In Sembène's terms, although the men are not responsible for their condition, they are implicated in the maintenance of events, complicit in the production of value, and only dimly aware of the terms of their complicity, though they are conscious of exploitation. As in *Emitai,* Sembène shows that there *is* also resistance, despite the fact that rebellion leads inexorably to the men's deaths.[45]

The narrative moves from one well-meaning character to the next—from the sympathetic Captain Raymond and Senegalese Sergeant Diatta to men of assorted ranks and nationalities. The sergeant, a reader of Paul Vercors, Jules Romain, and Roger Martin du Gard among others, a lover of French classical music and of jazz, and a polyglot, lives not in the margins but in the in-between of two cultures, unable to return to the past, fantasizing a future that is impossible under colonialism. Intermittently Diatta seems to understand his situation. Sembène does not present Diatta as naive or foolish. He is doubly victimized through both coercion and consent, through the violence enacted upon him and through his inability to understand the connection between the French culture he admires and its relation to the barbarism it produces. Diatta exemplifies the limits of individual merit, of reason, and above all of the role of the traditional intellectual. Common sense dictates either a return to his village or his assimilation into French culture, but the situation in the camp reveals the impossibility of choice under the brutal circumstances of colonialism. The French culture admired by Diatta is revealed to be something other than the romanticism invested in great books, in music, and in love letters to an absent wife. The French officers have no great knowledge or esteem for their own intellectuals and none at all for African intellectuals, accusing them of being communists. African culture, as it is expressed through the sergeant's family and through the other men at the camp, also seems to be inadequate to address the local and global changes that have taken place as a result of imperialism, colonialism, and their inevitable counterpart, war.

In probing the secrets and silences connecting fascism, war, and colonialism, Sembène is not interested in the psychology of the French colonizers, in apologizing for their actions, in excoriating them as individuals, or even in singling them out as a nation. He is more interested in how French nationalism is representative of the production and effects of colonialism. He is closer in Le Camp de Thiaroye than in any of his previous films to portraying the French multidimensionally, giving us a spectrum of the various figures that defend and maintain colonialism, from the liberal captain to the general who is totally committed to his country (whether Vichyist or not).[46] By presenting the liberal French captain, Raymond, sympathetically, Sembène moves away—as he does with Diatta—from the reductive and Manichaean nature of affect characteristic of certain forms of melodrama, from its binary designations of good and evil, and from humanistic notions of the "saving remnant" to focus instead on the systemic aspects of fascism and colonialism. Le Camp de Thiaroye is not an oedipal narrative of a bad father or a narrative of psychotic and crazed individuals. The film is not a narrative of bad Germans and good French or good Germans and bad French or bad English and good Americans. Rather, it exposes this form of melodramatic distinction that serves to create false expectations on the part of the people and a folklore of colonialism that is destructive and violent. The Sembène narrative takes a different look at history and sees sameness ("*kiff kiff*") where others see difference and sees difference where others see sameness.

By eschewing good and bad characters, by focusing on the terms of the situation under which the men find themselves in the camp, and by focusing in particular on the impersonality of the actions on the part of the French and on their anticommunist pronationalist "politics," Sembène produces a portrait that resembles what Pays, the silent one, has been trying to focus on and communicate: the imperative to mistrust the language and the behavior of the colonizer, to not be beguiled by false promises. A survivor of Buchenwald, Pays is the one character who immediately recognizes the similarities between Thiaroye and the German camp, and he recognizes the similarities between the French and the Germans. His inarticulate groans, his pointing out of comparisons—unheeded by the Africans—are unfortunately attributed by his comrades to the trauma of the war, not to his insight.

The material conditions of the men's situation—being kept behind barbed wire, being treated as prisoners of war even to the diet they are given, being deprived of their money and cheated on the exchange rate—are apparent to the spectator but not to the French. Through a proliferation of characters with differing national and class positions and through the film's evaluation of events, Le Camp de Thiaroye obstructs a reductive assessment of the characters or events. The major strategy of the film is one of interrogation rather than of assertion of sameness or difference. Diatta and the captain seem to want the same thing—justice—but they are powerless as individuals. The image toward the end of the film of the tanks rolling ominously toward the camp, guns pointed at and ready to destroy the huts, conveys more than the anticipated climax in violence. The moment dramatizes the mechanical nature of the system, its impersonality: the culmination of the hierarchical, systemic, and specifically racist nature of colonization. The French captain who crosses the divide between colonizer and colonized is stigmatized as a "communist," treated as an outcast, and only used as an intermediary by the French to convince the Africans to abandon their "unpatriotic" rebelliousness. His role dramatizes, as part of the melodrama of the system, the violence of identifying with one side or the other.

Sembène dramatizes the ways in which both coercion and consent function to keep things in place, presumably not just in the past but as a parable for the present. Again and again in Le Camp de Thiaroye (and as we shall see again most cogently in *Guelwaar*), this parable that connects past and present resides in the ongoing economic and cultural dependence of most Africans and in the use of force by the elites to maintain their hegemony. In *Le Camp de Thiaroye* the edicts of the French, as they seek to keep the men confined and placid, contrast sharply with the various meetings of the men in their attempts to gain differing objectives, underlining the ways in which the men attempt to maintain a sense of equilibrium, to stay focused on the immediate problems, and to plan and initiate a revolt. What the men underestimate—even when kidnapping the general—is the extent to which the French will go in order to maintain power, even to the point of violating their articulated ethos of honor, loyalty, obedience, and shared fate with their men. Not even Diatta, the intellectual and the aesthete, anticipates the degree to which the history of war at home, abroad, and in the prison camps has obscured for the Africans the inherent violence that supports the power of their adversary. This is where official history has done its job. The treatment of the Africans by the French seems more brutal on African soil than the seemingly more "benign" treatment they received on European soil, presenting a dilemma for the Africans in understanding their present plight.

The allegory that Sembène employs by returning to World War II and fascism is a history of and for the Africans, and Sembène returns to the past to dissect the tendency toward repetition. The French may be silent, as in postindependence *Xala*, or argumentative and aggressive, as in preindependence *Le Camp de Thiaroye*, but both films are critical of the power the French have wielded in the past and continue to wield. The film's allegory asks what, if any, the alternatives are to undergoing the same experiences again and again. The end of the film returns to the beginning, thus underscoring the presence of repetition. In using allegory, Sembène seems to be resisting the tightly structured narrative that leads toward a resolution. The men's ultimate failure to understand their situation suggests that Sembène's focus is not on producing a familiar wholesome narrative of success but on the audience's ability to work with the narrative of failure, to interrogate the nature of that failure.

Questions proliferate throughout the film: What is the actual failure of the revolt? Why did the men remain at the camp? Was the massacre inevitable? So much of this film plays with the affiliations and disaffiliations among Africans and between Africans and African Americans, but what are the obstacles that they confront in relation to survival and to resistance? The men can organize to get food when they are outraged about the food they are being served. They can organize to find sex for themselves out of frustration. They can organize to make the general a captive and they can organize to stand up to the French, but they cannot discern the more insidious linguistic traps that the French have in store for them and that lead to the final acts of destruction. Their failures are embedded as much in the problematics of culture as they are in the economics of this situation. In pragmatic terms, characteristic of common sense, the Africans understand when they are being cheated, but they understand neither what underpins the French refusal to grant them economic justice nor the duplicity of language that is an important key to their undoing.

The interconnectedness of language and identity is central to the film, since, in Sembène's terms, language is culture. The Africans speak the various languages of their regions and country. They also speak pidgin French ("*Francite*") to communicate with the French and with Africans from other regions. However, this rudimentary use of French does not enable them to understand the nuances, especially the nuances that would permit them to pick up the subtleties of the colonizer's intentions. The men's rudimentary use of German serves to reinforce the connections between their former experiences in the Nazi prison camp at Buchenwald and in the present French prison camp at Thiaroye. They use German to communicate a sense of impending danger. In contrast to the men's pragmatic uses of European languages, the language of the French officers is abstract and saturated with clichés involving law and order, with racist aphorisms about the inadequacies of Africans, and with slogans about war and patriotism. Among the many languages in the film, American English also plays a role as a way of dramatizing the differences and similarities between African-Americans and Africans. In the interchange between Diatta and an American soldier, Diatta's knowledge about Detroit and about jazz is revealed; however, the stilted conversation between the two men reveals limitations on both sides in discussing and understanding the political circumstances under which they meet.

Sergeant Diatta is multilingual. He speaks French, English, Diola, and like all the men a smattering of German. His knowledge of languages should put the French officers to shame but is instead a matter of annoyance to them. He is a source of perplexity and dismay to his family, who are not at all impressed by his Europeanization, his marriage to a European woman, and his adherence to Catholicism. According to them, by becoming a Francophile he has relinquished his past, becoming the Europeanized African. That Diatta is able to speak fluently in the language of the colonizer points to the legacy of colonialism with its imposed cultural norms. The use of the Diola language dramatizes the social and cultural differences between Diatta and his family. From them he receives the news of the village and of deaths. He treats his family with decorum and the news with indifference: the mark of the expatriate who has been transformed through his contacts with the Europeans. (In this respect, autobiographical elements continue to play a role in Sembène's work.) Likewise, his family has little understanding of Diatta's change, of the differences that the war has wrought in him. Their inability to communicate with each other is conspicuous in the silences between them. The linguistic/cultural/political divide between colonizer and colonized is evident in the fact that the colonizers are constantly in need of translators, since, not having made an effort to learn the men's language, they are unilingual. The role of translation signifies more than a paraphrase from one language to another. When Diatta is asked to translate the American English for the French officer, he wisely omits whatever is derogatory to the French, particularly the comment of an American officer who asserts in disgust that the French are losing their empire. The episode suggests that subalterns are not unaware of their condition, availing themselves whenever possible of the opportunity for expressing antagonism. However, Diatta's knowledge of French language and culture is also a reproach to the cultural limitations of the colonizers, and they are uncomfortable with his role as translator. In the context of common sense, it seems that Diatta, like the other men, has some vague glimmering of his situation, but despite the fact that he acts as translator, he ultimately has difficulty in translating that knowledge into a critical position. In Sembène's film the translator takes on the meaning of a cultural intermediary, raising questions about unwitting cultural complicity.

Diatta's situation is suggestive of Gramsci's distinction between traditional and organic intellectuals. Diatta has thrown his lot in with traditional intellectuals, in part because he is alienated from the indigenous culture. He does not yet envision a new way of producing knowledge as an organic intellectual, although through his character, the film discourse reveals *its* investment in producing organic intellectuals. In one sense, Diatta has become like his mentor, the captain, and as such he risks becoming politically impotent even if not traitorous. The traditional intellectual is faced with a binary situation in which he must either identify with the colonizer or escape to the past. The prospect of recognizing language and representation as an instrument of struggle is only barely perceived, seen more in terms of immediate survival than of sustained critical insight. Turning that knowledge in new and more fruitful directions is the problem. When the men agree to relinquish the general and celebrate their victory, suppressing the knowledge that his promises are merely evasions and a means for him to escape rather than a sign of his acquiescence to their demands, they reveal that they still do not understand their history and are doomed to repeat it. The brutal events that ended *Emitai*—the massacre of the men—are reproduced with in *Le Camp de Thiaroye* with more violence and without the hopeful presence of the militant women and children (*Emitai* did not actually show the deaths).

Thus *Le Camp de Thiaroye* reveals that postcolonial analysis demands something other than binary thinking. As Spivak writes: "You won't be able to dissolve everything into Black against White; there is also Black against Black, Brown against Brown and so forth."[47] And the film's challenge to the common sense of binarism forces a rethinking of difference against its leveling and abuses. The liberal humanist project of nominal equality presents this in the guise of benevolence. However, the liberal rhetoric of universalism is exposed in Sembène's film as the folklore of nationalism, a folklore that relies on forms of racism and sexism, and on the concomitant violence to both mind and body inherent in them. The film suggests that more than physical force is involved in the intricacies and subtleties of cultural dependency. The abilities to differentiate, to detect and resist repetition, to listen to and evaluate history, and to resist all forms of reduction that have been part of a history of epistemic and physical brutality are also necessary.

In one sense, despite their origins in different African countries, the men share a similar situation: going off and leaving African soil, being imprisoned in Europe, and returning to a situation that appears to be—but is not—the same as the one they left in Europe. The issue of sameness also functions for the colonizers, for whom all the men are "the same": childlike and ignorant of the ways of the world but also potential troublemakers. (The French vilify the embattled African as communists.) It is very evident as *Le Camp de Thiaroye* unfolds that

the men—Diatta, Diarra, Niger, Pays, Congo, Oubangui—are different in their countries of birth, religions, levels of education, languages,
social classes, occupations, and behaviors, but the French do not see
the differences. On the level of monetary value, the French insist that
there is little difference between the exchange rate they offer to the
Africans and the official exchange rate. This act of leveling underscores that the value of the Africans for the French is purely a matter
of exploiting the men and reducing the worth of their labor to the
lowest common denominator of value. In relation to the French and
the African intellectuals, it appears that the French captain and the
African sergeant share the same interests and admiration of European
culture. Again, the matter of difference recurs in the unfolding antagonisms, which reveal that the African men are not the same as each
other in their occupations, expectations, education, or religion, though
they have experienced similar hardships.

Among other differences that are invisible to the French but evident
to the film audience are religious differences. One is made aware of the
groups of men praying toward Mecca. The sergeant is a Catholic.
There is also evidence of residual indigenous ritual practices: the pour-
ing off of a portion of the palm wine onto the ground before drinking,
the ritualistic killing of a sheep, the "victory" dances of the men, and
the patterned mode of discourse in the African men's councils. The
film builds visual contrasts between the French and the Africans
through the contrast between the camp facilities and the officers' club
and between the men and the French officers, challenging the French
notion that French and African men were in the war together and
made similar investments. The issue of exchanging uniforms is a another way in which the film cues the audience to the problematic of
distinguishing sameness and difference, relating finally to the African's
confusion about repetition and change. When the men are first introduced in the films, they are in American uniforms, which they must
later change for French colonial uniforms, a signal of the difference between their status in Europe and their status in Africa, and the
sergeant's troubles begin with his being mistaken for an American by
the Americans because of his uniform. The attention to the uniforms—
American and African—serves allegorically to foreground the interrogation of the identity of the Africans: What is it to be an African?
What are the delusory dimensions of identity? How and to what ends
are such delusions fostered? With their return to French colonial

(African) uniforms, are the men returned to a more accurate assessment of their situation? And what about the situation of the women, of Bintum, the bride planned for Diatta, of the French and African prostitutes in the bar, and of Diatta's French bride? Can the women's situations be considered parallel to each other's and to those of the African men, or must further distinctions be made? Again, the question of sameness and difference is germane to the film's visual treatment of history. The audience is also given reminders of Buchenwald: Pays's helmet, the image of the camp with the close-up shots of the barbed wire, and the recurrent images of the watch towers seen through Pays's perspective. And thus further questions concerning difference arise: How different are Thiaroye from Buchenwald, the French from the Germans, fascism from colonialism? How different is the situation under neocolonialism?

What is the audience to make of the final terrifying image of the massacre of the men? In *Le Camp de Thiaroye* there is no consoling moment—except the consolation of memory offered by the film. There is no compensatory act; there is just the burials, the boarding of new recruits on their way to fight in Europe, and an image of the bag of coffee in the hands of the young woman Bintum, brought to the captain as the family had promised Diatta. Thus the life of the sergeant is ironically equated with a sack of coffee for his European widow, and thus the film disassembles the myth of the fully conscious subaltern who can save himself and the people and who is fully capable of articulating the "truth" of his situation to others. The film disarticulates common sense and melodramatic notions of heroism. Each of the characters exposes his imperfections. Neither totally pliable nor totally wise, each, though not responsible, is implicated in the final outcome. The terms of subalternity are tied to the constraints of common sense. The fragmented and disjointed knowledge that the men have is neither true nor false. Their situation and the terms in which they seek to combat it in the film are an indication of the limits against which they are struggling: official forms of historicizing, the limitations of the knowledge available to them, and the sheer physical power of the forces against which they must either struggle in order to survive or succumb. They are constrained by their underestimation of the nature of the enemy and the powerful resources at its disposal. The French opposition is massive, conjoining epistemic violence, physical violence, and economic exploitation.

In turning to film as a means of reaching a larger audience, especially audiences for whom language and literacy constitute both a political problem and a stage toward resolution, Sembène uses memory as a pedagogical instrument. But *Le Camp de Thiaroye* adopts a cautious and interrogative attitude toward politicizing and toward literacy. In the figure of Diatta, Sembène has raised a question about the nature and role of learning, about speaking, and about listening. The film suggests that the filmmaker has turned to his African audiences and asked them to reconsider their own state of knowledge, their history, the nature of their received knowledge, and their own capacity to look and listen. The question of what constitutes politics—particularly the politics of film—animates *Le Camp de Thiaroye*. Sembène has violated expectations of what a political film is as well as of what the role of history is in film. The film's utilization of narrative is not an end in itself but the pre-text for an essay, a prolegomenon and an invitation, to analyze the workings of historical narrative. While formally the film is not that of the Godardian/modernist variety, with its use of print, on-screen interview format, direct address, and extensive quotation, it shares certain theoretical objectives in its epistemological concerns. In its cultural allusions to writing, to music, and to language, *Le Camp de Thiaroye* interrogates representation, calling attention not to the forms of knowledge on which the characters' actions are based but to the forms of knowledge on which the film relies. *Le Camp de Thiaroye* uses a specific set of past events, the return of the men from Europe, as a pre-text to examining how to make sense of what passes for cultural knowledge; however, the film does not remain within the confines of African culture, though it takes place on African soil. The global dimension of the events reminds the spectator that Africa has never been insulated from the outside world and that cultural reminders of the colonialist past are scattered everywhere. The film attempts to pick up these shards and to place them before the viewer.

Sembène has employed every strategy at his disposal to call into question the means whereby European narratives of nationhood and people are inseparable from questions of colonialism and racism. As Balibar has reminded us, nationalism "never functions alone":[48] It relies on specific dimensions of historicizing that strive to produce a sense of commonality, a sameness in difference. What passes for universal history is based on the particularities of a national narrative predicated on the difference of the colonial other. In Sembène's narrative the excesses of history appear in a benign guise of culture, but they are instruments of domination. Sembène's return to history is an attempt to interrogate this culture and to identify its destructiveness. His film invites his audiences to probe and defamiliarize narratives that have been uncritically assimilated. *Le Camp de Thiaroye* reminds Africans of that history, but the allegory addresses the possibility of betrayal, failure, and repetition as a consequence of forgetting (or remembering inadequately).

## The Body Politic, *Guelwaar*, Folklore, and Postcoloniality

Sembène's film *Guelwaar*, though situated in a contemporary setting, maintains the concerns of *Le Camp de Thiaroye* to explore the historical nature and effects of political betrayal and failure. *Guelwaar* uses and critiques common sense and folklore as a means to enhance remembering and forgetting. *Guelwaar* is also an allegory and an essay in the form of a film. Significantly, the film ends with the title "An African Legend of the Twenty-First Century." If one reads the film backward, this title provides an entry to the mode of historicizing that animates the work, its pedagogical objectives, and its design on the future. It also offers an entry to a politics and style that are never comfortable and reassuring but consistently critical. Like *Le Camp de Thiaroye*, the film eschews the safety of conventional melodrama with its innocent victims and malevolent aggressors, in which the good are rewarded and the evil are punished, in which consolation is anticipated and desired. The film refuses the affective excesses of elegiac representation or nostalgia by refusing to idealize a past prior to colonialism.

The kind of melodrama that the film presents is alloyed with a critical and satiric look at the corruption of power. This analysis of power is not confined to a single exceptional individual or to one group alone; nor is it attributed to psychic derangement or delimited to one aberrant moment in history. Rather, the melodrama encompasses the entire society, tracing the ways in which the negative effects of power have historical resonance and are the effects of past knowledge and actions whose trace can be identified in present events and behavior. The effects of power are distributed through the various strata of society and through different institutions—the family, patriarchy, the police, diasporic intellectuals, the subordination of women, the corruption of bureaucrats, the traditional role of religion fused with the state, the role of international capital and its relation to local elites. Since he is interested in reaching his African audiences, Sembène's treatment of history depends on his confronting the people with the hard facts of their complicity, probing the multiple sources and effects whereby the people are betrayed and are also betrayers.

The melodrama adopted by the film works in centripetal rather than centrifugal fashion, leaving no aspect of the economic, cultural, social, and political life of Senegal untouched by critique. Sembène anastomoses different sectors of life to each other, dramatizing the inescapable hybridity that comes with the legacy of colonialism and constitutes the terrain of postcoloniality. Although the film tracks the failure of Senegal ("What a country," says one of the characters) and implicates all of the characters in its parable of power, it also differentiates degrees of complicity. Unlike *Le Camp de Thiaroye*, the film takes place in the present, but taking a cue from the printed title of the epilogue—"An African Legend of the Twenty-First Century"—it is reasonable to infer that, once again, the past is linked to the present and the future.

*Guelwaar* begins with the announcement of the death of Pierre Henri Thioune (Thiermo N'Diaye), "Guelwaar" in Wolof, signifying "the noble one." Aloys, one of Thioune's sons, comes in the night to report the news to his mother and to return Thioune's wedding ring to her. Through a flashback to the wedding, it is learned that the family is Christian rather than Muslim (the religion of the majority). One also learns that the son is lame; his lameness prefigures, as Pfaff describes it, the portrait of "a figuratively dismembered society handicapped by a limping dependent economy."[49] Allegory again provides Sembène with the means to connect different segments of his combined economic, social, and cultural concerns. The death of Thioune also introduces the disintegration of the traditional family and its economic and social effects on women. On the level of the diegesis as well as its theme, the announcement of the death introduces the enigma of the nature of Thioune's untimely death, an enigma that will take the entire film to be clarified. The cause of his death is buried like his body and will need to be exhumed.

The narrative centers on Thioune's erroneous burial in a Muslim cemetery and the attempts of the Christians to retrieve his body.[50] The idea for the narrative was derived from a newspaper article (much like Sembène's idea for his earlier *La noire de*). That the narrative is based

on an actual event recounted in a newspaper is also reminiscent of Ce-
sare Zavattini's claim that neorealism does not need elaborate plots
but can be based on a simple news story. In fact, another dimension of
the hybridity of Sembène's films derives from their fusion of actual
events and fiction based on neorealist modes of representation. Like
neorealism, the film's allegory will spin many threads out of this seemingly simple incident. Also like neorealism, the film relies on the dramas of everyday life. For example, Thioune's funeral early in the film
has the appearance of a serious but common event: a hearse bearing a
ribbon with "Nos condolences," the procession of mourners who
have come to express their respects to the widow, the presence of the
priest, Father Léon, and a discussion of Thioune's wishes to have a
Latin mass. This seriousness is finally undermined when it is learned
that the body has "disappeared." Now the family, including the son
who has returned from his home in Paris, and the entire village are involved in the attempts to retrieve the corpse. As in Sembène's earlier
film Ceddo, the religions of Senegal are represented as central to the
history of its cultural life, but the film reveals that this history has been
neither smooth nor unalloyed with political power. As in Ceddo, the
shape of and interactions among the various religions—Muslim,
Christian, and tribal—are due to the complexities of colonization, beginning first with colonization by Muslims and culminating later with
colonization by Christian Europe. Guelwaar thus inscribes the conflict
between these two religious groups in the film within a longer history;
an ironic strategy in that both are seen as the legacy of imperialism and
colonial power. The struggle to regain the body of Thioune thus trig-
gers the allegory, enabling the different economic, political, and social
levels to emerge. Religion becomes the film's vehicle for exploring political and economic betrayal.

The missing body of Thioune resonates not only on the level of the
body politic but on the level of the politics of the body. In relation to
the body politic, the Christians' attempt to recover the body constitutes their struggle to recover their collective political body. On the
level of the politics of the body, the missing body introduces the question of the body as a commodity. The commissioner tells Barthélémy,
another of Thioune's sons (N'Diawar Diop), that corpses are often
sold for fetishes. But the commodification of the body will become
even more explicit as the film explores the question of prostitution.
Early in the film we learn that Thioune's daughter, Sophie, earns her

livelihood as a prostitute in Dakar and that she has brought Hélène, one of her colleagues, home with her for the funeral. The lack of other employment has driven both women to prostitution in Dakar so that they can support themselves and their families. Thus the missing body generates an examination of values that includes the position of women's bodies as producers of value. The female body, like Thioune's Christian body, is linked to yet another issue in the film's examination of the economics of dependency: the question of foreign aid as the source of the deadly betrayal of Senegal by its local elites in complicity with some segments of the population. The issue is introduced innocuously enough by a sign on a truck that passes on the road. Gradually foreign aid comes to be connected to all the other issues in the film—social power, religion, the position of women, and political corruption on the part of the Muslim hierarchy in collusion with governmental authorities. Through another flashback the audience learns that Thioune had publicly denounced such aid as demeaning the people by making them dependent on foreign powers. Here again the connection is made between women's prostitution, the selling of the body of the nation, and the missing body of the dissenter Thioune. In confronting the police commissioner, Major Gora, Thioune had also complained about harassment of himself, his family, and the women in the community by government henchmen. Government harassment of oppositional figures is introduced even before we learn of the exact manner of Thioune's death.

*Guelwaar* is structured in a bifurcated fashion, alternating between scenes with the authorities in the various attempts to retrieve the body and scenes with the widow and the waiting villagers. This alternating structure allows for the introduction of different layers of information concerning the women, village life, and Thioune's background, all introducing different perspectives on power relations. While the women wait and mourn Thioune's death in the company of other villagers, the French-educated Barthélémy and the police commissioner travel to the village where Thioune has been buried in the Muslim cemetery. But the seemingly straightforward task of correcting the "administrative error" is not easily resolved, for the elders of that village refuse to believe that they have buried the wrong man. Rather than wanting to redress the problem, the Muslim elders insist that no error could have occurred and that it is their own man in the grave.

The question of property and identity in relation to the body is here made most explicit and generates Barthélémy's disgusted comment "What a country!" As a French national by adoption, he looks with disdain on the Senegalese, but his comments about the nature and degree of social corruption are penetrating. Initially, and not inappropriately, Major Gora describes him as "a black white man," a further index to the complex blurring of identities that the film entertains in its confounding of naming. Both Barthélémy and Major Gora are portrayed, as are the men in *Le Camp de Thiaroye,* as having a partial view of the social and cultural situation. In the film's portrayal of the history of colonialism and the persistence of its excesses and inequities in the present, the characters are themselves the repositories of the nature and effects of that history. Rather than relying on a spectacular mise-en-scène to convey past history, this film, like other Sembène films, relies on character, gesture, language, ritual, and clothing to dramatize the "presentness" of the past.

The Thioune family is itself a locus of the effects of colonialism. As Nagoy Marie, Thioune's wife (Astou N'Diaye), laments, she had seven children, only three of whom survived: a son, Barthélémy, who, like many young men, left Senegal for France; a daughter, Sophie, a prostitute; and Aloys, a handicapped son. In a scene that is visually reminiscent of a scene in *Un Chien Andalou* (1928) (and that hence reveals Sembène's awareness and uses of European cinema) in which a man's clothing—suit, shirt, tie, and shoes—is laid out on the bed like a fetish, Thioune's funeral gear is laid out in a similar fashion, and Nagoy addresses her complaints to it. The Western clothing is also a fetishistic reminder of the effects of Europeanization. The presence and use of both Wolof and French and the coexistence of tribal with Muslim and Christian rituals are further signs of the sheets of the past that are embedded in the present.

The culturally and economically precarious situation of women, also part of this problematic past, is reintroduced through Sophie's friend, Hélène. Wearing a European-style backless, tight-fitting dress, quite unlike the dresses worn by the other women, Hélène walks sinuously to a seat as the men gaze at her exposed body. The priest expresses his displeasure about the indecorousness of her clothes for a funeral, but then she tells him her history. Though educated, she tells him, she went to Dakar to find work and was unsuccessful. In order to support her brother in medical school, her younger brothers and sisters at home, and her father's religious pilgrimage, she became a regis-

tered prostitute. She lives with the threat of AIDS despite weekly exam-
inations. Her narrative encapsulates a number of issues central to the
film: the difficulty of surviving in the rural milieu, the precariousness
of life in the city, the lack of correspondence between education and
self-sufficiency, and the primary responsibilities that Senegalese
women must bear in maintaining their families. In this culture of dependence, they are forced to assume the financial burdens of the family and then are devalued for their work. Their condition is attributed
to the effects of foreign aid, which perpetuates the general system of
unemployment and the dependence on international capital that lines
the pockets of a few. Thus foreign aid is hardly altruistic. It signifies
something more than financial and alimentary support, constituting
the new form of colonialism whereby the African masses are kept in an
abject state of dependence, bereft of "self-sufficiency, and dignity."

From the vantage point of the Muslim village, the situation of
women is equally problematic. Their images are intercut with images
of hands shelling peanuts, the monoculture of the area and another
sign of dependence. The women are not privy to deliberations about
the mistaken burial though the man buried is purported by the village
elders to be the husband of two of them. As in *Xala,* which also explores polygamy, in *Guelwaar* we see a distinction between the two
Muslim wives that encodes different responses to the legacy of colonialism. One of the women, Aminta, the more traditional, counsels
resignation to the second wife, Oumy, who is more Westernized and
who announces that she would rather return to her village than marry.
(The man who offers her marriage is one with whom she had prior
adulterous relations.) She takes off her widow's clothing, picks up her
fashion magazines, and leaves. Familial relations are no more stable in
the Muslim village than in the Christian village.

More familial tensions become evident when Nagoy and the village
retinue arrive to reclaim Thioune's body. A flashback to a scene between Nagoy and Thioune reveals conflicts between the couple and
Nagoy's disaffection with the family. Nagoy complains about Sophie's
prostitution and woman's need for dignity. She insists that she would
rather live off charity than prostitution, a comment that Thioune
blithely dismisses: "Better a prostitute than a beggar." While he rails
about foreign aid, in his role as patriarch, Thioune does not confront
its debilitating effects in the domestic sphere and particularly on
women. Nor does Nagoy connect the problematic of woman's dignity

Thioune and Nagoy in Ousmane Sembène's *Guelwaar*. Courtesy of New Yorker Films.

to the demeaning role of charity. Both husband and wife dramatize the contradictions and limitations inherent in their situations, a situation that is the fruit of far-reaching economic and cultural changes over a long period of time and involving religion, the economics of dependence, the clash between tradition and modernity, and stark class oppositions.

The situation between Muslims and Christians worsens as the Muslims remain unwilling to cooperate with the Christians, presaging violence. In the midst of threats of a civil war, there is a flashback to Thioune's past that bears directly on the question of sexual politics. One of the Christian elders, Gor Mag, tells the story of Thioune's affair with a muezzin's wife. Disguised as a woman, Thioune would sneak into the Muslim village to have sex with her until the day he was caught and forced to run away stark naked. This episode offers more evidence of the politics of the body that the film explores to advantage. Sex, like death, levels difference, and Thioune has no more difficulty having relations with a woman of an opposing religion than any of the other men do—Christian or Muslim. In fact, like the other men, he has no qualms about engaging in adultery. Thus the seriousness of his Christian vows of monogamy—of religious vows in general—are also held up to question by the film. Pfaff describes this episode as typical of "situations a *griot* might use as comic relief in a pathetic or heroic story."[51] The "comic relief" that Pfaff refers to has serious implications. The issue of gender and sexual difference is central to *Guelwaar* and further dramatizes women's subordinate status. The narrator's allusion to "the weakness of the flesh" has a double meaning: It refers to men's sexuality as a substitute for power in the face of political impotence, and it also refers to death, exemplified by Thioune's rotting corpse disinterred by Biram, the imam. In a film whose conflicts rely on seemingly insurmountable religious and political differences, this reference to the weakness of the flesh acts as a reminder of sameness.

This scene and other scenes between Thioune and his wife undermine any notion of heroism—always undermined in Sembène's films—and contribute to a sense of the inevitable complicity, though not total debasement, of everyone living in a dependent culture. In the film's explorations of power, no character is left unscathed. Major Gora initially appears to be an indifferent bureaucrat, naive about the world outside of Senegal that Barthélémy describes to him. Gora does not seem at all sympathetic to the plight of Thioune's family—in fact, Barthélémy accuses him of favoring the Muslims. As a policeman Gora is involved in enforcing the laws of an inequitable society, yet the film also portrays his reliance on the law as instrumental in averting civil war and enabling a coming together of sorts between the antagonistic factions. In turn, Barthélémy "educates" Gora about international capital, telling him that despite the young French people who come to Senegal to help with harvests, French elites steal from the people and European banks misappropriate funds. Though their relationship begins antagonistically, the major and Barthélémy ultimately overcome their differences.

Like *Le Camp de Thiaroye, Guelwaar* probes history to understand difference. One of the Christian men asks his fellow villagers, "What is happening to our people?" Another responds that the people are "splitting apart." They shared similar origins, but "now the loss of tradition, of a common language, and the effects of the misappropriation of public funds" are all responsible for divisions. The question of complicity and betrayal on the part of the villagers comes to the foreground as the men castigate themselves for having kept silent while, to his detriment, Thioune condemned foreign aid. The role of "silence" adds another dimension to the question of responsibility. And as the men raise questions about the future, about what they will tell their

children—another link to the "legend of the twenty-first century"—
the importance of history and memory is reiterated but in the context
of a critical interrogation of events, tied to questions of language and
silence and to questions of power. When the mayor and the commissioner arrive to assess the situation and attempt to dissipate the conflict, they speak French, the official language of the bureaucracy and
the reminder of French hegemony. Major Gora speaks French to the
officials as he describes the state of affairs. Barthélémy also speaks
French, despite the fact that certain villagers express resentment about
the use of French rather than Wolof. Latin is introduced in the chanting by the women of the "Miserere" and in the allusions to the Latin
mass desired by Thioune. But the more profound political implications
of the language question have to do with the people's loss of voice and
with Thioune's punishment for speaking out.

At a ceremony celebrating the receipt of foreign aid, replete with
waving flags from European countries, Thioune attacks the concept of
foreign aid, introducing his critique in terms of language and silence.
He says: "We are a silent people, with no voice." At this point, the
mayor comes down from the platform and tells one of his henchmen
to "shut him up." The man responds, "He'll never speak again," and
later it is revealed that Thioune was silenced through murder, beaten
to death. Here memory comes into play, the recollection that the
mayor's actions are a reminder of the past, of the actions of former
colonizers. When cultural bribes fail, as in the form of aid, coercion
comes into play. Thioune is allowed to finish his speech, echoing other
African commentators on colonialism. He tells his audience that "this
negative state of affairs has been going on since Independence, and no
one has any dignity left," and that "the countries who send us aid,
laugh at us in their homes." In commonsensical terms, he stresses the
importance of self-reliance: "If you only keep taking from generation
to generation, people will only be able to say thank you." Ending on a
note of rage, he says, "This aid they're distributing to us will kill us. It
has killed all our dignity and pride. What shame! What humiliation!"

In his 1958 "Address on the Future of Africa," W. E. B. Du Bois,
warning in a similar vein about the importance of self-sufficiency, asked:

> Will you for temporary advantage—for automobiles, refrigerators, and
> Paris gowns—spend your income in paying interest on borrowed funds;
> or will you sacrifice your present comfort and the chance to shine before
> your neighbors in order to educate your children, develop such industry

as best serves the great mass of people and make your country strong in
ability, self-support, and self-defense? Such union of effort for strength
calls for sacrifice and self-denial, while the capital offered you at high
price by the colonial powers like Britain, Holland, Belgium, and the
United States will prolong fatal colonial imperialism, from which you
have suffered slavery, serfdom, and colonialism.[52]

In a similar vein, Julius K. Nyerere wrote:

Independence cannot be real if a nation depends upon gifts and loans
from another for its development. Even if there was a nation, or nations,
prepared to give us all the money we need for our development, it would
be improper for us to accept such assistance without asking ourselves
how much this would affect our independence and our very survival as
a nation.[53]

*Guelwaar* echoes these words, but its critique of foreign aid is not so
much a simple valorization of nationalism and Senegalese identity as a
harsh critique of foreign capital—both economic and cultural—which
masquerades in the guise of altruism and obscures the violence and
domination that lie beneath and reproduce the imperial "divide and
conquer" of the ruling elites, whose advantage lies in perpetuating religious, cultural, sexual, class, and racial conflicts. Again, the themes
in the film connect it to *Le Camp de Thiaroye*. *Guelwaar* also seems to
be intent on exposing the systemic violence of colonialism by stripping
away its benign appearance and revealing its destructiveness. Often in
the form of military aid, the "hand-outs [are offered] to corrupt oligarchies designed to ensure their loyalty."[54] And the film dramatizes
the corrupt nature of the local oligarchies and the massive cultural de-
moralization that a lack of self-sufficiency generates.

Despite their focus on failure—the suicide of Diouanna in *La Noir
de*, the shooting of the tribesmen in *Emitai*, the killing of the infantry-
men in *Le Camp de Thiaroye*, the brutal murder of Thioune in *Guelwaar*—Sembène's films also dramatize resistance even where that
resistance seems to have a limited effect in the short run. The examination of past and present failure is a lesson for the future. In *Guelwaar*, the outspoken role of Thioune dramatizes this lesson, as do
Major Gora's staunch defense of the law in averting civil war and especially the imam Biram's stance against the members of the Muslim
village and insistence on the opening of the grave and the return of the
Christian corpse. Biram aligns himself with the Christian woman
Nagoy, and in response to her comment "We share the same sorrow,"

the imam responds, "We all have to die." He opens the grave, covers the corrupted and ill-smelling body in dignified fashion, and, after the removal of the corpse, utters the proverbial wisdom of common sense: "When a vulture attacks your enemy's body, remember it might be you. Chase it away." Not only is this commonsensical language geared to a mode of building solidarity, but it also flies in the face of traditional notions of submission to the will of God. It can be compared to Thioune's earlier comment to the major that just because he is a Christian does not mean that he will turn the other cheek. The use of proverbs and clichés is another strategy for reappropriating lessons from the past—but with a difference—in the interests of change.

The final procession of the villagers with the shrouded body of Thioune shows another act of resistance. As a foreign aid truck appears, the cross carried by the young men of the Christian village is passed from one to another until it finally arrives, hand by hand, in the priest's arms. The youths run and rip open the sacks of flour and sugar, saying, "We can't grow up and live as beggars." Nagoy refuses to stop them, and when they are finished the funeral procession continues until, in typical Sembène fashion, there is a freeze frame as Thioune's words about foreign aid and cultural shame continue on the sound track, along with the singing of a song in Wolof.

## The Pedagogy of the Past

Sembène's films are a critique of the excesses of monumentalism and antiquarianism and a critique of forgetfulness and repetition. In the context of critical history, the films are wary of the dangers of being paralyzed by judgment and unable to assess past actions. Like Gramsci's writings on common sense and folklore, the films are empathetic to, though critical of, formulaic forms of knowledge. They dramatize the persistence of folklore in the light of the concern to interrogate its strengths and blind spots as a survival strategy of subaltern life. The analysis of power is attentive to the dissemination of power throughout the society, thus resisting a form of melodramatic scenario that polarizes and hierarchizes individuals and groups. While they are sensitive to pain and suffering, to the drama of loss, the texts are not trapped in an elegiac mode, mindful of the dangers of mourning that signal an unexamined relation to the past. Cognizant of the ways that history can be reduced to nostalgia, Sembène takes situations that could be treated melodramatically and uses history to question easy solutions, narratives of individual success, and binary thinking.

In tracing the causes and effects of colonialism and neocolonialism, Sembène's works interrogate the cultural forces that inhere in economic and political relations of power: the role of intellectuals; language; familial, sexual, and gender relations; commodity fetishism, and religion. The concern with history is not to reproduce factual "truth" but to explore how and for whom truth is constituted and the destructive consequences of relying on received knowledge. The films do not offer a unified version of the past; instead they present the past in an allegorical fashion to offer a striated rendition of history and memory. Through allusion to different cinematic styles and through the adoption of a broad range of cultural forms, including storytelling, traditional and popular music, dance, and photography, his films can probe different layers of the past. His cinema combines storytelling and essay. As essays, his films address complex issues of cultural politics and of postcoloniality involving the history of failure and the hope of resistance. The affect resides in Sembène's empathy for the people in the face of the exploitation, while he castigates them satirically for their failures. Resistance, though ending in death for the protagonists, is projected onto the survivors, the African and international audiences who are invited to reflect on the history of colonialism and its survival in neocolonialism.

# 2

## "Which Way Is West?": Americanism, History, and the Italian Western

"A historiography could be imagined," writes Nietzsche, "which had in it not a drop of common empirical truth and yet could lay claim to the highest degree of objectivity. . . . When the past speaks it always speaks as an oracle: only if you are an architect of the future and know the present will you understand it."[1] Nietzsche's comment diverts us from an emphasis on fidelity to fact to an examination of the ways in which knowledge and power are inextricable from historical representation. The investment in the past is related to the power to name, to determine what counts as history, and hence to identify differences between dominance and subordination, between inclusion and exclusion. The recording of the past is implicated in struggles over hegemony, legitimating the present in the light of the past. Nietzsche offers a position from which to distinguish competing versions of history.

From their different positions, Nietzsche and Gramsci chart forms of knowledge about the past and about identity that are heterogeneous and multifaceted analyses of cultural, political, and economic determinations. Their strands entail acknowledging what has seemingly been forgotten but remains residually in common sense, its contradictions evident in the textual excesses generated by ellipses, disjunctions, and juxtapositions that expose the impossibility of producing a coherent narration. The "excess" of historicizing, identified by Nietzsche as a surplus of attachment to the past, forecloses conditions of possibility for the present. The excess is dependent on strongly affective (e.g., melodramatic) relations to the past located in gendered, national, familial, and sexual representations.[2] Reliant on an established psychosocial lexicon, the melodramatic strategies of the historical film are both familiar and strange. Whereas the conventions of melodrama depend on a familiar affective relationship to history and memory, achieved through an often operatic valorization of image and sound over narrative, the spectacle can call attention to excess and frustrate strict causality.

67

Excess is detected in common sense in its unsettling penchant for anastomosing systems of thought from the past and the present. In its familiar dimensions, it draws on identity and experience; in its unfamiliar aspect it calls attention to ambiguity and undecidability. Commenting on the nature of excess in relation to the historical film *Ivan the Terrible*, Kristin Thompson writes: "The viewer is no longer constrained by conventions of reading to find a meaning or theme within the work as a solution to a sort of puzzle that has a correct answer."[3] Disruptive uses of image and of sound make evident the need to draw on different and unfamiliar strata of information that unevenly and obliquely force connections between past and present: "To a large extent, the spectator's ability to notice excess is dependent on his or her training in viewing films."[4] From my perspective, the problem is less one of the spectator's formal competence than of how excess is acknowledged and experienced. In Gramsci's words: "The popular element 'feels' but does not always know or understand; the intellectual element 'knows' but does not understand and in particular does not always feel."[5] This division between feeling and knowing is crucial for an understanding of how economic and cultural value—beyond quantitative economic measurement—relies on and encodes difference and sameness. For some viewers and in some instances, excess as affect is an inherent dimension of involvement in a commonsensical conception of the world that does not appear as surplus. For other viewers or for the same viewers in relation to certain texts, excess is a telltale sign of the institutional knowledges shared by different dominant and subaltern groups. This commonsensical knowledge—neither true nor false and productive of consensus and instrumental in survival—is never totally hidden. Its elusive and contradictory nature enables it to circulate in popular culture, appealing to disparate audiences.

More than mere ritual and cliché (though it is that too), common sense is a philosophy of history and of action, though not directly perceived as philosophical because of its reiterative, seemingly self-evident, and affective character. Since there is in Gramsci's terms no such thing as a nonintellectual, the critical project becomes one of understanding how and in whose interests common sense is constituted as history. Moreover, since common sense implies consent as opposed to coercion, it seems to promise certain material and psychic effects. It cannot appear both coercive and appropriate to action. In effect, since common sense presents itself as based on shared experience and pragmatic evidence of prior efficacy, it is regarded as a trustworthy basis for knowledge.

Common sense (or its simulacrum) as an instrument of hegemony aids the regrouping of social and political forces in the interests of restoration and containment, providing a sense of stable identification and a semblance of unity, but that unity constitutes "domination without that of leadership: dictatorship without hegemony,"[6] a situation characteristic of the Risorgimento and of fascism. The character of repetition discussed by Marx in *The Eighteenth Brumaire of Louis Napoleon* is a crucial element in common sense and is germane to the adaptability of common sense to a wide array of situations whose outcome (if not whose circumstances) is made to appear to be the same.

In this chapter, the popular cinema represented by the Italian "spaghetti western" will serve as a test case of the common sense of folklore and of folklore as history. Through an examination of the work of Sergio Leone and expressly through a close analysis of his film *Duck, You Sucker* (*Giù la testa*, released also in the United States as *A Fistful of Dynamite*, 1971), I inquire into common sense notions of Americanism and the role they have played in the Italian cinema of the 1960s. This chapter is not a study of the influences on the Italian western, especially not of Hollywood auteurs such as John Ford and their impact on the Italian western; nor is it a study of the genre. Such issues have been abundantly debated in the critical literature. I explore how Leone's films anastomose various textual strands, becoming "something else." In the uses of the United States and the trope of "the West," his films appear to be addressing a fusion of Europe and the United States (akin to Gramsci's discussions of Americanism) rather than creating a binary opposition between the two or subjecting one to the other. In relation to the question of nation formation, his spaghetti westerns reveal that despite their geographic and cultural boundedness, most modern discourses of nation are unstable constructions.

Common sense illuminates specific problems endemic to Leone's films: conflicts between different moments and versions of capitalism, relations between country and city, the nature of masculinity, the problematic of familial relations, the position of intellectuals and the nature of received knowledge, and the complex character of folklore (masquerading as fairy tale). Leone's treatment of "the West" blurs geographic boundaries between Europe and the United States, creating a more fluid sense of cultural transmission and of the past. Factors that complicate the cultural and historical role of Americanism in his films are the literal traffic between Europe and the United States in terms of demographic mobility entailed in the migration of peoples, capital, and cultural forms. The mobility that characterizes the films exceeds literal geography, becoming another instance of the instability of categories.

In examining the strategies that the films adopt in their violation of boundaries, I single out as especially symptomatic of common sense and folklore their incorporation of melodramatic, operatic, and comedic forms. My overarching assumption is that historical representation is less a matter of documenting than of identifying the fragmentary and even opposing elements that constitute a commonsensical conception of the past.

## Americanism and Fordism

In the *Prison Notebooks*, Gramsci devotes a series of notes to the role that U.S. capitalism and its corresponding cultural forms had begun to play in European culture. He was concerned with identifying a "new type of worker arising from the penetration of Fordism into the European context." He writes: "In America rationalisation has determined the need to elaborate a new type of man suited to the new type of work and production process."[7] Characteristic of Gramsci's nonreductive mode of simultaneously treating questions of capitalism and culture, he does not focus on a one-to-one relationship between base and superstructure; nor does he focus on the sole determining effects of economics, of value as money. His notion of capital includes cultural capital and what Gayatri Spivak has described as "affective value." Considerations of value are inextricable from representation in terms of the ways that value is constituted, affirmed, legitimated, and circulated through sexuality. Gramsci is at pains to point out in his notes that the "rationalisation of production," identified with Americanism, is intimately related to existing and possible changes for the "question of sex."[8] Of the elements that Gramsci singles out as the possible conditions of Americanism and Fordism, sexuality plays a major role, and he conjoins it to the economic dimensions of social reproduction that "operate within the smallest economic units, such as the family."[9]

Most striking in his discussions of Americanism is the importance he places on body politics: the effects of new forms of social life on the body and reciprocally the effects of new and different bodily constraints and possibilities on social life. His discussions of the body are not only manifest in his description of the new forms of work under Fordism in contrast to older patterns of production, but they are also apparent in his descriptions of increasing expressions of mechanization, antagonism, and brutality to which the social changes give rise. Thus he is concerned with patterns not only of femininity but also of masculinity. In his notes on rural and urban familial life, he notes the presence of such phenomena as "sex as sport," "animality," divorce, prostitution, and the rise in beauty competitions, which he compares to putting women up for auction. His interests in identifying sexual practices are tied to his examination of the different directions that culture and capital can take.

One means of attempting to ameliorate political, cultural, and economic crises is "passive revolution": revolution from above that restores the old order with minor revisions, giving the appearance of change. Another is the creation of a revolution that capitalizes on social antagonisms and on crisis to radically alter class relations and the relationship of the state to civil society. In both cases, Gramsci recognized that Americanism and Fordism were gradually introducing changes in the relationship of the state to civil society that required analysis. On the role of the state in relation to Americanism, he writes:

> Americanisation requires a particular environment, a particular social structure (or at least a determined intention to create it) and a certain type of State. This State is the liberal State, not in the sense of free-trade liberalism or of effective political liberty, but in the more fundamental sense of free initiative and of economic individualism, which with its own means, on the level of 'civil society,' through historical development, itself arrives at a régime of industrial concentration and monopoly.[10]

Gramsci adds that it is "claimed that Americanism is 'mechanicist,' crude, brutal—'pure action' in other words—and it is contrasted with tradition."[11] Dissatisfied with this type of reductionism, he insists that this "philosophy of action" requires further exploration and understanding. Gramsci writes: "[N]o attempt has been made to apply to Americanism Gentile's little formula about 'philosophy which is not expressed in verbal formulations, but is affirmed in action.'"[12] In Americanism and tradition Gramsci finds a contradiction in "the difference between real action on the one hand, which modifies in an essential way," and "on the other hand the gladiatorial futility which is self-declared action but modifies only the word, not things, the external gesture and not the man inside."13

Americanism is not an unalloyed evil destroying the heart of European culture. Rather, Gramsci sees possibilities introduced by Americanism for addressing the ancient and ritualized structures of European society and its potential for making manifest latent antagonisms in social and political life. His concern with a rereading of the philosophical implications of action is related especially to anti-intellectualism, to the exaltation of action for its own sake that characterized fascism, and thus he seeks distinctions that can help account for cultural changes that are more explicit in charting departures from traditional practices. His assessment of tradition and modernity—intrinsic to an analysis of Americanism and Fordism—is not binary. He is not positing cataclysmic cultural differences. Americanism has never been totally divorced from European civilization:

> What we are dealing with is an organic extension and an intensification of European civilisation, which has simply acquired a new coating in the American climate. Pirandello's observation on the opposition that Americanism encounters in Paris (but in Le Creusot?) and on the immediate welcome that it supposedly had in Berlin proves, in any case, that the difference between it and "Europeanism" is not one of nature but of degree.14

Americanism played an important role in the interwar and wartime periods in which he was writing. His identification of the merging of U.S. and European cultures in varying degrees is dependent on the role of modernization and its relation to new capital formations. Gramsci's comments on Americanism have extraordinary relevance for understanding the phenomenon of fascism as a passive revolution. As a reconsolidation of the dominant ruling groups, fascism created a "philosophy of action" based on the promise, not the actualization, of change in the name of both tradition and modernity. This philosophy of action was scornful of intellectuals and of theory, extolling (as exemplified in *1860*) spontaneity, nationalism, and action for its own sake. Thus Gramsci rejects the utopian dimensions of Americanism and Fordism while at the same time insisting on understanding what they have come to signify.

Americanism as a philosophy of action is germane to the ways the

Italian cinema has produced forms reliant on and ambivalent toward North American culture, specifically to representations of the state and civil society. The trope of Americanism is useful for probing the contradictory nature of this reliance on action and its destabilizing and transforming effects in the Italian and European context. The pre-occupations (if not the actual figure) of Gramsci are embedded in much of postwar Italian cinema and is evident in the works of such filmmakers as Pasolini, Visconti, and the Taviani brothers.[15] The issue that seems to recur most in the various cinematic dramatizations of Italian history, especially in films that treat the Risorgimento, fascism, and World War II, is the role of intellectuals in Italian cultural and political life deriving from distinctions that Gramsci makes between traditional and organic intellectuals. The films interrogate the role of common sense and folklore in their treatment of Italian history (e.g., *The Night of the Shooting Stars,* 1982, and *Fiorile,* 1993) as a means to understanding how, by whom, and in whose interests knowledge is disseminated. Prominent in so many films from the post–World War II era to the present is the theme of betrayal of revolution. Gramsci's complex comments on the nature of subalternity and his refusal to romanticize the conditions of subaltern life are also germane to many historical representations—Leone's *Duck, You Sucker,* the Tavianis' *Allonsanfan* (1974), Pasolini's *Salò* (1975), Bertolucci's *1900* (1976), and Ermanno Olmi's *The Tree of Wooden Clogs* (1978), to name only a few films.

If one goes further back to the Italian films of the 1930s—to the work of such directors as Mario Camerini and Ferdinando Maria Poggioli, for example—certain concerns are evident that do not have a Marxist orientation but that nonetheless corroborate problematics relating to Americanism: the precarious relations between northern and southern Italy, conflicting attitudes toward modernity and tradition, and a consistent folklore about subaltern life, which can take the form of populism and containment or can suggest antagonistic class relations. The ambiguous role of intellectuals is seen in such historical films as Blasetti's *1860,* which dramatizes one form of the "philosophy of action" to which Gramsci links Americanism. If common sense and folklore in these films is not treated in the self-conscious mode of later filmmakers (such as the Tavianis or Leone), it is nevertheless the basis for the history that is enacted in earlier Italian films.

## History in and of the Italian Cinema

Putting the decade of neorealism aside, an overview of the Italian cinema reveals the popularity of the historical film and a penchant for representations of history. From biblical epics, costume dramas, Roman spectacles and biopics to the numerous films that have sought to unravel the nature and effects of the fascist era and of World War II, historical concerns have animated Italian film forms, and historical genres have constituted a staple of Italian cinema. The appearance of the Italian western in the 1960s on the heels of the resurgence of Roman and biblical spectacles is yet another manifestation of a return to history in filmmaking and to a form of genre production, despite neorealist antipathy to this form of filmmaking.

The neorealists were a conduit for the dissemination of a stringent critique of existing film production. Their film aesthetic was geared toward a clearing away of fascist cultural production and toward introducing what they regarded as more realistic and hence anti-hegemonic styles and themes into a cinema that exemplified for them the excesses and perniciousness of fascist cultural production. In their quest for an alternative cinema, they turned to writers and critics whom they believed had a concern for the ethical and everyday dimension of reality in relation to politics and representation.[16] Certain critics and filmmakers would cite precursors in the verismo writings of Giovanni Verga in early cinema, in such films as *Sperduti nel buio* (Nino Martoglio, 1914), and in the writings of the Americans John Dos Passos, James M. Cain, William Faulkner, and Ernest Hemingway. In seeking "an alternative to the clichés and falsehoods of the Fascist film industry, [they] found in the Sicily of verismo the authenticity so lacking in contemporary cultural models."[17] Despite stylistic differences, there were common points of reference for those who claimed a neorealist position, and the commonality resided in a commitment to a moral and ethical stance, to social change, and to exposing contemporary social antagonisms. The neorealists' hostility to the cultural products of the fascist years is understandable in the light of their own commitment to what they believed should be new and different attitudes toward cultural representation. In certain ways, their dismissal of the work of the prior twenty years was too monolithic, occluding an understanding of the social and political problems they sought to address.

Nonetheless, neorealism as a worldwide phenomenon made a lasting impact on cinematic and television production, and an examination of the genre cinema of the 1960s—including the Italian western—reveals traces of neorealism in style and in social concerns. The decline of interest in neorealist subjects by the mid-1950s signaled economic and political changes for the Italian cinema that are crucial to understanding the work of directors such as Leone. But given the antagonism of the neorealists to the Italian genre film, which was associated with the fascist era—with escapism and with legitimation of the regime[18]—what accounts for the appearance of genre films after the hiatus of a decade? Do they signify a forgetfulness of the past?

Answers to these questions may be sought in the postwar settlement: the victory of the Christian Democrats, the heightened "Americanization" of Italian culture and of European culture in general, increased industrialization, and the growth of consumer capitalism. In part because of the Cold War and the economic and political intervention of the United States, Europe underwent an economic transformation from a devastated wartime economy to the economic miracle of the 1950s. Paul Ginsborg writes that "an extraordinary process of transformation . . . was taking place in the everyday life of Italians—in the culture, family life, leisure-time activities, consumption habits, even the language they spoke and their cultural mores."[19] And of changes in the Italian cinema, Peter Bondanella writes: "The decade between 1958 and 1968 may in retrospect be accurately described as the golden age of Italian cinema, for in no other single period was the artistic quality, the international prestige, or its economic strength so consistently high."[20] Bondanella attributes this boom to economic problems in Hollywood that resulted in the reduction of the number of Hollywood films exported to Italy. While neorealism downplayed the star system, this period saw the international popularity of such Italian stars as Monica Vitti, Sophia Loren, Gina Lollobrigida, and Marcello Mastroianni and of such directors as Federico Fellini, Michelangelo Antonioni, and Luchino Visconti.

To many, neorealism may in retrospect seem to have been more inclined toward a melodramatic than a comic mode with its portraits of the effects of fascist bureaucracy, war, and rural and urban poverty, but it was not without its comic side. Ernesto G. Laura cites the popularity of Luigi Zampa's films, the performance of such comedians as Totò and Erminio Macario, and in later decades the rise to popularity of comic actors such as Alberto Sordi, Nino Manfredi, and Ugo Tognazzi. Moreover, Laura reminds the reader that Italian comedy was closely tied to historical subjects: "[I]n the Italian cinema, so bound up with contemporary events, a fondness for looking back and for resorting to humor to recount stories of distant centuries pops up frequently."[21] This comic style is manifest from the 1950s through the 1960s, from *Il cappotto* (1953) to *L'armata Brancaleone* (1966) and *Brancaleone alle crociate* (1969). This was also a time when films such as Ettore Scola's *We All Loved Each Other Very Much* (1974) reflected (in retrospect) on a distancing from social commitment characteristic of the immediate postwar era and took a critical, even cynical, look at the growing consumerism of Italian society, not dissimilar to what was happening throughout the rest of Europe and the United States.

The 1950s and 1960s films, whether comic or melodramatic, addressed contemporary preoccupations with urban anomie, industrial—not wartime—blight, familial disintegration, divorce, marriage, and new sexual mores. In commenting on this time, Pierre Sorlin asserts that filmmakers found "no necessity . . . to bring in social issues since neorealism had already introduced them to the cinema."[22] This does not mean that there was an abandonment of "social issues" in the cinemas of Italy and Great Britain. There was abundant evidence of an ongoing investment in social concerns in the British "social problem" films as well as in the Italian historical films and spaghetti westerns of this era, but the treatment of political and social issues in the films was much less direct and much less melodramatic, even antimelodramatic. The texts were hybrid and often self-reflexive in their use of preexisting cinematic genres and forms, offering themselves as "artificial creations rather than windows opened on reality."[23] Many of the films straddled the critical divide between auteurist, New Wave forms of filmmaking and popular cinema. However, in his concern to move away from the exclusive critical preoccupation with individual national cinema production so as to identify concerns and problems common to European cinemas, Sorlin pays scant attention to the character and impact of such popular forms as the historical "peplum" films set in ancient Greece and Rome and the highly successful European western, thus perpetuating the same critical neglect that has characterized critical relations to the popular cinema.

This time period was rich in films with historical settings that drew on such diverse contexts as ancient Rome, the Middle Ages, and the eighteenth and nineteenth centuries. Italian modernist filmmakers, such as Fellini in his *Satyricon* (1969), also offered versions of history in film. The spaghetti western appeared at this moment. The popularity of the western form began slowly and crested in the late 1960s and early 1970s. Peter Bondanella writes that before Leone's *A Fistful of Dollars* (1964), "some 25 westerns had been produced at Cinecittà."[24] Though largely associated with Leone, Italian westerns were also made by such filmmakers as Sergio Corbucci, Sergio Sollima, and Tonino Valerii, among others. An extensive discussion and analysis of the individuals involved and of the films, their modes of production, themes, style, and politics can be found in Christopher Frayling's *Spaghetti Westerns*.[25] The Italian western can be characterized by its eclecticism—it draws on different genres, on different national film traditions, and on international casts—by its combination of comedy and melodrama, and by its innovative approach to the cinematic medium. According to Frayling, who acknowledges and attempts to account for this eclecticism, an understanding of international as well as national film culture is essential for an understanding of the films. Leone himself has cited the importance of such films as *Yojimbo* (1961), *Sanjuro* (1962), *Shane* (1953), and *Vera Cruz* (1954) to his work.[26]

One layer of history subtending the Italian western involves the concept of "westernness," that is, what the designation "the West" signifies, how this signification circulates throughout European and Asian culture, and how it inflects and is inflected by other indigenous forms. From their earliest manifestation in the silent era, the historical film in general and the western in particular have been closely linked to nation formation, and this link persists even when the uses of history are aimed at undermining discourses of nation. In the analysis of the impact of Americanism on European culture today, there are two major conflicting positions that can account for this phenomenon. The weighty presence of U.S. films and television can be taken as prime evidence for the ubiquitous and devastating nature of North American economic and cultural imperialism. Alternatively, Americanism can be interpreted as a selective appropriation of the host culture by the foreign culture for its own uses. Americanism can signify, for better or for worse, the hybridity attendant on an increasing global interdependence that reveals a historical and hence changing relation to the circulation of capital.

In an examination of the culture of Americanism, it is necessary to understand its "third meaning," that is, not as a signification of the geographic United States or Europe but as a phenomenon that has existed since the turn of the century and that has undergone various permutations. For example, in the 1880s Nietzsche wrote: "There is something of the American Indians, something of the ferocity peculiar to the Indian blood, in the American lust for gold, and the breathless haste with which they work—the distinctive vice of the new world— [which] is beginning to infect old Europe with its ferocity and is spreading a lack of spirituality like a blanket."[27] Nietzsche's comments reveal, as do Gramsci's later (if in a different vein), that Americanism was a force to be reckoned with in accounting for changes in European culture. It is significant too that Nietzsche cites the lust for gold (presumably referring to the Gold Rush of 1849) as an important factor in Americanism. Nietzsche's comments, in conjunction with Frayling's discussion of the importance of the influential writings of Karl May, foreground two themes that are part of the European construction of North America: that of the "noble savage" and that of "Gold."[28] That the themes persist is evident in the German sauerkraut westerns of the late 1950s and 1960s.

Americanism has been an integral part of Italian history, bound to the effects of waves of immigration, starting in the middle of the nineteenth century, from Italy to the United States and Latin America. Immigration was intimately tied to long-standing economic and political problems in Italy that were exacerbated by the Risorgimento, relating especially to stark inequities between northern and southern Italy.[29] The move westward by Italians in the nineteenth century, first from Abruzzi and Calabria and later from Sicily, carried with it profound changes for those regions and for the families that it often parted (but who might still be privy to news from across the ocean). And the United States figures prominently in Italian literature and cinema. (Conversely, Italy has also figured prominently in Hollywood and in U.S. literature.) The drama of emigration figures in such films as Guido Brignone's *Passaporto rosso* (1935). The 1930s comedies of Mario Camerini contain American themes and characters. Postwar dramatizations of Americans in Italy are prominent in films by Roberto Rossellini and Vittorio de Sica, among many others.

More recently, the Tavianis' *Kaos* (1984) and *Good Morning, Babylon* (1987) address the effects of emigration. It is not at all unusual or surprising that the Italian westerns have assimilated and appropriated Americanism to their own ends. There is a congenial union between the themes and styles attributed to the North American western, involving the North American continent both north and south of the U.S.–Mexican border, and portrayals of Italian life—in representations of the *Mezzogiorno* in particular. The emphasis on landscape and on demographic mobility—the movement from east to west—the focus on brutality, brigandage, revenge, and criminality, the decomposition of villages, the ambiguous role of the Catholic church, and the stark competition for economic power are all conditions that inhere in Italian folklore but that can be grafted onto prevailing representations of Americanism. (This grafting is not restricted to the western genre but is also evident in the Italian-American crime film.)

Frayling describes Leone's uses of history as "populist rather than materialist,"[30] though not didactic. Leone's films are engaged with the subject of historicizing. The role that history plays resides in the complex ways the films draw on an orchestration of European, U.S., and Italian folklore, on Hollywood film, and on earlier and contemporary Italian cinema, bespeaking the changing nature of spectatorship and patterns of consumption. The hallmark of the films is their heterogeneity, their hybridity, and their popular qualities. Pamela Falkenburg, in writing on *Once upon a Time in the West* (1969), has insisted on the openness of the text: "The openness of *Once Upon a Time in the West* is perhaps most evident in its intertextuality. . . . However, rather than serving as an occasion for an analysis of the ununifiable heterogeneity and the fragmented multiplicity of the textuality of *Once Upon a Time in the West*, this openness is seized upon only in order to give it a unitary reading."[31] In her effort to maintain multiplicity and openness of meaning, Falkenburg would resist the unitary naming of a text as populist or materialist as she would resist assigning it an origin. Her argument against totalizing is a cautionary note about historicism with its emphasis on teleology, coherence, and foundations. The emphasis on the fragmentary and provisional nature of textuality is useful in trying to reconfigure the historical and social contradictions that unitary readings tend to foreclose. Leone himself has articulated his position concerning politics and representation: "We have no right to prick the political conscience of our contemporaries. We are not *magisters*. The films we make ought to make people think. We are professional 'exciters.' But we are not directors of conscience. The audience should be allowed to draw their own conclusions."[32] Contrary to reductive notions of spectatorship, the "audience" is not a monolith, and its members will draw what they can or what they desire from the texts. Leone's comments acknowledge his recognition that audiences cannot be coerced into responding properly, but the reaction against tendentiousness can be construed as a reaction not against politics or history but against the imposition of forms of historicism and forms of politics. Hence there seems to be—again referring to Gramsci—a different notion of pedagogy at work through Leone's films as social text. This pedagogy entails a more reciprocal and heuristic relation to the spectator. The uses of history are not fixed but become the pre-text to a narrativization and philosophizing in nonpolemic and interrogative fashion. In this context, Gramsci blurs the boundaries between philosophy and history. He writes: "The philosophy of an age is not the philosophy of this or that philosophy, of this or that group of intellectuals, of this or that broad section of the popular masses. It is a process of combination of all these elements."[33]

## Leone Alias "Bob Robertson": Which Way Is West?

Born in Naples in 1929, Sergio Leone came to cinema by way of a family that was professionally involved in the cinema. His mother was a film actress; his father, Vincenzo Leone, a director, remembered mostly for his silent films under the name of Roberto Roberti, though he did direct a handful of sound films. The actress Carla del Poggio recalls seeing the young Sergio Leone following his father around on the set of *La bocca sulla strada* (1941), which also starred the popular actor Armando Falconi.[34] In the silent era, the elder Leone had worked on several films with the famous diva Francesca Bertini. He later ran afoul of the fascist bureaucracy, forcing him and his family into rustication for a period of time. This memory of fascism was to resurface in the films of his son Sergio, as well as in the films of Sergio's contemporaries.

According to the actor Aldo Fabrizzi, Sergio Leone's first work in cinema in the 1940s was as assistant to well-known directors such as Mario Bonnard.[35] Leone also worked with such popular directors of the time as Mario Camerini and Carmine Gallone. In the post–World War II period, when neorealism was still in full sway, reaching audiences that the filmmakers of the *Ventennio,* the two decades of fascism, could only strive for but never realize in their attempts to garner international acclaim, Leone acted in a bit part in *The Bicycle Thief.* However, his career was to move not toward acting but toward directing. After apprenticing himself to various Italian directors in the 1950s and working in various capacities as an assistant to Hollywood directors, he turned to directing his own films; he worked on about fifty films in a supportive capacity until 1959, helping to direct such historical spectacles as *The Last Days of Pompeii* (1959), *The Colossus of Rhodes* (1960), and *Sodom and Gomorrah* (1962), all inexpensive costume films that featured international casts and abundant physical action. The films, based either on biblical themes or on ancient Greece or Rome, seemed to be a throwback to earlier Italian silent film spectacles such as Mario Caserini's *The Last Days of Pompeii* (1913) and Giovanni Pastrone's *Cabiria* (1913), with such heroes as Ursus and Maciste, and to Hollywood-type Cecil B. DeMille epics. In fact, the films were closer to *Ben Hur* (1959) and *Spartacus* (1960) in their dramatization of power conflicts between tyrannical figures and the social groups they seek to exploit. In this critically neglected genre,[36] the protagonist as outsider—as Jew, as slave, or as both—works to solidify the embattled community in its fight against hostile forces. The preoccupation of the films with power, masculinity, and greed is in many ways related to the themes of many other Italian and European melodramatic and comic films of the era, and it certainly comes to inflect the Italian western.

The popular films of the era, including the western, share a preoccupation with history, adventure, and masculine derring-do. They are also similar in their use of an international cast of stars (especially lesser-known Hollywood actors and stars whose careers are in decline), their inexpensive mode of production, and their preoccupation with physical movement; crowd scenes, acrobatics, choreography, violence, and fistfights. The films emphasized the conflict between "insiders" and "outsiders," with insiders representing institutionalized authority, and outsiders, the struggle for freedom and recognition. The films are intertextual, drawing on Roman, biblical, and North American history. They make a link with the popular cinema of the past—including silent adventure films—in their narratives, styles, and types of characters, which are altered to suit contemporary audiences. In the multilingual nature of the personnel, in their use of international casts, dubbing, and location settings all over the world, the films signaled the increased internationalization of filmmaking and Americanism as the metaphor for globalization. This globalization went beyond the actual mechanics of assembling the films to shared concerns across national boundaries: the preoccupation with historical representation, the cultural merging of East and West on the level of cinematic forms, a greater recognition of cultural interdependency, and a recognition of mass powerlessness. Before 1968, it is possible to see in the films a commonality of antagonisms toward prevailing power structures, a concern with militarism and its deleterious effects, and a mistrust of state structures.

The Italian westerns represented trends in cinematic representation that were taking place on a worldwide scale. In the post–World War II era, the Japanese made inroads into the West with the films of Akira Kurosawa and later Yasujiro Ozu. Popular Japanese science fiction films also crossed international boundaries. The genre system that had been associated with so many popular national cinemas, from Hollywood and Great Britain to Japan and India, was undergoing a transformation because of economic, cultural, and political conditions. The old forms were being injected with more social (though not necessarily revolutionary) content. "Art" forms were contesting with popular forms, and a new form—a hybrid—was emerging that drew on both art and popular cinema. Not only did genre boundaries become blurred, but the images of old established stars gave way to new and different national and international icons (as we shall see with the stars that emerged from the Italian westerns such as Clint Eastwood). Thus the filmmaking of this era reveals that "the West" is no longer the United States; rather, Americanism is a phenomenon that is larger than the geographic and cultural boundaries of the United States and its Cold War domination, coming to represent worldwide transformations and conflicts. The uses of history in that era—whether of feudal Japan, the India of the zamindars, ancient Rome, or the American West—signal the contest over domination.

When Sergio Leone and his team of actors, musicians, camera persons, and technicians undertook the series of Italian westerns that were to make such an impact on popular filmmaking, they were not working without precedent. They were operating within a cultural climate congenial to the themes and styles of their work.

## He Went Thataway: The Form and Style of Leone's Italian Westerns

The western is a literary and cinematic form that has received a lot of commentary in American Studies and more recently in film studies. Like the treatment of much popular and mass culture, the attitudes toward history represented by writers on the western have been problematic. If there is a common denominator among the various discussions of the western, the commonality resides in the persistence of an adherence to seminal texts that treat the western as mythological discourse, valorizing, in one form or another, such works as Henry Nash Smith's *Virgin Land,* Frederick Jackson Turner's essays on the frontier, and lesser-cited but parallel works such as Leo Marx's *The Machine in the Garden* and R. W. B. Lewis's *The American Adam.*[37]

In the influential studies of the film western—such as Jim Kitses's *Horizons West* and Will Wright's *Six Guns and Society*—mythology has not disappeared but the western has been subjected to the rigors of structuralist analysis, which schematizes and codifies elements of the narrative according to the variant expressions of myth and to the concept of genre.[38] Nonetheless, the status of the discourse of history haunts discussions of the western, revealing, as with other forms of representation, the current crisis of historicizing. In George Fenin's and William Everson's study of the western, there is a bifurcation between the history of the settlement of the American frontier and the mythology to which it gave rise. Fenin and Everson complain that "reconstruction of historical events was and still is changed to suit the script," and they refer to the lack of "realistic pictures" and "authentic traditions."[39] Kitses argues that westward expansionism is inscribed in the larger ideological project of nation formation and that "the western is American history," though the idea of the West is "an ambiguous mercurial concept."[40]

In his study of Clint Eastwood, Paul Smith addresses the ways in which the concept of the "real" has now shifted from the earlier binary conflict between two notions of history, one real and the other fantasmatic, to a conception of a "cultural and social imaginary" that subsumes the division between the real and the fictional, allowing for a more flexible and less monolithic conception of genre.[41] While there is little doubt about the variability of the forms adopted by the western (which can allow for Italian, German, Japanese, and Indian production), there lingers the sense that these forms are a North American property. The notion of a social imaginary comes closer to redressing complaints about lack of historical accuracy in the popular cinema and in the western in particular, opening the way for rethinking notions of myth and ideology that are all-encompassing, abstract, dismissive of countermemory, and useless for entertaining the historicity and heterogeneity of popular culture. Writings on the western, whether the authors' positions are overt or not, draw on some theory of the nature and role of history, and their models will inevitably reiterate positions concerning the status of knowledge and its relation to the dynamics of change.

In discussing the Italian western, it has become customary to make parallels between that form and the Hollywood western by comparing them to such films as *Stagecoach* (1939) or *My Darling Clementine* (1946) and to later films such as *Shane, Vera Cruz,* and *The Man Who Shot Liberty Valance* (1962). Discussions of the North American western stress abiding elements of structure, theme, and style. One of the most prominent motifs discussed by Thomas Schatz is the foundational narrative, or the struggle to create a civilization in the wilderness, as in *Stagecoach*. This narrative entails, along with the drama of forging a community, a struggle between the individual and the collectivity, the motif of "moral regeneration," and the archetypal binary conflict "between nature and civilization."[42] John Cawelti cites further the inappropriateness of European/Eastern values to the frontier, but the "basic premise of the classic western was a recognition of the inevitable passing of the old order of things, reflected in the myth of the 'old West,' together with an attempt to affirm that the new society would somehow be based on the older values."[43] According to Cawelti this formula was not suited to the exigencies of the post–World War II world and even less to the "more polarized social and political atmosphere of the 1960s."[44]

Much stress has been laid on the importance of community in relation to a savior figure who, for reasons of altruism, revenge, romance, or profit, becomes embroiled in the society for a period of time and who either stays or moves on after his goals are accomplished. The protagonist may enter the community as an agent of transformation, though he may ultimately choose not to be assimilated into it (as in *My Darling Clementine*). Or conversely, the community can assimilate the hero, as in *The Virginian* (1946) or *Stagecoach*. The male couple—the protagonist and his sidekick—who work in tandem for or against the community is also a familiar convention. It is customary in the critical literature to associate, as Cawelti has done, the earlier forms of the western with more idealistic notions of nation and to see a rupture in representation concomitant with the postwar era and with the Cold War. Genre lines begin to blur, even to the extent of grafting the crime genre and film noir onto the western. Psychosocial and sexual treatments become increasingly evident.[45] A transformation in the ethical values can be detected, particularly in the more sympathetic treatment of the outlaw. The professional protagonist often replaces the idealist, "in the right place at the right time," as exemplified by *The Wild Bunch* (1969) and *Butch Cassidy and the Sundance Kid* (1969). This "job happens to be fighting whether for the law or against it."[46] Representatives of the law are also presented in more ambiguous terms.

Such general descriptions, however, can apply to any Hollywood genre, allowing for variations in the use of landscape, in the typology of the characters, in the use of stars, and in representations of the other. In a similar sense, the narrative schema can be read as characteristic of national narratives generally, allowing for the specificity of language and local customs. The problem is the inert nature of genre classification and the static nature of myth and archetype. The problem is also that foundational narratives rely on notions of linearity and progress, but instead of movement from disorder to order, the narrative trajectory often moves from order to disorder. A commitment to narratives of progression or regression occludes the possibility of seeing contradiction, of identifying the "excesses" of history. The insertion of a modernist perspective, the notion of increasing self-consciousness, Hegelian style, serves to impose a new narrative of progress, replacing action with self-awareness on the part of the auteur and his handling of genre.

To read Sergio Leone's films as remakes, as mere deconstruction of the Hollywood western, or as modernist in the vein of Antonioni and Fellini—though all such elements may be imbricated in the text—is to address cinema history and history in cinema schematically and reductively rather than analytically and interrogatively, univalently rather than heterogeneously. To read and judge the films from the unique position of auteurism is also problematic. For example, Sergio Leone has been regarded as an "opportunist" who has "simply yoked samurai gestures to western iconography."[47] His films deserve better; they deserve to be understood as repositories of social and cultural knowledge. They have gone a different route than most critical judgments of his use of the western genre assume, broadly engaging the moral concerns of neorealism in their dramatization of protagonists who struggle to survive in societies that are hostile to change and to collective practices. The films interrogate masculinity and its discontents, its complicity with violence and power, and they pose, though they do not resolve, ethical dilemmas about the forms of power similar in many ways to the historical investments of the Tavianis' films—especially *Padre Padrone* (1977)—which orchestrate the problematics of language, patriarchy, subalternity, masculinity, the family, social power, and the clash between rural and urban life and between tradition and modernity.

The Leone films rely on a certain dry and dusty desert landscape that comes to signify "the West" but that provides an arena of open space for action. This landscape is rarely associated with domestic space. Occasionally we see a contrast between open, contested public space and closed domestic space in *For a Few Dollars More* (1965) and *Once upon a Time in the West* (a film that particularly capitalizes on this disjunction). The images of towns such as Tucumcari, Agua Caliente, Sweetwater, and El Paso convey the sense of dirt, grime, and poverty that could apply just as easily to the underdeveloped terrains of Latin America, Africa, Sicily, or Sardinia as to the North American West. The ubiquitous fly (the most notorious example is seen in the opening of *Once upon a Time in the West*) serves as a synecdoche, a specific marker of the annoyances and discomforts inherent in this life and also of the physicality of the characters and of the mise-en-scène. The protagonists—Clint Eastwood with his familiar poncho and facial stubble, Eli Wallach in his stained clothing, the contrast between the meticulous Lee Van Cleef and the casual Eastwood, between the coarse Rod Steiger and the suave James Coburn—bespeak an attention to the relation between characters and environment.

The minutiae of this world are a distinctive dimension of Leone's film: the choreography of movement; the stylized use of faces; and the aversive uses of sound, represented by the grating sounds of wheels, the extra-loud noise of oncoming or departing trains, the ubiquitous buzz of flies, the sounds of eating, belching, and farting. These sounds fuse with the music, so that it is often difficult to know which are "natural" and which are "manufactured." Chanting, orchestral music, whistling, guitar music, the sounds of a flute or piccolo, and choral and instrumental themes mingle to provide a complex narration that acts as more than mere support to the narrative, more than mere atmosphere or filler. All of the critical work on the Italian western has singled out the music of Ennio Morricone for analysis (and for praise).[48] The scores for Leone's films serve a number of functions: as affective commentary on a character's actions or state of mind; as mockery, cliché, leitmotiv, thematic continuity; and hence as a comment on repetition, variation, or ironic reversal in the narrative. The music is a major carrier of the historical excess that creates the sense of openness and heterogeneity of narration. It enhances the melodrama and directs its affective strategies toward antimelodrama. As in opera, there is a union between verbal and gestural language and the music. The dialogue is often sparse, with the exception of *Duck, You Sucker,* which seems most committed to the use of words. Where there is dialogue, it is often restricted to one-liners, something Clint Eastwood will employ to advantage in both his western and nonwestern films (e.g., the infamous "Make my day"). There is a sense too that the dialogue, composed as it is of clichés, truisms, proverbs, one-liners, and commonsensical wisdom, works with the music and sound to punctuate, mock, comment on, or correct the banality of language. In many instances, the sparsity of dialogue is a sign that this world is more one of action than of thought.

In their dependence on physical action, Leone's films draw on traditions from Italian theatrical comedy and film comedy. The importance of farce, slapstick, and satiric allegory are evident in such films as *Once upon a Time in the West* and *Duck, You Sucker.* Moreover, the residual elements of the commedia dell' arte are evident in character typification and in the uses of gags, stylized gestures, *lazzi* (physical and verbal tricks), and repartee. Frayling has noted the relations between the Italian art of puppetry and the staging of the action in the Italian western. In the musical scores of Ennio Morricone in particular and in the choreography of body movement generally the films also evoke the characteristics of comic opera. Commenting on the persistence of the operatic in Italian culture, Gramsci linked the stylization of the operatic to a penchant for oratory, especially funeral oratory, and to the spectacle of district magistrate's courts, in which "the hall is always full of . . . people who memorize the turns of phrase and the solemn words, feed on them and remember them."[49] The turns of phrase and the instances of mock solemnity in Italian comedy have this mnemonic and oratorical attribute that is also evident in spaghetti westerns.

The fairy tale, "once upon a time" quality in Sergio Leone films[50] is related to Gramsci's conception of folklore. The films' dependence on the past, on "the West," is more than schematic and supra-historical myth: As folklore, it is "tied to the culture of the dominant class and, in its own way, has drawn from it the motifs which have then become inserted into combination with the previous traditions. Besides, there is nothing more contradictory and fragmentary than folklore."[51] Folklore, in the guise of fairy tale narration, in Leone's films calls attention to the commonsensical positions of the characters as a form of popular wisdom that is often revealed to be contradictory.

The strongly affective nature of Leone's treatment of the western has been described as emotional, "perhaps too emotional, for the audiences of Britain and America." While such comments may be more applicable to British than North American audiences, their invocation of the melodramatic and the operatic invites a comparison between Italian westerns and "Weepies, women's films."[52] Many of the spaghetti westerns are male melodramas, involving conflicts over identity and homosocial bonding. The films validate the connection between folklore, melodrama, and the operatic that I claim is central to popular representations of history. The nonverbal and affective strategies of melodrama and opera are conveyed in the iconography, in bodily movement (especially in the choreography), and in the use of intense close-up, particularly of the face. Bodies in motion are a hallmark of the films. Instead of the ballets of grand opera, there is the choreography of the shoot-out, of men riding through the landscape, of processionals; there is the choreography of ritual scenes, such as that in *Once upon a Time in the West* in which Jill and the other mourners observe the bodies of the dead McBains, and of the various ritual forms of violence itself interspersed throughout the film. The camera movement—pans, tilts, the use of handheld equipment—conveys the sense of a world of energy and motion, a world of bodies that collide. The music also serves to render the affective intensity of the bodily interactions. The choreography and the music call attention to the body politics of the films—more to the sexuality of the masculine body than to that of the feminine, since femininity seems confined to the few instances in which women are fantasized or dreamed about, or in which the homosocial relations suggest traces of tenderness in the brutal and violent environment.

Heterosexual romance is not a central motif and is subordinated to the motif of homosocial bonding. The relations between men—Mr. Mortimer and Monco in a *For a Few Dollars More,* Cheyenne and Harmonica in *Once upon a Time in the West,* Tuco and Blondie in *The Good, the Bad, and the Ugly* (1966), and especially Juan and Sean in *Duck, You Sucker*—are central and complex, involving a form of coupling that is ambivalent. The relations are based on economic competition but also on something else that entails grudging admiration and respect, even if not affection and tenderness. Sex between men and women is circumscribed in this environment, and when present it is likely to be coercive and brutal. When women are present, they are usually carriers of economic value as kept women, prostitutes, or heirs to property, like Jill in *Once upon a Time in the West,* or figures of nostalgia, as in *Duck, You Sucker.* Maternal figures are either conspicuously placed in the background or entirely absent, or they violate conventional notions of service. Eroticism is conveyed primarily through scenes of eating, sparring, or killing.

The faces in close-up, so much identified with Italian westerns, contribute in many ways to an understanding of the world in the films. They serve a triple function: to intensify the affect, to interrogate the character and the situation, and to render them ambiguous. The close-ups are not reserved for the protagonists alone but are dispersed, associated with antagonists and with silent observers of the action.[53] Close-ups also contribute to the tragicomic nature of the situation, since characters are identified by their unshaven faces: dirt, moles, and in some cases spittle that is clearly visible. In the early part of *Duck, You Sucker,* the agonizing close-ups focus on fragments, on facial parts; especially the leering eyes and the masticating mouths filled with crushed and oozing food. The alternation between full-body shots and close-ups serves to underscore a conflict between the head and the body—a primary tension in Leone's films that centers on the relation between intelligence and force, creating questions about the dominance of one over the other.

The body mechanics are reminiscent of physical movement in Vsevolod Pudovkin and Sergei Eisenstein. They recall too the comic choreography of Chaplin—an icon of Americanism for many Europeans. Body movement in the films can be fruitfully identified with the Italian tradition of the commedia dell'arte. In contrast to opera,

> the body in the commedia seems more in tune with a bustling street life caught unawares, even when performed indoors. The body in the commedia also expresses a paradox. While it refers to the slow-moving, deep structures of daily life, it is in constant motion. The body in the commedia, with its agility of a dancer and its careful choreography, nonetheless produces an effect of spontaneity. By virtue of movement, the body in the commedia resembles more a living document than a still monument.[54]

Leone's films mix the melodramatic and the comic, the monumental and the everyday. The foregrounding of the body communicates the constraints on the conforming body via an eruption of unruly antagonisms that signify the impossibility of total submission. The physical action in the Leone films, their emphasis on trickery and on violence, recalls the *lazzi* of the commedia as the characters engage in a range of physical actions and verbal wit to antagonize and outsmart their opponents.[55] The *lazzi* refer to "comic routines that were planned or unplanned," and they "allude to any discrete or independent, comic and repeatable activity that guaranteed laughs for its participants."[56] The *lazzi* were associated with "athleticism and clowning . . . tumbling, stilt walking, diving, and tightrope balancing."[57]

This masculine form of clowning is not only slapstick but also serves as a means of aggressiveness in attacking another or protecting oneself against attack. An instance of a *lazzi* is a scene in *The Good, the Bad, and the Ugly*: Clint Eastwood is cleaning his gun as Eli Wallach's hired assassins attempt to sneak up on him; with great agility and sangfroid he manages to dispatch them all. In the same film, the repeated gag of Tuco and Blondie taking turns hanging each other and then shooting through the rope, causing the victim to fall, recapitulates in humorous fashion the double-crossing tricks that Eastwood and Wallach play on each other. *Once upon a Time in the West* and *Duck, You Sucker* are filled with repetitive gags and reversals based on fast movement and legerdemain. A more bizarre episode of this trickery occurs in *A Fistful of Dollars*: The Man with No Name inserts himself between the Rojo and the Baxter families, propping up two dead bodies to lure the warring groups into fighting with each other. The play with repetition of physical objects as vehicles of recognition, revenge, and trickery can be seen in the use of the armor in this film or in the use of the locket in *For a Few Dollars More*. The repetition of routines works, along with the music, to highlight ironic reversals as well as narrative transformations.

The typology of the characters in the Italian western also resembles commedia types. For example, vestigial remnants of the braggart captain can be seen in such figures as Tuco in *The Good, the Bad, and the Ugly* and as Cheyenne in *Once upon a Time in the West* and in the rivalry between the two bounty hunters—Mr. Mortimer and Monco—in *For a Few Dollars More*. The pairing of figures, their competitiveness, and their exchange of serious and comic qualities are also reminiscent of the relations between *zanni*, the various clowning figures. According to Allardyce Nicoll, the *zanni* of the commedia (sometimes referred to as John) "appears as a stupid booby, but more commonly he mingles with his folly an element of wit, an element of liveliness, of good fun, of grotesquerie."[58] Also evident in the Leone films are the interchangeable figures of the *Dottore* and Pantalone: the older professional men who should be wise but who are pedants, traitors, or sunk in folly, such as Doctor Villega in *Duck, You Sucker*.

The comedy relies on common sense as a guide for action only to reveal the inadequacy of common sense in contexts that require innovation and wit. If common sense as folklore involves a stylized and naturalized commitment to past actions and behavior, the melodramatic and comic treatment of character and situation in the films serves to foreground historical excess. The dependence on physical action, on the body, and on the face sets up a tension between historical stasis and dynamic movement, between mechanization and spontaneity, and between the containing and the release of energy. Common sense is not a matter merely of words but of gesture and behavior, intimately related to the politics of the body and, therefore, to the body politic. While the Russian formalists objected to the mechanization of modern Fordist industrialism, Gramsci saw its possibilities for freeing the mind from the repetitive routines of production. Physical action in a Leone film can signify static repetition and routine mechanization, but it can also signify mental alertness.

The world created in the Italian westerns is not one of simple heroes and villains, though there are many Machiavellian characters. This is not the familiar Manichaean world of melodrama, though at times it appears to be binary. There is abundant affect and melodrama, but this melodrama coexists with the comedy; and the comedy tempers the melodrama but does not overwhelm it. Common sense is not defeated; it is shown in its contradictory dimensions: as a form of wisdom in the short run and as more questionable knowledge that requires interrogation in the long run. Clint Eastwood's comment in *A Fistful of Dollars* that "[e]very town has a boss. When there are two around I'd say there's one too many" is conducive to an understanding of the wisdom necessary for survival, but it also raises more questions than it answers: Why can there not be two? How does one know who is the boss? The statements may adequately characterize the competitiveness and violence that results from two bosses—the Rojos and the Baxters—but the resolution, getting rid of both, although it solves one problem, introduces more fundamental problems about power. There is no doubt that the pragmatic assessment of power works in immediate terms to both describe and diagnose problems that are integral to survival. The uses of history, the road taken by the films, does not lead to a future that is mapped but to one that is open, like the roads that the protagonists take as they ride out of town, alone as when they arrived.

## Common Sense and *Duck, You Sucker*

Leone's films have encouraged allegorical readings, and most work along such lines has been done regarding *Once upon a Time in the West*, its title alone inviting this type of encounter. I choose to discuss *Duck, You Sucker* because of its orchestration of Gramscian issues relating to Americanism, common sense, the role of intellectuals, the nature of subalternity, the characteristics of passive revolution, and above all its uses of history to inform these issues. Inscribed in his films are regional antagonisms that have played an ongoing role in the cultural and political life of Italy—in the distribution of economic and political power, in the hierarchization of racial and ethnic characteristics, in linguistic differences, in condescending attitudes by northern intellectuals toward southern culture, and especially in the association of the southern peasant with primitivism, brutality, and brigandage. Therefore a mere assessment of the influences of the American western in style and theme is barely adequate to an understanding of the form and preoccupation of the film, its treatment of difference.[59]

From the opening moments of *Duck, You Sucker* when Juan attempts to hitch a ride in a passing stagecoach, concealing his identity and the objective of his journey, the film presents a number of questions that are common to Leone films. Who is this man? Why is he at this deserted stop along the road? How long has he been here? Why is he important enough to open the film? The film will play with questions of identity. The character is obviously not a minor figure. Those who recognize Rod Steiger from the film credits know that this is an important character, though they do not know what course his role will take. Familiarity with other Leone films alerts the spectator to the possibility that appearance is not a reliable guide to character identification. For initiates, the excess will soon cue the spectator to distinctions.

Juan Miranda allows himself to be kicked and taunted by the driver and be sent into the coach as a source of entertainment. Inside he is the silent subaltern, and this lengthy sequence plays with familiar images of subalternity. He is totally passive, victimized, verbally abused, humiliated, and the physical mistreatment he receives at the hands of the drivers is matched by the cruel treatment he receives at the hands of the patricians inside the coach. The close-ups of the assembled passengers are accompanied by a relay of gazes from them to Juan and from the silent Juan to the camera. The camera isolates each of the passengers and allows each in turn an opportunity to vilify peasant life, which they characterize as bestial, inarticulate, and promiscuous: Peasants breed "like rats," are stupid, and have no sense of genealogy or family. Juan's silence seems to confirm their assessments. But the taut editing of the close-ups escalates in speed, intensity, and tightness. As the camera dissects their faces, the group becomes an Eisensteinian montage of leering eyes, drooling mouths, and tearing teeth, transforming them into images of the beasts they consider peasants to be.

When the stagecoach is attacked by Juan Miranda's gang and his "family," the tables are turned, and ironically Juan fulfills the passengers' and perhaps the audience's expectations of peasants in his indifference to life through his casual shooting of one of the passengers, his thievery, and his rape of the woman on the coach. There is one exception: he has a genealogy. He introduces his father to the passengers and informs them that his mother had "the pure blood of the Aztecs which was before your people." Thus the question underpinning this episode and the entire film (and other Leone films), "Who are you?" involves more than a proper name but is positional in relation to access to knowledge and to the exercise of power.

In coming across another "John," John H. Mallory or Sean (James Coburn), another set of reversals comes into play to characterize the seesaw relationship between the two characters. Sean appears like a magician or a trickster, materializing from the smoke of the explosion he has produced. As with Juan, Sean's abrupt entry into the narrative raises more questions: What is an Irishman doing in the Mexican countryside? Why is he riding a motorcycle in this barren and uninhabited environment? Why is he causing explosions? Differences between Sean and Juan become evident—one is an intellectual, the other a peasant; one is a reader of books, the other has a hostility toward readers of books; one is a committed revolutionary, the other a brigand and a lumpen. The contrasts also raise the problem of detecting sameness and difference in relation to identity and to history. Are the two men with the same name, merely expressed in different languages, the same or different? What is the importance attached to those differences? More questions proliferate from these: What are the similarities and differences between the Mexican revolution, the Irish revolution, or any revolution (including the Risorgimento)? What is revolution? And what constitutes relations among men in a situation identified as revolutionary?

The sound track from the beginning of the film is a montage of chants: "Sean, Sean, Sean" and "Waa, Waa, Waa" as mocking responses to many of the questions that are posed. The choral and orchestral music become what Robert C. Cumbow describes as "hymnlike," often in conjunction with religious images, since the ironic role of religion is embedded in this film. The commonsensical aspects of religion, related to strategies of survival, of wish fulfillment, and of the fusion of the secular and the commercial, are evident in this film, especially in the surreal images of the bank at Mesa Verde lit up (through Juan's perspective) to look like a religious reliquary. Before he blew up the stage coach, Sean had knelt to pray inside the coach before a "shrine": a small statue of a Madonna and a replica of the bank with a candle beneath it. Juan's speech is peppered with allusions to a God he does not believe in as much as he believes in the bank and in America. An organ accompanies Sean's practicing his exploding skills in what Juan describes as "a miracle of God"—the miracle that will get him the money from the bank at Mesa Verde.

Sean is in the superior position by virtue of his class status and especially by virtue of his skill with explosives. Recognizing and accepting this inequality for the moment, Juan offers a partnership between them, suggesting they share the loot from the banks that they rob:

"My name is Juan and your name is John. That is destiny." This assertion is accompanied by the sound of a woman's voice singing, introducing the first of the five flashbacks in the film to Sean's past in Ireland. He is seen in a pastoral setting with another young man and a woman. There is no dialogue, only music. In the contrast of landscape and character, the lush green of the Irish countryside and the well-dressed, clean appearance of the three young people contrasted to the rocky, barren "Mexican" landscape with its dirty and disheveled inhabitants, the scene poses questions of sameness and difference that deepen with the flashbacks to come. Despite the visual contrasts, how different is Sean's recollection of the past from the present? This sequence introduces Juan's commonsensical attitude toward history and toward revolutionary struggle:

> Seems to me there are revolutions all over the world. They are like the crops. We had a revolution here. When it started all the brave people were in it and what it did to them was terrible. Pancho Villa the best bandit chief in the world, you know that this man had two balls like the bull. He went in like a great bandit and he came out as what? Nothing, a general. That to me is the bullshit.

This speech poses the Gramscian problematic of passive revolution, which addresses the redirection and containment of revolution, through a co-opting of its leaders. Pancho Villa's "two balls like the bull" is a graphic physical invocation of the emasculation of revolution, an index to this film's preoccupation with masculinity and virility and its connection to the "philosophy of action."

Questions concerning sameness and difference arise too from the objectives of Juan and Sean. What is the difference between robbing a bank and making a revolution when the revolution turns out to maintain the status quo, of existing property and social relations? The film's interrogation of revolution is further problematized through the figure of Doctor Villega (Romolo Valli). A physician who appears to have compassion for his revolutionary compatriots, he is shown to be capable of killing his enemies in cold blood when he dispatches the soldiers on the train who threaten Juan. A traditional intellectual and a traitor, he assumes a position of leadership but is incapable of withstanding torture and thus becomes an informer. His first appearance on the train borders on the comic: his black suit like that of a priest, crisp white shirt, white hat with a black band, and pince-nez. Giving the appearance of a mild, middle-class, bookish man, he speaks to no one and continues to be absorbed in his book even after he has disposed of the soldier. Like the *Dottore* of the commedia and of opera, he is also characterized by his "bookish affectations and his academic excesses."[60] Also comparable to the *Dottore* are his naiveté, his unsubtle manipulation of others, and his posturing as one who "desires to be up to date."

While Villega does not appear to be a clown or a blatant fool, it becomes obvious that his claims to leadership are more dependent on his professional status as physician than on his knowledge of people and events. He is shown to be as self-serving as the other characters when he shrinks from battle and when he informs on his colleagues because of his fear of bodily harm. In this respect, he contrasts with Sean, with the Mexican officer, Guttierez, and with other Leone characters who do not shrink from physical confrontation. However, distinctions among the characters are not clear-cut. Juan shares certain characteristics with the doctor, a near relation to the Braggart Captain of the commedia, namely, a tendency toward cowardice. In the commedia, the Braggart Captain is often identified with Spain, coincidentally the setting of most spaghetti westerns. Like the Braggart Captain of the commedia, Juan is the offspring of the *miles gloriosus*. The Braggart Captain shares with the *Dottore* an air of bravado that easily degenerates into reticence. In Juan's case, this behavior is exemplified in his urging Sean to avoid a confrontation with the Mexican army and instead escape with him to the United States, a reiterative plea on his part. But Juan also shares with Sean a mistrust of the motives of revolutionaries.

In the working out of the narrative, especially in the crossing over of characteristics between the two men with the same name, Juan appears to gain respect for Sean's abilities and Sean begins to adopt certain of Juan's positions. At first Sean is condescending toward Juan, laughing at Juan's ambitions. He toys with Juan as if Juan were a fool, and Juan, like a *zanni*, provokes laughter by his appearance, egregious behavior, and grandiose language, and by his "cruel, libidinous, cynically witty, and self-seeking actions."[61] Sean frequently smiles at Juan's speeches and behavior, occasionally laughing raucously, especially at Juan's dreams of going to the United States and of the "big future" that Juan imagines to be ahead of them as bank robbers.

A seriocomic aspect of *Duck, You Sucker* arises from the motif of confusion, which Sean articulates as "Where there's confusion a man who knows what he wants stands a good chance of getting it," a proverbial bit of common sense that invites examination. Confusion comes to stand in for the blurring of boundaries between characters and the firmness of their positions and for the contingent dimensions of political struggle. Its dominant metaphor appears to reside in the imagery of explosions generated by Sean, producing confusion and the inability to see clearly, but emblematized in the reversal of events that turn out contrary to expectations. Like comedy, melodrama is closely tied to narrative confusion. Predicated on conceptions of victimization, of order restored, and of innocence vindicated and on the expectation of justice, melodrama's affect is generated from the precariousness of social identity, the fear of loss of position, the disappearance of moral and ethical boundaries, and disjunctions between expectations and outcome. The melodramatic moments in the Leone film are especially concerned with death—evident in the horrible Goya-like scene in which Sean and Juan witness the devastation of the revolutionaries in the grotto and in the scene in which Juan confronts the death of his sons. The melodrama of loss is further dramatized through the scenes of masses of people gratuitously shot down by the troops. Sean's adage "Revolution is confusion" solidifies the link between the melodramatic and comic elements in the film. Melodrama is interdigitated with scenes of comic confusion—the most notable being the robbing of the bank, which was to turn Juan into a rich man but instead makes him a poor hero. This episode begins with one of Juan's sons pulling a toy train containing explosives. Then, in the manner of an Ealing comedy, Juan's men burst into the bank, shooting down waves of guards in their quest for gold, opening door after door (accompanied by a range of musical sounds including orchestral theme music intercut with jaunty pipe sounds and with the omnipresent "Waa, Waa" sounds) only to find men standing in the vaults instead of gold. Juan is informed by Sean that the bank was being used as a prison and that the valuables had been taken away and lodged in Mexico City. The scene compounds irony: The "gold" in the vaults turns out to be the revolutionaries, and Juan's elevation from a bank robber to, in Sean's terms, "a grand hero of the revolution" runs counter to his own material objectives: "I don't want to be a hero. I just want the money." From a melodramatic perspective of heroism, Juan's situation marks him as self-deluded. Yet the subsequent scenes provide evidence for his strong

The reluctant revolutionary Juan (Rod Steiger), in *Duck, You Sucker*. Courtesy of New York Museum of Modern Art, Film Stills Archive.

distrust of revolutionary enthusiasm in showing his resentment of being manipulated by intellectuals. His preference for gold and for escape to the United States does not seem foolish when compared with what he is offered as a revolutionary puppet.

In the encampment where the revolutionaries are based, waiting for the federal troops to come, Juan lies down on a map of Mexico, only to be told by Sean, "It's your country you're lying all over," another indication of Juan's mistrust, based on experience, of the nation-state and its apparatuses. His riposte to Sean is "My country is only me and my family." The characterization of familialism in conflict with nationalism seems to be an instance of the insertion of Italian regional and national discourses into Leone's films, perhaps an instance of the "amoral familism" attributed to southern Italians.[62] And here the notion of "*la famiglia*" is tenuous. It is a site of harassment by regional and state authority and by brigands out for economic or personal gain. Juan's comments on self and family are characteristic of his other commonsensical formulations: Although they are not false, neither are they true; they are a strategy for undermining the inflexible and seemingly impersonal positions of revolutionary intellectuals. Perhaps this is the film's opportunity to take a satiric jab at vanguardism and the refusal of many revolutionaries to confront the question of subjectivity and the consequences of such a failure.

In an unusually lengthy verbal passage for a Leone film, Juan lets loose with another barrage of invectives against the revolution and the role of intellectuals: "Don't tell me about revolution. The people that read the books they go to the people who don't read the books and they tell them the time has come to have a change and the people who read the books sit around the big polished table and talk and talk and eat and eat but what has happened to the poor people. They're dead." Recalling the peasants' attitudes toward revolution in *1900*, the scene is important because it dramatizes—not merely in Juan's words but in the nature of interactions between Sean and him—the gap between intellectuals and subaltern groups. Juan has consistently referred to a connection between revolution and intellectuals as an instance of the betrayal of the "people." The Gramscian distinction between organic and traditional intellectuals underpins Juan's commonsensical characterization of intellectuals. Maintaining his superiority, Sean tries to silence Juan, showing his disdain and condescension toward him, but after the speech he throws his copy of Mikhail Bakunin's *Patriotism*, a major anarchist document on the state, into a muddy puddle and does not laugh at Juan's words.

Juan is also presented as altered. In a subsequent scene, he remains with Sean to fight the *federales*, shouting at him "You listen to me, you piece of shit. You think you are the only man in the world who has balls. Well, you are wrong. I have the balls and I stay." Juan's brash invocation of masculinity appears to be a mixture of *onore* and machismo, suggesting that his motives are no less contradictory than Sean's. Aside from his reference to his male organs, Juan's decision to remain raises but does not answer the question of why he stays with Sean in this dangerous venture. Is the homosocial bond stronger than their ideological differences? Juan seems to have somewhat relinquished his earlier obsession of exploiting this "firecracker," as he calls Sean. Or are we to believe that Juan has been infected by Sean's revolutionary attitudes? His refusal to engage with Sean's seemingly wild plans to remain, explode the bridge, and single-handedly route the *federales* vanishes despite his reservations. The contrast between the affective responses of the two men toward this suicidal rearguard action is reinforced by Juan's observations as he looks, through binoc-

The "firecracker" Sean (James Coburn), in *Duck, You Sucker*. Courtesy New York Museum of Modern Art, Film Stills Archive.

ulars, at Sean calmly setting up his gun and his explosives, then lying down to rest and wait for the columns of troops. Juan compares the unemotional Sean to a tourist "who is going somewhere only he's staying. I'm glad he's having fun, God, because I'm not having fun." Juan is like a tourist peering through binoculars (in comic fashion through the wrong end at first) and watching events at a remove. The image of tourism as applied to Sean captures the sense of his lack of engagement with people and points up his class difference from Juan and the "revolutionary masses." The reference to tourism also connects to the film's focus on mobility, on the role of trains, on the movement of populations, and on the the globalization of even the most remote corners of the world, and it provides yet another complication to Juan's question "Which way is America?"

The film abandons its satiric treatment in its portrayal of the massacre of the revolutionaries in the grotto where they have taken refuge while Sean and Juan have been attacking the *federales*. In this elegiac segment, the camera slowly pans the rows of dead bodies, intercutting Juan and Sean's gaze at the corpses, accompanied by slow orchestral music, blended with sounds of whistling and of a guitar. Finally Juan says, "All of them. I never counted them before." Here as in his earlier farewell to his sons at the encampment, Juan displays an emotional response in striking contrast to his earlier mockery and callousness. This spectacle of death provides visual confirmation of Juan's warnings about the betrayal of the people by both the state and by traditional intellectuals. Again, through death, Juan and Sean are bonded.

The episodes involving the destructiveness of the troops, the representatives of the state, evoke connections with the cinema of the post–World War II era. The figure of the blonde, blue-eyed Mexican federal officer especially conjures up representations of that time. In his uniform as well as in his behavior he is more familiar as a representation of a Nazi than of a Mexican officer from the early part of the century. The way he is filmed in his armored transport seems to have more connection to a World War II panzer commander than to a military officer from 1913. Moreover, his appearance in his impeccable uniform, his effete attention to his bodily needs, and the close-ups of him sucking an egg and later brushing his teeth also suggest parallels with the portrayal of the Nazi officer in Rossellini's *Rome, Open City*. Does the Leone film also contain a similar implication of effeminacy, an implication that the federal officer has "no balls," to use Juan's designation of masculinity? Does the film therefore imply that sexual politics in the form of the overvaluation of masculinity is responsible for the violence of those who represent the authority of the state (and also those that would challenge it)?

The scenes of the torture and shooting of the revolutionaries while the federal officer sits observing the massacre from behind the wheel of his vehicle through the rain on the windshield (with Doctor Villega at his side as informer) connect this episode to *Rome, Open City* and its dramatization of Nazi brutality. But although there is a parallel, there is also an important difference. Whereas Manfredi, the engineer, and Don Pietro, the priest, do not break down under torture and inform on the people, Doctor Villega does. *Duck, You Sucker* both supplements Rossellini's portrayal of the fascist state and its barbarism and reflects on the lessons of history, especially the betrayal of the Italian Resistance in the post–World War II period. Here Leone's film interrogates revolutionary heroism, suggesting either that representations of heroism are too idealistic and dissonant with the actual confrontation of power or, in contrasting Doctor Villega and the Irish informer with Sean and Juan, that critical recognition of complicity, betrayal, and bodily needs, if not foolhardiness, is a requisite in political struggle.

A further doubling of Sean and Juan is cemented when Sean saves Juan's life by producing yet another explosion, enabling the men to take advantage of the confusion and to disappear on Sean's motorcycle. From this point on, the relations between the men become less combative and less hierarchical. Juan's changed position is dramatized most graphically in another train scene, in which he and Sean confront Don Jaime, the governor escaping from the revolutionaries. The governor is first alluded to when Juan arrives in Mesa Verde, where the politician's image on a poster is plastered all over the walls of the town with the caption "The governor loves the people and the people love the governor." No love is manifest when the governor, clutching a bag containing money and jewels, shouts at Sean and Juan, "You scum, let me by." Sean throws a gun to Juan, presenting him with the opportunity to kill Don Jaime, who offers the bag to Juan, but Juan hesitates.

Melodramatic affect becomes central as flashbacks of the governor's poster and of Juan's dead sons are intercut with images of Juan's face in close-up. There is no dialogue—only the sound of chickens, a bird, machine-gun fire, and slow music—which heightens the tension of the moment but which does not simplify the nature of the affect Juan expresses. Sean observes Juan's conflict as Juan looks at the bag of valuables and then at the governor but still does not shoot. Only when the governor opens the door does Juan shoot, but the revolutionaries have also shot at him. In a scene that would have been unbelievable at the beginning of the film, Juan looks at his shaking hands, while Sean observes, through a slat, a scene of carnage outside. Now Juan asks, "Hey, which way is America?" Watching Juan fingering a silver necklace, Sean responds ambiguously, "Surely not that way," and for the first time says, "Let's go," a further indication of the changed relations between the men. America, it appears, is not a geographic place after all, but present in the figure of the governor and the violence of the men. However, Juan's question, "Which way is America?" suggests that another form of Americanism also exists: a cultural phantasm tied to the idea of movement and escape.

Despite his renewed desire to escape to the United States, Juan, through another ironic twist, is celebrated for a second time as "a great, grand, glorious hero of the Revolution." But the ensuing scenes are focused on Sean and his confrontation with Villega, whom he selects, despite Juan's offer, to assist him in blowing up the oncoming train of *federales*. Sean prods Villega to physical work, urging him to help provide sufficient steam for the train with its explosives, and Villega accuses Sean of having "judged and condemned him." He attempts to justify his act of becoming an informer: "It's easy to judge. Have you ever been tortured. Are you sure you wouldn't talk?" He asks if he should have killed himself, but his death would not have resurrected the murdered men. His words occasion another flashback, in which Sean's Irish friend, having broken down under torture, is seen in a pub with a British officer, identifying Irish revolutionaries. In this flashback, after an exchange of close-ups between Sean and his friend, Sean shoots both the British officer who was ready to arrest him and the informer. Confronting Villega now, Sean tells him, "When I started using dynamite, I believed in many things. Finally I believe only in dynamite. I don't judge you, Villega. I did that only once in my life." In fact he tells Villega to jump from the train that is about to collide with the troop train, but Villega refuses. Is this another act of cowardice? Has Villega judged himself? Is this another instance of revolutionary melodrama and heroics, when he should have learned to "Duck, you sucker?" This episode increases the confusion rather than clarifying and assigning a specific meaning to the actions and the actors in revolutionary struggle.

In the final moments of the film, a number of further reversals take place. When Sean exposes himself in hand-to-hand combat during his pursuit of the federal officer, he appears to be ignoring his own dictum to "Duck, you sucker." This act seems to be either particularly foolhardy, the essence of romantic heroism and martyrdom, or suicidal. Why does he choose to die along with the Mexican officer? There is a great deal of the operatic involved in this final death scene. While Sean is breathing his last, Juan is ministering to him, trying to keep him alive. Here their relationship can be characterized as a form of homosocial love. There is little mockery or boasting, only Juan's tender and vain ministrations and Sean's lapsing into a flashback in which he is once again in the Irish countryside and once again with a young woman, whom he is kissing. This scene is more complex and open-ended in relation to Juan and Sean than "a Leone effort to recapture lost innocence—to return perhaps to the sweetness of life 'before the revolution.'"[63] Once again, it introduces questions: Has Juan retained his subordinate role? Will he become a revolutionary leader? Did Sean die for the people or for his balls? Has Juan been betrayed by the intellectual who would rather have his climax than his life? The film remains interrogative to the end. Juan is left alone, like the spectator, with the question, "What about me?"

## Which Way Is History?

The film's ending is emblematic of Leone's open-ended uses of the past. The history of the West involves not only North and South America but Europe, as the grafting of the Irish uprising onto the Mexican revolution suggests. The treatment of history is striated, addressing many layers and different orders of questions. *Duck, You Sucker* does not nostalgically enshrine the history that it probes. The film does not abandon history for the ahistorical realm of "once upon a time." The "once upon a time" in all of Leone's films is not a golden age, not an untroubled pastoral world. The narratives begin in a past that is crisis driven, not orderly and peaceful.

The historical interrogation involves distinctions between repetition and change, sameness and difference, especially in the pairing of masculine characters like Juan and Sean, Mr. Mortimer and Monco, Tuco and Blondie, and Cheyenne and Harmonica. Uppermost is the question of recognition. Is there a way of distinguishing the good from the bad, the opportunist from the man with a score to settle, the revolutionary from the bandit? They seem to share or to acquire similar attitudes despite differences in their physical appearances, and they appear to be obsessively attached to each other despite apparent antagonisms. The antagonisms arise from the men's immersion in the struggle for economic gain, though ostensibly—as their individual histories come to dramatize—for different historical reasons. The apparent repetitiveness of their actions as well as of those of their opponents generates the problematic for the narrative (and perhaps for the audience) of discriminating among individuals and events. The repeated concern of the films with the question of identity—as represented by Frank's repeated statement to Harmonica, "I have to know who you are," in *Once upon a Time in the West*—can be taken as emblematic of the preoccupation with knowledge posed by Leone's films. Any answer is always partial, and the knowledge may produce failure rather than unqualified success. The essence of this knowledge is related to the commonsensical valorization of "experience" with its pragmatic reliance on the past as a guide to action in the present. Since the trajectory of the film does not seem to be resolution but investigation, the narratives and the "confusion" they dramatize highlight the indeterminacy of knowledge.

In its address of revolutionary struggle to probe such issues, *Duck, You Sucker* seems to take for granted the strengths of capital and the inequalities it produces (unlike *Once upon a Time in the West,* which bristles with conflict over forms of capitalism) in order to explore the power and brutality of the state and the tenuousness of the forces that seek to challenge state power. In that exploration, different moments of the past collide—1913, the 1940s, and the present. In this conjoining of moments certain issues overlap: the pervasiveness of the violence of the state, the capacity for fascism, the ubiquitous conflicts over property and ownership, and the problematic nature of revolutionary struggles to challenge power and inequality. While force seems incontrovertible, what is interrogated in the unwitting strategies of consent is the composition, the identity of the individuals and groups that regard themselves as revolutionary. *Duck, You Sucker* does not lend itself to easy political labeling as revolutionary or reactionary. What we are given is an encyclopedic interrogation of intellectuals, heroism, economism, common sense, and history in a Gramscian vein. This type of interrogation frustrates binary distinctions of aggressor and victim and performs a critique of traditional conceptions of power and their relation to historicizing.

Gramsci wrote that "one cannot have a critical and coherent conception of the world without having a consciousness of its historicity." And he asked, "How is it possible to consider the present, and the quite specific present, with a mode of thought elaborated for a past which is often remote and superseded. When someone does this it means that he is a walking anachronism, a fossil, and not living in the modern world, or at the least that he is strangely composite."[64] In its question, "Which way is America?," in its references to tourism, and in its abundant images of confusion, the film's uses of the past suggest that antagonism and crisis are apparent and associated with the contradictory phenomenon of Americanism.

The film suggests that the characters in their words and actions are located between past and present. (As the Man with No Name is in *A Fistful of Dollars,* the characters are in the middle, in the in-between.)

They are mired in repetition, and the events are also characterized by repetition. It is not that the characters do not move in some fashion to confront their past; rather, the film questions the disparity between the attitudes they carry from their past and the exigencies of the situations with which they are confronted. For the traditional intellectual, dramatized in the film through Doctor Villega, this entails attachment to one's status and class in relation to subaltern groups and a refusal to confront inevitable violence and physicality. In the case of Sean, this attachment to the past appears to involve youthfulness, romanticism, a pragmatic mistrust of everyone, and a commitment to action. In the case of Juan, subalternity teaches the common sense of self-interest, mistrust of intellectuals, and physical survival. The characters share versions of the past, which they apply to the present, though in each instance there is the recognition of failure in this confrontation. Moreover, in this film the question of writing history in terms of failure rather than success—in ways reminiscent of postcolonial theory—challenges conventional forms of historicizing.

The issue of hybridity is important to the dramatization of history in *Duck, You Sucker* and other Italian westerns where the United States is also Europe, where the characters begin to merge in perspective, where clear-cut divisions begin to blur, where statements are really questions, and where indeterminacy is essential for understanding the changing character of the present, for understanding its ties to and departures from the past. In particular, *Duck, You Sucker* seems timely to the early 1970s when competing notions about revolutionary change were everywhere evident in Europe and in the United States, where confusion—not necessarily unproductive confusion—seemed to be dominant. While the spaghetti westerns are set in the American past, the particular preoccupation with materialism, the role of intellectuals and of knowledge, and the violence of the state places the films in dialogue with concerns that are identified with the European and specifically Italian political struggles. The use of history in the films brings past and present together for a still vital critique about social identity and political change.

# 3

# The Operatic as History:
# Two Risorgimento Narratives

From the silent cinema to the sound era, from classic Hollywood texts and European narrative cinema to avant garde films, the cinema has been drawn to opera despite prevailing misconceptions that opera is solely an elite form and that cinema is merely mass entertainment. As early as 1903 audiences saw a film rendition of Charles Gounod's *Faust*. In 1909 a French version of *Rigoletto* using Victor Hugo's *Le Roi s'amuse* and Giuseppe Verdi's *Rigoletto* appeared in an American translation, *The Fool's Revenge*. The following year witnessed two *Carmen* films, and 1911 saw a French *Aida* and a Russian *A Life for the Tsar*. In 1914 Cecil B. DeMille directed *Carmen* starring Geraldine Farrar, who had appeared the previous year in *Manon Lescaut*, and in 1918 Pola Negri starred in Ernst Lubitsch's German production of *Carmen*. In addition, Mary Garden performed in *Thais* (1917).[1]

Opera singers also took major roles in narrative films. Enrico Caruso appeared in *My Cousin* (1918), and it was not unusual to see Geraldine Farrar and Mary Garden in nonoperatic dramatic roles. The sound cinema expanded on the uses of opera. The 1930s and 1940s saw film appearances by notable opera stars such as Grace Moore in *Louise* (1939), Jarmila Novotna in *The Bartered Bride* (1922), and Fyodor Shalyapin in *Don Quixote* (1923). Other opera singers who appeared in nonoperatic film roles, lending their names, popularity, and prestige to the cinematic medium, included Lily Pons, Lauritz Melchior, Lawrence Tibbetts, Beniamino Gigli, Tito Schipa, Tito Gobbi, and Ezio Pinza.[2] Divas like Conchita Supervia also appeared in cameo roles, as in Victor Savile's *Evensong* (1934), based on the life of opera singer Nellie Melba.

Hollywood musicals have contained their share of the operatic. The extremely popular films of Deanna Durbin, Kathryn Grayson, Jeannette MacDonald and Nelson Eddy, and Mario Lanza were often based on operettas or included arias from various operas. Several versions of *Tosca*, *La traviata*, *La bohème*, and *Madama Butterfly* appeared between the two World Wars. The ongoing production of movie melodramas based on operas (often derived from novels, plays, or short stories) was exemplified in Italy by films such as Castellani's *Zazà* (1942) and Palermi's *Cavalleria rusticana* (1939) and in the United States, *The Loves of Carmen* (1948), starring Rita Hayworth. The biographical film was also dependent on opera, with such films as Carmine Gallone's *Giuseppe Verdi* (1938), Alfred Hitchcock's *Waltzes from Vienna* (1934), a British biopic, *The Great Mr. Handel* (1942), and Hollywood's *The Great Caruso* (1951)

Two of the most discussed operatic segments in narrative film are from *Citizen Kane* (1941), with its sequences involving *The Barber of Seville* and *Salammbò*. The opening of Visconti's *Senso* is set in the La Fenice opera house and stages the "All'armi" from *Il trovatore*. So recent a film as *Philadelphia* (1993) places great thematic and affective emphasis on Callas's rendition of Maddalena's aria "La mamma morta" from Giordano's *Andrea Chénier*. Jean-Jacques Beineix's *Diva* (1982), Norman Jewison's *Moonstruck* (1987), Francis Ford Coppola's *Godfather III* (1992), and Martin Scorsese's *Age of Innocence* (1993) are further instances of films that draw on opera. Two prominent examples of the uses of the operatic in avant-garde cinema are Germaine Dulac's *The Smiling Madame Beudet* (1923) and more recently Sally Potter's *Thriller* (1979).

Beyond these examples of cinema's indebtedness to opera narratives and of their performance on film, there are the countless historical and costume dramas, biopics, women's films, male oedipal melodramas, and family melodramas that resemble opera in their diegetic and extradiegetic uses of music, extravagant gestures, tableaux, and rhetorical flourishes, and their penchant for spectacle in the lavishness of costume and mise-en-scène. Their scenarios of seduction, enchantment, suffering, loss, and dying exquisitely are intrinsic to the operatic in cinema and indicative to many critics of the problematic nature of "pleasure in viewing this spectacle of (feigned) humiliation."[3] The operatic relies too on affinities between the star and the opera diva. Not surprisingly, critical reactions to opera and popular cinema are often similar. In addressing the operatic, Jean Starobinski writes: "[W]e restore opera to a little bit of its original quality when we admit that there is no innocent pleasure, that opera leads us astray to chimerical shores where we become the toys of a powerful enchantment."[4] And

Theodor Adorno was concerned with the "ideological element of opera, the affirmative element."[5]

What accounts for the various forms of the operatic and melodramatic in historical films, and how can they be identified and understood? According to Christine Gledhill:

> [T]he melodramatic mode . . . has served artists throughout the 19th century for the depiction of a variety of themes and social phenomena. . . . Industrialisation, urbanisation, and nascent entrepreneurial capitalism have found their most telling embodiment in a type of novel indebted to the melodrama, and the national liberals in Italy during the *Risorgimento*, for example, saw their political aspirations reflected in Verdi's operas (cf. the opening of Visconti's *Senso*).[6]

Important cultural and political connections between melodrama and music, and their role in the formation of national and popular conceptions, have also been commented on by Gramsci.[7]

In this chapter, I explore the operatic qualities of two Italian historical films on the Risorgimento: Alessandro Blasetti's *1860*, an Italian film that appeared in 1933, and Luchino Visconti's *The Leopard,* which appeared thirty years later. Operatic techniques, though not music from opera, are used in *1860*. Its reliance on the operatic resides in its uses of spectacle, music, choreography, and characterization. Its use of operatic conventions—not direct allusion to opera—reinforces nationalist mythology and traditionally sanctioned conceptions of power and politics. By contrast, the Visconti film both draws on opera music as well as on operatic conventions in its themes, characterization, and diegetic and nondiegetic uses of music to dramatize a very different conception of the Risorgimento. What, beyond the passage of 30 years, accounts for these different appropriations of the operatic?

## "Passion That Sings": The Operatic in the Historical Film

Cinema and opera are united in their dependence on several media—drama, music, painting, and spectacle. David Littlejohn's description of opera is applicable to cinema: "Opera has the ability to attack us with the combined power of three or four art forms (and popular spectacles) at once. A full-length play, a three-hour orchestral concert, frequently a ballet, a pageant or parade, a choral concert, and (depending on the designer) a certain amount of painting and sculpture may be contained within one ordinary opera."[8] Operatic narratives are also indebted to historical novels and plays,[9] relying on historical settings that cannot be reduced to the notion of empty spectacle but that must be seen, in the complex fashion of Verdi operas, as bearing social, historical, and political consequence. Like opera, the cinema has drawn on history for different ideological and aesthetic motives, and like cinema, opera has been criticized for the ways it misrepresents history. Historical films seem to be united in their attraction to the operatic, and the operatic, as melodrama, owes everything to spectacle, gesture, and music.

One of the charges often leveled against both opera and the historical film is that these forms are mere spectacle and that meaning is elusive, absurd, or irrelevant to them. The same critique has been applied to melodrama, a form of theatricality that is more dependent on gesture and music than on speech. In nineteenth-century theater, silent cinema, and opera, music and drama are interdependent. In his discussion of the transposition of melodrama from stage to screen, Nicholas Vardac affirms the importance of the relationship between music and spectacle, which are often far more important than dialogue: the music "enhanc[ed] the spectacle and heighten[ed] emotional sequences."[10] In particular, David Belasco's melodramas relied on spectacular "pictorial values, architectural settings, costumes, lights, supernatural effects, fireworks, and tableau . . . [accompanied by] the strains of a continuous musical accompaniment."[11] Similarly, Peter Brooks and Thomas Elsaesser have commented on the expressive use of music in all forms of melodramatic representation. And in her discussion of *Humoresque* (1946), Mary Ann Doane comments on "its reliance on music as the privileged signifier of affect. . . . [T]here are extended segments of *Humoresque* which stake out a space of signification almost totally outside language—language in any form, whether dialogue, voice-over, or graphics."[12] These critics exemplify a trend in recent film research that has sought to counteract the dismissive treatment of melodrama and to identify its specific modes of signification.

In melodrama as in opera, sights and sounds compete with verbal utterance. Speeches often are more important for their affect and delivery than for any innovation of meaning. In deciphering the strategies of melodrama, one must look to less rational and familiar sources of explanation for an understanding of spectacle's relation to common sense as folklore. The significance of the images and sounds, their relation to certain commonsensical apprehensions of the culture (or conversely their disruption of the commonsensical nature of phenomena), resides in the use of spectacle, choreography, and music, specifically in the ways they depend on past traditions of representation but also in the ways they depend on folklore—often described as magic or sorcery—that draws "from mysterious sources the power of making desire's injunction triumph."[13] Perhaps these sources are not mysterious, perhaps the common sense of folklore makes the texts' designs historically accessible and exposes their imbrication in notions of power and national, perhaps imperial, aspirations.[14] The "excess" of monumentalism derives from an inordinate veneration of past heroic figures and overvaluation of past events. The "great man" view of history relies on monumentalism and a grand scale of representation. In films such as *The Birth of a Nation, Napoléon* (1927), *October* (1927), and *Gone with the Wind* (1939) and in operas such as *Les Troyens* and *Aida*, one is impressed by the affective nature of spectacle: the emphasis on architecture, statuary, ancient monuments, the copying of the mise-en-scène from paintings of the period, the identification of the heroic protagonists with sculptures, the vastness of crowds, and the choreography of dances, processions, and military formations.

In the music of the films and in operas, especially Verdian opera, one hears brilliant fanfares of trumpets and trombones. Orchestras, like choruses, function in both literal and metaphoric fashion to provide the necessary musical accompaniment and to generate the proper solemn, ritual, or ceremonial affect. Orchestral and choral music also functions as a means of distinguishing between the individual and the collectivity, especially of distinguishing the great individual from the masses. The use of many instruments contributes further to this sense of monumentality, adding to a sense of the vastness and greatness of the individuals and the events. Orchestration also contributes to the illusion of transcendence, of surpassing both individual and collective struggles, where the interests of the state is visible as a major producer of monumental national images consumed through visual and aural media.[15]

In its uncritical and repetitive cannibalization of cultural sights and sounds, monumentality is affectively moving and reassuringly familiar:

> [M]onumental history . . . will always have to deal in approximations and generalities, in making what is dissimilar look similar; it will always have to diminish the differences of motives and instigations so as to exhibit the *effectus* monumentally, that is to say as something exemplary and worthy of imitation, at the expense of the *causae*, so that, since it as far as possible ignores causes, one might with only slight exaggeration call it a collection of "effects in themselves," of events which will produce an effect upon all future ages.[16]

At the same time, in its recognizable linking of the singular to the plural, the present to the past, in its very form and substance, it broadcasts its artifice. Monumentalism is assumed to partake of the sublime and the inarticulate and hence to overwhelm any critical sense. Unless one is ready to assume that audiences are completely hoodwinked into the belief that what they see is real, one must produce a more complex accounting of the affective relationship to "monuments." The operatic—even in its most monumental forms—actually relies on the most banal of commonsensical thinking. Composed of pastiches of elements from the past, verbal and visual clichés, folklore, and proverbial wisdom, monumental representations are paradoxically unmonumental in the immediacy of the affects they seek to invoke: patriotism, service, maternal sacrifice, paternal discipline, and youthful enthusiasm. Monumentality in all the arts addresses the construction of subjectivity, but in far more subtle ways than does propaganda. The valorization of sound functions in operatic terms to beguile auditors with a sense of presence and authenticity, thus diverting them—at least momentarily—from the knowledge of death, finitude, and contingency. The operatic and melodramatic sense relies on the *ars moriendi*, the fascination with death and with dying well.

Antiquarianism as another "excess" of attachment to the past is central to operatic and cinematic representations. Like monumentalism, this form of historicizing makes a fetish of past objects, people, and events and dramatizes the impossibility of living in the present; but unlike monumentalism, antiquarianism strives to create the illusion of things as they "really were" in the past. Monumentalism is willing to sacrifice fidelity for immediate effects. By contrast, antiquarianism is nostalgic in its attachment to exactitude :

> The fact that something has grown old now gives rise to the demand that it be made immortal; for when one considers all that such an antiquity—an ancient custom of the ancestors, a religious belief, an inherited

political privilege—has experienced during the course of its existence, how great a sum of piety and reverence on the part of individuals and generations, then it must seem arrogant or even wicked to replace such an antiquity with a novelty and to set against such a numerical accumulation of acts of piety and reverence the single unit of that which is evolving and has just arrived.[17]

In the reproduction of historical scenarios in the cinema, excessive reverence for the past can be identified in films like *Young Mr. Pitt* (1942) and *Young Mr. Lincoln* (1939) and operas like *Die Meistersinger von Nürnberg* with their painstaking historical research into the past.

Critical history in excess poses a danger that is the reverse of the other two historical forms. Identified with modernity, critical history tends to be judgmental and iconoclastic, disregarding what may be important for understanding the past,[18] interacting with monumentalism and antiquarianism in its inverted attachment to the past. The other two forms are affectively tied to the past through artifacts and documentation; critical history is tied to it in psychological fashion. In the cinema, such films as *Queen Christina, Catherine the Great* (1934), *The Scarlet Empress,* and *Camille* (1936) are instances of the fusion of psychology and history. Verdi's work also exemplifies this fusion in *Don Carlo,* the Shakespearean operas, and *La traviata.* From George Frideric Handel to John Corigliano, Western opera and cinema have willfully appropriated scenarios that dramatize the emotive, affective dimensions of social class and sexual and national relations. Portraits of wronged women are the lifeblood of opera and cinema, and the images seem to cut across tragedy and comedy, across historical moments, and across composers. Catherine Clément's study of opera heroines identifies the centrality of women—or more accurately, of prevailing conceptions of femininity—within the narratives: the kind of music with which they are identified and the relationship of the operatic narratives to forms of storytelling in Western culture.[19]

This melodramatic world is preoccupied with incest, the family and its terrible parents, the motif of madness, the ubiquity of unfulfilled desire, and the fascination with death and violence. The proliferation of scenarios involves conflicts between fathers and daughters, conflicts between mothers and sons, fratricide, matricide, patricide, suicide, infanticide, class betrayal, exploitation of the underclasses by the upperclasses, marriages of convenience that end in a cataclysm of violence. Whether the dramas are transplanted to Babylon, the Egypt of the pharaohs, the world of the crusades, or the time of Joan of Arc, the uses of the past are not empty spectacle or unchanging representations of a universal human condition; in their styles and modes of production and in their excessiveness, they flaunt their historical designs, as Edward Said has shown in his discussion of Verdi's *Aida* in *Culture and Imperialism.* He situates *Aida* within the discourse of imperialism with the caveat that the opera is "not so much *about* but *of* imperial power."[20] His discussion of the opera's production and of its text validates the presence of the history of imperialism. The rewriting of history "uses narrative to dispel contradictory memories and occlude violence—the exotic replaces the impress of power with the blandishments of curiosity—with the imperial presence so dominating as to make impossible any effort to separate it from historical necessity."[21]

The carriers of melodramatic excess are often the operatic diva and the film star as actress, spectacle, character, and personality. Though cinematic and operatic representation are collective forms, involving librettists/script writers, actors/singers, directors, conductors, composers, costumers, designers, and painters, the individuals recognized and adulated are the stars/divas. Divas—such as Maria Callas or Greta Garbo—become known not merely for their technical proficiency but for qualities that extend beyond the roles they perform and into the narratives of their personal lives. The diva exemplifies the figure of femininity, both as subject and object of melodramatic narrative, and its dependence on history. Inextricably tied to melodrama, the movie star and diva are associated with theatricality, with artifice, and with difference.

But what role does masculinity play in the operatic? The opera and cinema are inhabited by a range of masculine types: the ineffectual senex, the stock elderly figure of classical drama; the not-always-wise paternal figure; the tyrannical patriarch; the naive and youthful enthusiast called upon to save the nation (often the son of a tyrant or madman); the other-worldly magician; the misguided lover; and the scheming and unscrupulous malcontent or subverter. Despite their complicity in the restoration of political and social order, these figures are doomed to "power, loneliness, and death," thus dramatizing the cost of being implicated in conflicts over domination. The dramas involving masculinity are often conversion dramas wherein the protagonist undergoes a series of trials from which he emerges transformed. However, the operatic and melodramatic cannot be seen in binary terms. Femininity determines, secures, but also problematizes conceptions of masculinity. While femininity relies on historical narration, its affective dimensions exceed narration and temporality, signaling the protean, parasitic, and excessive nature that attaches it to all forms of gender and sexual identification.

David Littlejohn has described the role of the soprano as "at once ethereally (like E-string notes above the finger board on the violin) and, by the standards of most human beings superhumanly powerful."[22] Of the diva, Wayne Koestenbaum writes:

> [We] love her for intruding, via magisterial discipline, such a range of mannerisms—a control of how a phrase might always, every moment, *mean* something. This control made her an avatar of speakability, of the ability to say painful and illuminating truths and to shroud those truths in a medium that leaves its message shadowy and subliminal. . . . Sometimes her singing sounds like weeping. The suffering seems to arise from the discipline of music-making, and the discipline of woman-making.[23]

In accounting for a certain gay male fascination with the diva, Koestenbaum locates its source in the ways the diva is intimately associated with the transgression of sexual and gender expectations.[24]

Gender distinctions and transgressions are evident not only through singers' roles within the narrative but through their voices. For example, in the Verdi operas, Paul Robinson identifies the "power voices," those of the high baritone and the mezzo-soprano. The high baritone is associated with political roles and the mezzo-soprano with sexual roles. In both cases, Robinson asserts, the roles' tessituras are unnatural: unnaturally high for the baritone, as in the roles of Nabucco, Don Carlo, and Macbeth, and unnaturally low for the mezzo-soprano, as in the case of Abigaille in *Nabucco*, Lady Macbeth, Eboli in *Don Carlo*, and Amneris in *Aida*. This unnaturalness contributes to the heightened intensity of Verdi's melodramas in contrast, for example, to Mozart's comedies.[25] Most significantly, the voices' unnaturalness calls attention to the singers' artifice and so to the unnaturalness of conventional gender expectations. In the interdigitation of film melodrama and history, such figures convey a "sense of sexual ambiguity."[26] This sexual ambiguity has its counterpart in the cinema: in roles that undermine conventional familial and gender positions, in the iconography of stars, and in the narratives' obsessions with conflicts over power in both the public and private spheres.

Historical dramas in opera and cinema are highly rhetorical. In opera, this rhetoric is signaled by stilted expressions, archaisms, contorted syntax, double entendres, internal monologues, soliloquies, stichomythia, anaphora, and sighs, groans, weeping, and other affective sounds. Paralleling the rhetoricity of the language, the music and the narrative construction are rife with repetition as a dominant mode of organization: parallelism and antithesis, prolepsis and realization of prophecy, rising and falling action. Jeremy Tambling cites the use of palindromism—the patterned doing and ensuing of undoing of actions—which provides a forward and backward movement.[27] This palindromism is evident in the music, in the visual effects, and in events. The use of flashback techniques—visually or through speech and song—serves as a means of enhancing memory, providing information about the past, and offering a means of entry to the character's state of mind and to the outcome of events.

The role of dance in opera has its analogue in theatrical and cinematic melodrama. In Baroque opera, where it could occupy up to one-third of the performance, dance served a variety of functions: to further the action, to extend the dramatic tension, as celebration and ritual, as choric commentary, to convey "different passions or states of mind, and to communicate 'philosophic' positions."[28] The use of ballet and other dances, such as musettes, chaconnes, sarabandes, contredanses, and minuets, enhances themes, serving as a commentary on the state of the community or offering a dramatization of the protagonist's conflicts through fantasies, dreams, and hallucinations.[29] From the Renaissance to the present, dance has been a metaphor for social relations. Dance offers a portrait of integrating or disintegrating elements within the community, often by means of ballroom scenes in historical films and in opera. As an enhancement of spectacle, dance calls attention to cultural artifice. In its emphasis on bodily movement and on music, it enhances monumentality, and in the verbally limited expressive milieu of melodrama, gesture communicates affect for which there is no verbal analogue. Cinema and opera rely on posture, hand gestures, stiff and unyielding stances, slow and measured gait, surprising and protean shifts in movement, and the obvious and deliberate covering of areas of the face and body as standard melodramatic techniques. The antithesis between presence and absence, nature and culture, unity and fragmentation, and intimacy and remoteness are conveyed through the melodramatic "text of muteness."[30] This text invents and stages identities rather than merely imitating "reality."

The use of music other than arias in both opera and film can have the effect of heightening or undermining the visual representation. A critical assessment of the use of music in film reveals the composite sense of spectacle, music, sound, and silence, bringing cinema closer to opera. From accompaniments to silent film to fully developed musical scores, cinema offers a history of the varied use of music as a way of providing clues to the story; as narration; as counterpoint and emotive amplification providing access to the character's state of mind; and as a way of identifying context.[31] More than mere ancillary support for narratives, film music functions to express the limits of verbal and visual representation. Verbal utterances, especially the heightened language of melodrama, resonate with psychosocial significance, functioning to create a circuitry of affect that brings audience and text together in a bond of commonality. In the range of possible affects, they can serve as a reiteration of a commonsensical reception of the world or they can call into question programmatic and clichéd responses. The most seemingly banal sentiment can be transfigured or parodied.

In discussing the historical film as operatic (and keeping in mind Nietzsche's useful taxonomy of the uses and abuses of history), the next two sections will examine how operatic films work both with and against notions of historicism. Through a discussion of the films' use of iconography, painting, architecture, music, rhetoric, and dance, I will test the hypothesis that melodramatic affect is the currency that gives the historical narratives their credibility and value.

## Blasetti's *1860*, Fascism, the Historical Film, and the Risorgimento

The historical film has a conventional trajectory. At the outset, it offers a prolepsis, a foreshadowing of the events to come: a sense of foreboding, a foretaste of disaster, a sense of fatality, but also a foretaste of victory. The introduction to the protagonists involves an orchestration of images and sounds that document events, linking characters to a specific moment in history. The use of paintings, familiar classical or popular music, and especially patriotic hymns identify national context, landscape, and political themes. Stereotypical facial and physical qualities, drawn from a lexicon of class, gender, and ethnic characteristics, identify admirable or reprehensible qualities: "Cinematic history looks a bit like school history. . . . Classical history films were artifacts which attempted to reenact, recreate, dead events. The scenery had to be accurate and to conform to the models already offered by pictures or engravings. . . . Actors recited elaborate texts which were lectures on history and encapsulated what was considered the 'spirit' of an epoch."[32] The conjunction of artifice with the emphasis on accuracy, the cohabitation of the false and the "authentic," is also one of the major characteristics of opera. The historical film announces itself as both "possible and fallacious"; these are charges often made against melodrama, which has the same dual relation to fantasy and realism. As an instance of the "possible and fallacious" historical film, Pierre Sorlin cites Visconti's *Senso* and its portrait of the Risorgimento. The most blatantly patriotic type of historical film rubs shoulders with more subtle and critical types of representation in this dependence on documents, maps, paintings, landscapes, costumes, geography, and character treatment.

The *Ventennio* was a moment when the historical film offered opportunities to serve the fascist regime as well as opportunities to be critical of the regime. Alessandro Blasetti was one of the most prolific and popular historical filmmakers of the era. His historical films ranged from costume dramas, such as *La cena delle beffe* (1941) and *La corona di ferro* (1941), to biopics, such as *Un' avventura di Salvator Rosa* (1940), to Risorgimento epics, such as *1860*. In an interview with Francesco Savio, Blasetti, echoing the sentiments of other makers of historical films, stressed the authenticity of *1860*: "I protagonisti erano assolutamente presi proprio nelle compagne, nelle montagne siciliane. La gran masse dei personaggi era presi proprio dalla realtà." [The protagonists were actually taken from the countryside, from the Sicilian mountains. The majority of characters were taken from reality.][33]

The film focuses on the anticipation of Giuseppe Garibaldi's victory at Catalfimi, and according to Blasetti, the narration is consonant with fascist ideology: "Con l' inno di Mameli si concludeva il film, con questa adesione al regime. Che lo feci senza alcuno sforzo e senza alcuna vergogna. Lo dichiarò perchè ero convintamente fascista e credevo che effettivamente fosse giusto che la generazione attuale fosse indicata come la prosecuzione della tradizione garibaldina." [The film concludes with Mameli's hymn, with adherence to the regime. I did this without coercion and without shame. I say this because I was a convinced fascist and really believed it correct that the current generation should be shown the Garibaldian tradition.][34]

Blasetti's *1860* is a picture without stars and without professional actors, a phenomenon unusual for films of the early 1930s. In his earlier sound films, such as *Terra madre* (1931), and in most of his later films Blasetti used professional actors. However, in the later vein of neorealism, in *1860*, as his comments on the film indicate, he chose to work with local figures. The film was not shot exclusively in the studio but was made on location in Sicily. Though not a regular practice in Italy, the use of location settings was characteristic of the Soviet cinema of that era, to which Blasetti's work is indebted in style even if not in theme. The narrative is also a national rather than a domestic melodrama, featuring Garibaldi as its mythic protagonist, but he is remote, visible only in a few long shots. Though the film's differences from dominant commercial cinema are evident, they lead in a direction other than neorealism. The landscape is highly stylized, shot from long distances, and often in angular fashion. The characters are not seen from the vantage point of their daily activities or in a psychological treatment. Rather, they are shot in a fashion reminiscent of the paintings of the period. Appropriate to the commonsensical treatment of the Risorgimento in relation to fascism, the dialogue is meant to seem mundane and (ultimately) to convey the common interests of the various classes. The speeches of the peasant couple, Carmeniddu (Giuseppe Gulino) and Gesuzza (Aida Bellia), are sparse; they are made to appear representative of their social class and affiliation, as are the priest and other villagers.

From its opening moments, the film enunciates its operatic and monumental concerns. The music functions there (and throughout the film) as a signifier for the intense emotions invested in the struggle for national unity. The music will also be identified with nature and with the innocence of the Sicilians, and the orchestration serves as a bridge to the setting, connecting nature to revolution. Variations in tempo, volume, and intensity enhance contrasts in mood, character, and moral position. The images of heroic paintings of the battle of Catalfimi under the titles are accompanied by the sounds of trumpets and drums as well as by the sound of guns. A printed prologue announces the film's political designs on history: "Sicily was still under the rule of the Bourbons, who opposed the growing hatred of the people with regiments of foreign mercenaries. The revolt of Palermo was suppressed by blood and violence, but the destruction and the attacks only increased the actions of the 'pisciotti.' The rebel bands organized in the mountains in anticipation of their liberator GIUSEPPE GARIBALDI." Images of the gallows, of hangings, and of foreign flags are juxtaposed with images of a landscape, of mountains, trees, and earth.

In the vein of monumentalism, the images of the landscape assume a mystical significance, reinforced by music, that transcends their specificity to become part of the film's dialectical structure of the opposition between the foreigners and the Sicilian (soon to be Italian) population. Chiaroscuro lighting distinguishes the enemy from the heroic villagers, shown in a clear light. The choreography contrasts the unnaturalness of the Austrian mercenaries—moving rigidly and mechanically in columns—to the fluid and random movement of the Sicilians identified with nature.

Visual and auditory distinctions serve in monumental fashion to paint a melodramatic canvas in which lines are clearly drawn between friend and foe, patriot and interloper. The assignment of horizontal and vertical positions is metaphoric. The images of reclining and rising, like movement and stasis, measure progress but are also proleptic insofar as the notion of rising is associated with the notion of the Risorgimento. The enemy is also identified by jarring sounds, abrupt interruptions, entrances, and exits, whereas softly played patriotic music identifies the Sicilians. To enhance the stages of the conflict, a voice-over narration describes the course of events, the losses and gains, commenting on the changes in the action, serving as oracle, explanation, and historical authority.

The film does not depend on suspense. The emphasis falls on the realization of the already known, on the rehearsal of events that are drawn from history, a rehearsal that relies on reiteration and heroic embellishment. A moving camera records the panorama, the sense of the forces arrayed, and the rhythm of events. The camera movements are accompanied by loud or soft orchestral music, depending on the rise or fall of action. The use of tableaux, so characteristic of historical films, militates against the very naturalness the film seeks to espouse, enhancing its operatic features. The first image of Carmeniddu and Gesuzza, lying affectionately next to each other until awakened at the priest's behest to serve the cause, is like a painting that comes to life.

The various groups of villagers are also drawn from pastoral paintings, as are the later scenes in the church. The rhythm of the peasants'
lives is marked by tableaux of collectivity that are disrupted by the
enemy. Time in the film is directed to the future and to the anticipated
arrival of Garibaldi announced at the outset. The titles underscore the
notion of waiting, reiterating the phrase "Patience . . . Garibaldi is
coming," and the titles—like the voice-over—are reiterated at significant moments in the action until the final victory in battle.

The costumes by Nino Vittorio Novarese are instrumental in developing the dramatic class and national opposition that the film pursues
in relation to the peasants, the Bourbons, and the middle-class intellectuals that Carmeniddu meets on his journey to Garibaldi. As befits
her peasant status, Gesuzza is dressed simply, but she is filmed in a
highly stylized manner. Despite her apparent similarity to the other
women, she is frequently distinguished from them as an icon of familial and conjugal devotion through the use of low camera angles and
through close-up. Carmeniddu, who is also shot in similar fashion,
is—in relation to the other men and to Gesuzza—an icon of national
purity and devotion. The Bourbons are encased in their tightly fitting,
ornate uniforms, while the Sicilian men are seen in their coarsely
woven shirts and fleece pants, which, like the rocky landscape they inhabit, suggest primitiveness. One is reminded of Antonio Gramsci's
critique of Alessandro Manzoni's treatment of the peasants in *I
promessi sposi*; Gramsci describes their portrayal as typical of ways in
which subalterns are represented: childlike, inarticulate, and innocent.

The treatment of the passage of time is characterized by contrast.
The importance to them of the brief ten days that the couple has been
married before being forced to separate for reasons of political exi-
gency contrasts with the overriding urgency of this moment in national history. Carmeniddu's father-in-law reminds him that he "has
time" for Gesuzza after he has served his country. The inordinate
length of time that the Bourbons have occupied Sicily is juxtaposed to
the soon-to-be-experienced arrival of Garibaldi to free the people. The
journey that Carmeniddu will undertake will mark the time between
the people's continued suffering at the hands of the Bourbons, who are
seeking vengeance for a lost patrol, and his return with Garibaldi.

Children are significant figures in the films of the fascist era, as can
be seen in such films as *Vecchia guardia* (1935) and *I bambini ci
guardano* (1942); the child is a signifier of martyrdom, a vehicle for

The Sicilian heroes in Blasetti's *1860*. Courtesy of New York Museum of Modern Art, Film Stills Archive.

the legitimation of vengeance. The barbarism of the Bourbons is conveyed by their wanton killing of a young boy, a victim in this Manichaean struggle between good and evil. The slow movement of the horse that brings the boy's body back to the village conveys a further reproach to the inhumanity of the enemy. The music swells as the animal approaches the waiting priest (Gianfranco Giachetti). The priest's slow and methodical laying out of the boy's body under the impatient observation of the Bourbon officer dramatizes that the church is aligned with the people and that the cause for which they fight is sacred. The tableau of the people chanting their prayers in the church further enhances the unity between the church and emergent state.

Carmeniddu is accompanied by low lyrical music as he rides off, saying, "Ritorno con Garibaldi," and he is associated with water images, which act as a metaphoric bridge between Sicily and Genoa, his destination, and the return journey with Garibaldi and his men. The journey is intercut several times with scenes of battle between Bourbons and peasants that culminate in the brutal roundup of the peasants, underscoring the urgency of Carmeniddu's journey. Unconscious on his small boat, Carmeniddu is saved by a French ship that brings him to port.

Spoken language and dialect work as a strategy of political differentiation. The coexistence of Italian, German, and French functions as a reminder of foreign domination and as a means for distinguishing friend from foe. Unlike in a neorealist film, in *1860* the Sicilians for the most part speak not the Sicilian dialect but Italian, as if marking their assimilation into the future national landscape. The film makes a distinction between the plain style of communication of the peasants and of Carmeniddu, in particular, and the style of communication of the middle- and upper-class intellectuals whom he meets on his arrival in Civitavecchia. Carmeniddu is unable to understand the French of the captain who has saved him. Carmeniddu's role as silent subaltern is underscored as he listens to men arguing about the number of French troops present and listing the atrocities committed against women and children and the destruction of churches. Later he is also an audience to men of differing political persuasions arguing over the best course of events for the emerging nation: union between church and state, monarchy with Victor Emanuel, or a republic headed by Giuseppe Mazzini. The oppositions will be resolved in the victory of Garibaldi, who will be identified with the triumph of the monarchy under the house of Savoy. Carmeniddu breaks his silence only to ask penetrating questions about Garibaldi. His questions do not only underscore his peasant origins and hence his lack of sophistication, his distance from the political machinations and sophistry of the various groups struggling for control, his difference from quarrelsome intellectuals; they also dramatize his single-minded commitment to Garibaldi.

The use of posters and graffiti documents distinctions between Italians and foreigners. Graffiti on the walls of buildings reveal support for Victor Emanuel and the "revolution." By contrast, a picture of Napoleon is dissolved to a title, "Italia." A portrait of the Bourbon queen of the Kingdom of the Two Sicilies dissolves to a scene of a roundup of the peasants which then dissolves to a scene of the priest and Gesuzza, who are being threatened in an attempt to get them to provide information about the reasons for Carmeniddu's journey. Silence then comes to play a major role as the peasants refuse—even at the cost of their lives—to give the Bourbons the information they demand. The rhythm of the narrative quickens as the intercutting between the village and the city dramatizes the urgency of action, not dialogue. A delay in the inevitable resolution occurs when Carmeniddu learns that Garibaldi is tired and "ready to give up" and may not, after all, come to Sicily but go instead to Point Caprera. The setting of the military headquarters—the paintings on the wall, the furniture, the billiard room—contrasts with the dusty, rocky, and simple images of the village and with the threatened condition of its inhabitants. Further divisions among the soon-to-be-unified men of different regions are dramatized in the regional conflicts between Genoese, Piedmontese, and Sicilians. Throughout the episodes, the film employs folk songs from the various regions to call attention to regional antagonisms, which will be resolved in the news that Garibaldi will indeed make the trip to Sicily. Patriotic songs mark the end of this episode as one man says, "We can rejoice. Italy is unified."

Tableaux common to opera portray the familiar leave-taking between volunteers and their families. This lengthy episode, the prologue to the ultimate return of the men to Sicily and to the scenes of battle, is drawn out as two young man are shown, one saying his good-bye to his sweetheart, the other to his mother. The mother and son are filmed from various angles, especially low angle, and in medium close-up as he receives food from her and wipes away her tears. He is then filmed alone, immobile, like a statue in a low-angle shot. Carmeniddu's perspective is then recorded as he observes the various constituencies.

The high point of the scene of the departure to Sicily is the brief appearance of Garibaldi, who is announced by a group of people shouting his name. Then in a long shot, a male figure—Garibaldi—waves to the gathered group. An important commentary on the ideology and style of the film emerges at this point as men debate the merits of thought as opposed to action. One of the men asserts that one should not think too much about the events that are transpiring: "Action is better. Thinking leads to differences." These comments illuminate the film's strategy of highlighting differences only as a means to overcoming them in the interests of national unity. The specifically contemporary (and fascist) perspective in the film's valorization of action over thought is reminiscent of Gramsci's discussions of how "philosophy is affirmed in action" without regard even for tradition.[35] The commonsensical rejection of thought (and hence the rejection of difference) serves in this context of force to underline the impossibility of making difference disappear. In the work of concealing differences, the film only further exposes the nature and degree of the differences that exist. The film's uses of Risorgimento history come more clearly into focus as that earlier history is read as the true origin for the fascist emphasis on national unity, and especially as the basis for the overcoming of differences between north and south. The figures of Carmeniddu and the peasants, the emphasis on their lack of complexity, their loyalty, and their single-minded devotion, become the standard for action rather than contemplation. The scene ends with the image of the men heading toward their destined battle as the masses of spectators cheer them on.

Images and sounds escalate with the men's arrival in Sicily. The Bourbons abandon the villagers to fight Garibaldi. Freed, the peasants stream out in all directions, bells are rung, and the theme music rises slowly as the men mobilize. Statues of the patron saints of the church are paraded forth as the columns of men and women merge. The "painterly" dimensions of the ensuing scenes are evoked in the panoramic images of the landscape. The sight of the approaching Bourbon troops is accompanied by the sounds of drums. The moving camera also embraces the assembled group of villagers, intercutting those shots with isolated shots of Gesuzza observing the events. Images in profile of Gesuzza and then of the other assembled women, standing in worshipful attention, have an iconic quality.

Resorting to visual documentation, the film titles show a proclamation signed by Garibaldi that states: "Considering that in time of war it is necessary that civil and military power be concentrated in one man, I assume the dictatorship of Sicily in the name of Victor Emanuel, King of Italy." This document brings past and present together, suggesting a connection between the figure of Garibaldi and his assumption of power and the implied figure of Mussolini and his regime. The final scenes of the film are choreographed in monumental fashion, reminiscent of the paintings of battle shown at the beginning of the film. The film choreographs the opposing and diagonal movements of the two groups, the Bourbons and the Garibaldians. Interspersed are shots of Carmeniddu seeking Gesuzza, whose father had kept her away from the battle through subterfuge. Also intercut are images of flowers and trees, signifying rebirth, juxtaposed to scenes of combat.

Shots of the Italian flag are accompanied by the ever swelling theme music. The Garibaldians sing as they go to fight, and music (especially the sound of trumpets) is skillfully edited to advance or retard the various lines of group movement. The sound is interspersed with moments of silence. An elegiac tableau is intercut with scenes of intense fighting as Gesuzza comes across a dying soldier—the boy shown earlier with his mother at the men's departure for Sicily. Gesuzza cradles his head, and as he dies Carmeniddu comes running to her, shouting, "Italy has been saved." The film ends with the waving of banners, a painting of the famous battle, and the playing of the national anthem. Thus the film itself becomes monumentalized through the fusion of the national anthem and the image of the heroic painting, linking present to past and enshrining the actions of the men involved.

Drawing on the heroic traditions associated with the Risorgimento and the mythic figure of Garibaldi, the film seeks not to analyze the discourse of nation but rather to enact it in terms of a public melodrama that pits the forces of national and ethnic identity against the demonic forces of a foreign empire. The film reveals that the enterprise of nation building is highly dependent on the celebration of the union of family, church, and social classes and that this union is based on affective ties that are derived from part of the cultural and political landscape of the nineteenth century as reproduced in its paintings, novels, music, and opera. In particular, the operatic work of Verdi is relevant to the film's historical subject and treatment. In his *Opera and Ideas*, Paul Robinson discusses the political currents embedded in Verdi's operas, situating Verdi's work squarely in the context of the creation and realization of the nation-state. Accounting for Verdi's interests in historical subjects, subjects ranging from the fourteenth to the eighteenth centuries, Robinson identifies Verdi's settings as moments when the "important political entities were fashioned out of the feudal remnants of the middle ages."[36] Thus a drama of power is enacted in Verdi operas: "When the curtain goes up on a Verdi opera, we can expect to find ourselves in a political landscape and often in the midst of a struggle for power. We are made intensely conscious of the state and its reasons."[37] The political struggles in the operas bear on the failures of 1848, the renewed conflicts in the following decade, and the ultimate unification of 1870.

Instances of monumentalism and its rhetorical effects can be seen in Verdi's predilection for individual and group voices, interdigitation between speed and slowness, strident and subdued states, lyric and militant moments, and thematically the notion of "sacrificial leadership,"[38] which is also evident in *1860*. Blasetti's film focuses on the rhetoric of consensus that binds leader and people. The relations of power are not articulated polemically but are visually and musically conveyed in the way the film choreographs the dialectical oppositions between the protagonists (individual and collective) and their antago-

nists and in the way these oppositions are resolved through the elimination of foreign elements. Spectacle overrides narrative. As in opera,
it is not the narrative but the spectacle, music, and choreography that
drive the film. The iconography, tableaux, and choreography serve
rhetorical ends. Overriding the narrative are the numerous intertextual references that conjoin past and present, leaders and followers,
Sicily and the north of Italy, self-interest and sacrifice. The romanticiz-
ing of the leader (even to the point of making him inaccessible to view
like a divinity) makes *1860* a hagiographic exercise in combining religion and nationalism, a not uncommon strategy in certain historical
representations of the *Ventennio*. As in opera too, the masses as cho-
rus and as protagonists and the internal and external audiences are
united in the spirit of the Risorgimento in the final unifying ritualistic
moment of the Garibaldians and in the playing of Mameli's hymn and
in the image of the flag. The film draws heavily on commonsensical
knowledge broadly available in the culture to provide the audience
with a version of history wherein "their previous knowledge . . . will
be confirmed and improved."[39] In the terms of Gramscian common
sense, folklore acts to confirm, perhaps even domesticate, that knowledge. In Blasetti's film common sense unifies family, villagers, priest,
military leader, and political leader in a common fate. Does not history
sanction their relationships? Melodrama, with its ties to the family
and the corresponding ties of the family to the emergent state, is the
glue that cements the nation. The film confirms how the ideology of
nation formation anastomoses religious, familial, and ethnic discourses, transmitted through an iconography and language derived
from nineteenth-century operatic conceptions of politics and power.[40]

## Critical History and the Operatic:
## The Case of *The Leopard*

Luchino Visconti has been quoted as saying, "Verdi and Italian opera
were my first love. My work always betrays a touch of the operatic
whether in my films or in my plays."[41] Visconti's florid style reveals his
dependence on the operatic, if not on opera itself. From *Ossessione*
(1942) to *The Damned* (1970), Visconti's film work has not only been
identified with the operatic but also with the uses of history and spectacle. Two of his films, *Senso* and *The Leopard,* deal directly with the
Risorgimento. In the case of the former film, the text opens with the

presentation of a moment from *Il trovatore* in La Fenice opera house. The production of Verdi's opera becomes an occasion for patriotic demonstrations on behalf of Italian unity and of rebelliousness against the Austrians. This episode leads directly to the mainspring of the plot and to the relationship between the Countess Livia Serpieri (Allida Valli) and her Austrian lover, Franz (Farley Granger), through whom the failure of the Risorgimento is enacted. Visconti uses the operatic to expose the romanticism of nationalism, particularly the tension between the politics of family and of nation.

Despite Visconti's comments and those of his critics, how valid is an attempt to link film, opera, and historicizing and to describe Visconti's work from this vantage point? That Italy has been the home of major composers and singers and that Visconti was a director of opera is hardly a sufficient ground for making such connections. Angela Dalle Vacche has cautioned that the "connection with opera is an appropriate but limited one" in accounting for the penchant in Italian cinema for a "spectacular-allegorical style."[42] She identifies the style as Rankean history, "a history of great men, crucial battles, and memorable events," and suggests rather that the commedia dell'arte "historicizes not only the lives of the rich and famous, but can also turn its attention to the interface of body and history, of subjective experience and public events."[43] Dalle Vacche's position concerning opera reminds us of opera's hybrid nature and alerts us to the need to examine the multifarious ways in which spectacle—not merely narration and theme—functions to bridge "the interface between the body and history."

In contrast to the style of *1860*, one of the major features of the style of *The Leopard* is its reflexive uses of the operatic, producing an ironic treatment of the commonsensical nature of monumental historicizing. The film seems to be acknowledging its debt to Antonio Gramsci's concern for reading history critically: not for its successes but for its failures, not for its unifying effects but for its disunifying effects.[44] The operatic—including the literal borrowings from opera—serves satiric and hence antipopular ends, disarticulating conventional connections between the politics of nationalism and of familialism. The film, imbued as it is with a concerted play on the diegetic and non-diegetic possibilities of cinema, utilizes music, song, dance, gesture, physiognomy, architecture, costume, painting, melodrama, and satire. The excessively mannered presentation highlights theatricality. Narrative is minimal. The fetishized attachment to things and exaggerated sentiment call attention to the erotic experience of opera and cinema.[45]

Visconti's film was the result of a collaboration with the composer, Nino Rota, and the photographer, Giuseppe Rotunno. As usual for Visconti's films, Piero Tosi did the costumes. The script, faithfully based on the Lampedusa novel, was cowritten by Suso Cecchi d'Amico, Enrico Medioli, Pasquale Festa Campanile, Massimo Franciosa, and Visconti himself. The major actors were international stars: Burt Lancaster and Alain Delon; the Italian actors were people who had worked with Visconti before and were familiar faces in Italian cinema: Claudia Cardinale, Paolo Stoppa, Massimo Girotti, and Rina Morelli, among others. The Lampedusa novel was the inspiration for the work, though there is no doubt that, as in other of his films, Visconti embroidered elements from his own personal history onto the text. Though the operatic style of *The Leopard* is inextricably tied to certain familiar conventions of the historical film, opera is also incorporated through the ironic use of music from Vincenzo Bellini and Verdi to dramatize the machinations of power: the theme of succession, of family continuity and disruption, of inheritance, of romance. The violation of classical film narration, the slower pace of the narrative, and the characters' excessively mannered posturing function as distancing, as commentary, and as object for critical contemplation. The effect of the slowing down of the action is to undermine fascination with public performance and ritualized actions.

The speeches function less as oration and more as recitative. They move in the direction of deflating rather than melodramatically inflating sentiment. Despite the presence of operatic and melodramatic motifs—unrequited love, political betrayal, misrecognition, and loss of power—which should bind spectators to the text, these motifs are derailed by unresolvable contrasts and a self-conscious use of spectatorship (an emphasis on seeing and being seen) that inhibits any comfortable sense that the spectators are witnessing a representation that is transparent and uncomplicated. As if further to forestall any sense of Nietzschean monumental history, the film complicates the spectator's relation to both sound and image by placing a character or objects between the spectator and the filmed events. The dialogue and speeches—Don Fabrizio's, Chevalley's, Don Ciccio's, and Colonel Pallavicino's—are highly mannered, less in a conversational mode, more in a self-conscious rhetorical mode. However, *The Leopard* is not a reduc-

tive polemic on history. Through melodrama, history is subtly transformed into a critical instrument for enhancing the demystification of
official historical narratives of the Risorgimento. The fluid nature of
the music and the incremental and florid use of images serve to conjoin
Lampedusa's text to the film text, Verdi's operas to the Risorgimento,
Bellini's operas to Sicily, Visconti's films to Gramsci's writings, and the
Risorgimento to fascism and even to the post–World War II era. As a
historical text, the film's obsession with time is not unidirectional—
neither backward in time nor forward—but alternates between past
and present by means of its dialectical movement. In contrast to *1860*,
which moves linearly, this film, despite the wide-screen projection, undermines monumentality by also using images of paintings to undercut
any sense of inevitability and of progress.

The initial shots of the film act as a prologue; they establish the setting and the particular tone of the film. Shots from a slow-moving
camera accompanied by Rota's music will serve as the leitmotiv for the
work and will be used in different contexts. Houses are an index to the
film's treatment of character, the architecture serving to identify class
relations. The film opens with an image of a princely house, partially
obscured by trees and a statue. The camera continues to move into the
house, linking outside to inside and linking the architecture and statuary to the people as if they too were artifacts. Music gives way to the
chanting of prayers even before the tableau of Don Fabrizio, prince of
Salina (Burt Lancaster), and his family are seen. The seriousness of the
scene is undercut by images of a blowing curtain, by the bored stance
of the prince, and by the monotonous sounds of chanting. His slam-
ming closed his prayer book disrupts any illusion of piety. The session
is cut short by noises outside the room, which the prince learns have to
do with the discovery of a dead Garibaldian soldier in the garden and
with the news that Garibaldi and his men have arrived in Palermo.

In this film, as in *1860*, the figure of Garibaldi looms large, though
he is never seen, only talked about. As in *Senso*, Garibaldi is a figure
betrayed rather than the heroic leader of Blasetti's film, but the history
of the Risorgimento takes on new perspectives in *The Leopard*. For
the characters in *The Leopard*, Garibaldi becomes a threatening figure
and ultimately a figure to be contained and neutralized. The events of
the film will trace the ways the Risorgimento is a history of "passive
revolution" in Gramsci's terms. Don Fabrizio, whose motto is "All
must change, so that all can remain the same," is intent on collaborat-

ing with the revolution for his own and his family's self-interest rather than from idealistic conceptions of nationalism.

The contrast between the wife's (Rina Morelli) excessive affect in her fear of Garibaldi and the prince's aloof disdain (as in the Lampedusa novel) serves as a distancing and restraining effect on the melodrama.[46] In general, melodramatic affect is constantly undermined through contrasts between Don Fabrizio and the other characters. Contrasts become immediately apparent in the first scenes: between the prince's large body and the smallness of the princess's, the emphasis on closed and open spaces, and the contrast between movement and stasis. The differences will linger throughout the film as keys to the characters' subjective states and to the film's ironic invocation of sentiment. Other visual motifs, introduced early on in the film, will contribute to a sense of the various levels of affective interaction among the characters that the audience is invited to process. The recurring image of the coach ride—Don Fabrizio's nocturnal ride to visit his mistress in Palermo, the journey of the family to Donnafugata, and the coach ride with Angelica, Don Calogero Sedara, and Tancredi in the final moments of the film—does more than punctuate the various moments in the narrative; it is identified with temporality though not with progress.

Mirrors function as an index to the self-preoccupation of the characters and as a measure of the increasing nature of the prince's self-division. One of the first scenes between the prince and his nephew, Tancredi (Alain Delon), occurs before a mirror as Don Fabrizio orates on his political resistance to the Risorgimento, referring to the supporters of Italian unity as mafiosi and troublemakers. Tancredi, who has joined with the Garibaldian Red Shirts, will be the prince's unreliable instrument for realizing his plans for frustrating change. Through Tancredi the prince will ensure that power remains in the hands of the upper classes by a necessary class realignment with bourgeois wealth. This scene affords an ironic play on the use of mirrors: While the prince's reflection is one of "aristocracy incarnate," the view of Tancredi in another mirror projects the young man's opportunism. The two different mirror images reveal Tancredi's "duplicity not only to the revolutionary cause that he joins only to exploit, but to the uncle who stands to be hoodwinked by Tancredi's seeming commitment to the status quo."[47] The mirror shots will be contrasted later to shots of the prince at the ball, where he sees an impotent and dying man in the place of the earlier self-satisfied embodiment of power.

Sexuality and power will underpin the film's dramatization of the actors in what turns out to be an elegy for a dying conception of aristocracy and a satire on the birth of a new class reconstituted on the ruins of the old. The textual strands that weave discourses of family, sexuality, social class, and nation are consummated in the marriage of Tancredi to Angelica, the beautiful and seductive daughter of Don Calogero Sedara, the symbolic representative of the rising moneyed class. Don Fabrizio is the visual battleground for the conflict of the subjective and social forces that animate the historical analysis.

Nino Rota's musical theme for the House of Salina and for the prince's person is only evoked for other characters when the events involve the fate of Don Fabrizio. This music accompanies the images of landscape, the visible sign of the prince's property and power. The prince's eloquent comments to Padre Pirrone (Romolo Valli) on the mortality of his social class in contrast to the immortality of the church are presented like a recitative accompanied by the theme music. Similarly, his lengthy conversations in the hunting scenes with Don Ciccio, the organist, delivered in high oratorical fashion, are accompanied by the theme music.

The film is organized by place: Palermo, the journey to Donnafugata, the ball, and the final, brief epilogue on the street after the ball. As do the scenes in the prologue, this division serves not merely as a device for setting the historical context but as a means of integrating characters with events. Each of the "acts" and the spectacles to which they are conjoined invite a reading that probes relations between the public and the private, the present and the past, the folkloric and the critical, and the individual and the collective.

The Battle of Palermo, a sequence not in the novel, is presented in completely different fashion from the battle scenes in Blasetti's *1860*; Visconti chooses to underplay heroism and to stress carnage. The movement is choreographed so as to convey not the Manichaean battle between the forces of light and darkness but the ebb and flow of the attacks. The shots are not edited in an elaborate montage but are often continuous. The moving camera forces the spectator to view the spectacle but shows the brutality of the struggle. The sound of trumpets is heard, but so is the sound of the weeping, not celebration, as the women come to collect their wounded and dead. The heroic dimensions of the battle are further undercut by the entrance of Tancredi, whose motives are hardly idealistic, thus making the deaths seem all the more gratuitous and consonant with the film's unmasking of patriotic mythology.

In the literal and symbolic movement of the film, the journey to Donnafugata utilizes the spectacle of the journey by carriage (much as in Livia's long carriage ride in *Senso*) to dramatize the privileged position of the prince as he travels through the landscape, enabled by his princely position to cross boundaries with impunity. Alongside shots of the Sicilian landscape, the episode of the family in the countryside shows their dependence on subordinates for their pleasure. The picnic scene also provides a vignette of Concetta's and Tancredi's relationship, a relationship that is undone by Don Fabrizio's and Tancredi's power maneuver, foreshadowing the ideological gap between Concetta's adherence to traditional forms of feminine behavior and Tancredi's self-interested pursuit of power and erotic pleasure. This scene, another addition to the novel, said by Visconti's biographers to be a recollection from the Visconti album of memories, is interrupted by two flashbacks to Palermo that clarify the rationale for the journey, providing another family tableau and an opportunity to develop the film's elegiac motifs.

In the first flashback, the arrival of Tancredi and his fellow officers lets the viewer know that Tancredi has used his position to arrange for the family's safe passage from Palermo to their country estate. In an unusual direct address, Tancredi winks at the camera, smiling while saying that he has broken a rule of Garibaldi's; and his statement reverberates with ironic meaning in this drama of betrayal. The scene also provides further images of the spectacle that is such an integral dimension of this aristocratic life, as Don Fabrizio shows his frescoes to the men and expounds on their mythological significance. Property, spectacle, and sensuality are intertwined in the visual image of the frescoes and in the manner of Don Fabrizio's exegesis on the genealogy of this work of art and its relation to the Salina family genealogy and property.

In the second flashback, opera and operatic style merge as an officer sings an aria from Bellini's *La sonnambula*, Vi ravviso, o luoghi ameni":

> Vi ravviso, o luoghi ameni
> In cui lieti, in cui sereni
> Si tranquillo, i di passai
> Dello prima, gioventù!
> Cari luoghi, io vi ritrovai
> Ma quei di non trovo più![48]

The nostalgic aria enhances the *ars moriendi* motif associated with the prince, a motif that deepens as the film progresses. The aria also underscores the contrast between Bellini, a Sicilian, and Verdi and the drama of the betrayal of the south that is being enacted. And as with the other artifacts in the film—architecture, painting, sculpture, and house furnishings—this scene identifies the aristocracy as patrons of the arts, another autobiographical link between Visconti, who was duke of Modrone, and the arts, particularly theater, opera, and film.

Upon arrival at Donnafugata, the family is greeted by music from *La traviata,* "Noi siamo le zingarelle," played by the local band. There is a leisurely descent from the carriage and a ceremonial procession accompanied by the Verdi music as the group wends their way into the church. Inside the church, the music switches from the band to an organ and to the Verdian aria "Amami Alfredo." The camera glides slowly around the church, picking out architectural details, then moves to the priests officiating. The sound of bells and the singing of the choir are heard as the camera pans the family and assembled dignitaries. The camera pans the immobile members of the House of Salina propped upright in their elaborately carved high-backed wooden seats, looking as if they too are carved wooden statues.

Finally, at Donnafugata, the terms of the class collaboration in the passive revolution will be enacted. When Padre Pirrone, interrupting Don Fabrizio as the prince is bathing, explores the possibility of a marriage between Concetta and Tancredi, the prince greets the suggestion with scorn. A sensualist, Don Fabrizio asks the priest to dry his back as he lifts himself from the tub, provocatively commenting on the innocence of naked bodies. His paganism contrasts with the priest's admonitions about wanton sexuality. In the prince's explanation for his discouragement of Concetta's love for Tancredi and his encouragement of a union between Tancredi and Angelica can be seen the contradictory politics that animate him, his willingness to collaborate with the bourgeoisie rather than see the demise of his house. But it is this collaboration that will spell out his own fate and the fate of the aristocracy: the demise of his way of life, and the rise of opportunists like Don Calogero Sedara in the new national formation.

A family dinner is the context for introducing Sedara and his daughter. Sedara's awkward appearance and behavior, mocked by one of Don Fabrizio's sons, is a counterpoint to the lilting and ceremonial music that accompanies the men's entrance to the sitting room and to

The Salina family enshrined in church, in *The Leopard*. Courtesy of New York Museum of Modern Art, Film Stills Archive.

the dinner table. Don Calogero's presence, as acted by Paolo Stoppa, is a burlesque disruption in this scene of pageantry, abundance, and tasteful decorum. However, the late and dramatic entrance of his daughter, Angelica (Claudia Cardinale), introduces a new element into the politics of the family. The awesome spectacle of her beauty, conveyed through close-up and through simplicity of dress, which reveals her shapely figure, is registered on the faces of both Don Fabrizio and Tancredi. Angelica will realize the heights of Don Calogero's ambitions: an alliance with the illustrious House of Salina. Her beauty masks the collaboration and betrayal that underpin the Risorgimento.

The scenes between Angelica and Tancredi at the dinner table as he tells risqué stories about his military exploits in a convent indicate that this couple are united—in contrast to Tancredi and Concetta—by bonds of eroticism, self-interest, and cynicism. Angelica's raucous and indecorous laughter disrupts the dinner party. It also serves as a comment on the hypocrisy and pretensions of the occasion and reveals that her encounter with the upper class is a pleasurable game that Angelica, in contrast to her father, can handle. Group scenes, like this dinner party, are reminiscent of group gatherings in opera, carefully orchestrated and choreographed, offering clues to the melodramatic relations among the characters.

Another musical episode follows in the scenes where the election results are to be broadcast, determining whether Sicily will join the new Italian nation. The prince, framed by red curtains, hears young men singing a Sicilian folk song. The men on the street are joined by other young men, and the prince, who steps out with Padre Pirrone, still to the accompaniment of the music, tells the priest, "This is not a funeral." However, their subdued mood contrasts to that of Don Calogero, the orchestrator of this scene. Don Calogero appears on the balcony and attempts to announce the results to the assembled throng, but a band keeps interrupting his pompous speech. As Calogero speaks in the name of "the people" and of their wish for "an indivisible nation with Victor Emanuel as their monarch," the band once again blares out loud discordant sounds and Don Fabrizio laughs. Don Fabrizio's negative attitude toward Don Calogero and the monarchy are further developed in a hunting scene with Don Ciccio. The prince's cynical and amused stance is contrasted to Don Ciccio's passionate denunciation of the new Italian nation. When the organist hears of Don Fabrizio's plans to marry Tancredi to Angelica, he is horrified (as the princess will be later) about this misalliance and the betrayal of the House of Salina. Fabrizio's comments are the most clearly articulated when he reiterates the motif of the film, "All must change, so that all can remain the same." He tells Don Ciccio that the House of Salina's union with the Sedara family is important because Don Calogero is "very rich and influential" and that Sedara will "end up as the biggest landowner in the district." He is the "man of the future."

While Don Fabrizio is aware of the necessity of uniting wealth to power, he is also conscious of the threat that men like Don Calogero will pose to his own position. In contrast to the hysterical organist, Don Fabrizio acts realistically. His obstruction of revolution is his means of protecting his own class interests: He is not at all interested in change that would extend the power of the people. For him, "to follow the times," the creation of the nation-state under the reign of Victor Emanuel, appears to be the only solution for his class. Don Fabrizio and Don Calogero seal the marriage of Tancredi and Angelica, the future of the House of Salina, and the fate of Italy, bargaining over how much money and property Don Calogero will deliver as his entrance fee into the House of Salina. In the background, Padre Pirrone observes the business transactions. The camera glides to maps of the prince's holding and to paintings, underlining the "squalid reality of this engagement," bringing together "'pedigree in search of property' with 'property in search of pedigree'—a truth that Visconti reinforces visually by cutting to the painting of the once-glorious Donnafugata as Calogero triumphantly inventories the wealthy fiefdoms of Settisoli and Gibildolce which will constitute the landed part of Angelica's dowry."[49] After the contract is sealed, the prince releases Don Ciccio from the hiding place where he had been confined, saying merely, "I had to do it," and Rota's musical theme for the film is again introduced, this time played slowly and funereally.

That class continuity is at stake and linked to family is underlined in yet another family gathering. Tancredi arrives, no longer in the uniform of the Garibaldians but in the official uniform of the monarchy, with a fellow officer, Cavriaghi, a potential suitor for Concetta's hand. A storm is raging, and the atmosphere serves as a portent and an ironic commentary on the changing vicissitudes of the family. Angelica's dramatic entrance out of the storm in her wet cape contrasts with the subdued interactions between Concetta and Cavriaghi. Having given Concetta a book of poems by Aleardo Aleardi and inscribed in it "sempre sorda" [always deaf], Cavriaghi explains to her that she is deaf to his entreaties. By contrast, the greeting between Angelica and Tancredi is accompanied by lyrical music and a passionate embrace. The next episode underlines further the disjunction between the lovers' passion and their indifference to the past. They move through old rooms in the palace that are full of decaying paintings, dusty bits of furniture, and other mementos from the past. The dialogue is minimal, but the music is pervasive throughout this lengthy scene, which has little narrative relevance but which serves as a means to develop the lovers' sensuality and their indifference to others and to distinguish them as the founders of a new way of life. The loudness and intensity of the music, the close-ups of their faces, and the emphasis on their physical movement convey their youth and beauty, self-absorption, and energy in contrast to others in the family.

One of the most critical episodes, this scene highlights the sense in which class realignments between aristocracy and bourgeoisie are integral to the new nation-state. Chevalley, the secretary to the prefecture of Girgenti, comes to the House of Salina to urge the prince to take a political role in the new government by running for the Senate. A card game sets the scene for the interview to come between the two men. Don Fabrizio's son taunts Chevalley with stories of the barbarism of Sicilian life, telling him of a murder by brigands in which they dismembered a man. A liberal and a rationalist, Chevalley is horrified by what he hears, convinced that things will change with the new government. Persisting in this liberal discourse in his audience with the prince, Chevalley tells Don Fabrizio that he can aid his "lovely island" where there "are so many wounds to be healed" and asks the prince if he would like to see the elimination of squalor. The prince, in a long and highly oratorical speech derived from the novel, responds that the Sicilians do not want to be helped, that they are in love with death. The speech has multiple ironies: It seals Don Fabrizio to his own past. It perpetuates a familiar prejudice about Sicily as wild, primitive, and unmanageable. And it casts legitimate doubts on Chevalley's rationalistic discourse and on the notion that the new state, headed by people like Don Calogero and Tancredi, will ever be able to redress the "wounds" and eradicate the "squalor." When Chevalley leaves in his carriage, the prince says in elegiac fashion: "We were the leopards. . . . those who'll take our place will be little jackals, hyenas, and the whole lot of us, leopards, jackals, and sheep, we'll all go on thinking of ourselves as the salt of the earth." In keeping with the film's preoccupation, in theme and style, with listening and with obstructions to hearing, Chevalley cannot hear the prince as the carriage rides off to the swelling sounds of the theme music.

The climax of this drama opens with Verdian waltz music as the camera pans the landscape and the workers in the fields. By contrast, the scene dissolves to a palace, and the final third of the film is largely devoted to a ball where the cream of society is gathered. In Claretta Tonetti's words: "Against a background of fleshy flowers, gold-rimmed mirrors, precious candelabras, palm trees, and polychromatic marble, an elegantly dressed multitude dances the hours away and unknowingly celebrates the passing of an era."[50] From the initial moments of the processions of the guests as they greet the Prince and Princess Ponteleone to the strains of the last dance music, the scene is devoted to documenting the artifice, mannerisms, and material splendor of this world that will pass into the hands of the new landowners. Providing his own elegy for Sicily, the prince intones to a guest, "We are old.

2500 years we have been a colony. We are tired . . . sleep, eternal sleep is what the Sicilians want, and they will always hate anyone who tries to wake them. I have strong doubts whether the new kingdom will have many gifts for us." Though the last of the statements is prophetic, the prince is inured to the duplicitous role he has played in bringing this new kingdom to pass. The constant scenes of movement—not only of the dancers but of the prince's perambulation through the fourteen rooms—are, like so many scenes of the film, nondiegetic. The scenes serve, as in opera, to conjoin a number of motifs, with the prince always at the center. This passing world, its opulence, its excessiveness, its obliviousness to the world beyond its walls, is most fully realized through sound and image at the moment when it is most threatened with extinction. The ball episodes are the most operatic of the film. The music is unceasing. Either it drowns out the banal dialogue, or it remains in the background, but in both cases the music acts along with the movement and stasis of the characters to highlight the alienation of the prince from the others. When contrasted to images of courtly gatherings in earlier literature, such as in Baldassare Castiglione's *The Courtier,* the prince's perspective on the proceedings seems all the more moribund.[51]

From the Renaissance to the present, the image of dancing has signified social order: patterned and ritualized existence. Of dance, Sir John Davies writes:

> All sacred orgies and religious rites,
> All pomps and triumphs and solemnities,
> All funerals, nuptials, and like public sights,
> All parliaments of peace, and warlike fights,
> All learnèd arts, and every great affair,
> A lively shape of dancing seems to bear."[52]

Yet the ball scene in Visconti's film uses the dance to dramatize the emptiness of these rituals and to highlight the film's *ars moriendi* perspective by exposing this simulacrum of social order, one that is tied to commodification. Commenting on this scene, Millicent Marcus writes that the "[d]ance itself retells the story of the marriage contract, in all its social and moral ramifications, from acceptance to compromise to inner corruption and decay."[53]

The camera's attentiveness to the artifacts in the rooms—the paintings, the potted plants, and the tables burdened with the food—provides a visual reminder of the decadent opulence of the surroundings, as does Don Calogero's presence. Although given little dialogue, Don Calogero, the outsider, in his surveying of the objects in the house, seems like a property appraiser. His medal of the Order of the Crown of Italy is removed by Tancredi with the cryptic comment "Here it does not suffice." The scenes are a combination of masque, pantomime, and dumb show, played against the ubiquitous music and dance. By contrast, the prince's increasingly immobile stance is emphasized through the visual tableaux and linked to his declining political and historical role in this "new order."

Generational differences are prominent and center particularly on the stellar radiance of Angelica: All around her are dazzled by her beauty, which contrasts to the mummified appearance of the older members of the gathering. If the dance serves to signify social order, the emergence of the nation-state, and its founding moment in the new family, then Angelica and Tancredi are admired by all not merely for their beauty but for their centrality to the new order. Thus the prince's wandering on the edges of the ball signifies his peripheral nature and serves as a prolegomenon to his meditation on death in the library. In a scene derived from an episode in the novel, he retreats from the ball and sits and gazes at a painting, "Death of the Just Man" by Jean-Baptiste Greuze. Throughout the film, paintings have measured the progress of family affairs. This painting does not abandon the technique. In the tradition of the *ars moriendi*, it portrays the traditional preparation for death. The dying man in the portrait is surrounded by his family as the prince is surrounded by Angelica and Tancredi, who enter the library during his meditation. The irony of the portrait of Fabrizio as the "just man" surrounded by his family, Tancredi and Angelica, is not lost, since Angelica and Tancredi are preoccupied with themselves. Observing them, the prince tells Tancredi that "young people cannot understand death. For them death does not exist." Their silence validates his comment, and Angelica is instead eager to have a dance with Don Fabrizio. Tancredi, recognizing an erotic interchange between the old man and the young woman, gives his permission "this once." On the dance floor, the couple is observed by Tancredi and Don Calogero as if to underscore, despite the men's difference in birth and upbringing, their complicity in betrayal. The dance itself is like a *danse macabre*, as if the young woman were dancing with a corpse as the others look on. In relation to this scene, Mar-

The ball scene in *The Leopard*. Courtesy of New York Museum of Modern Art, Film Stills Archive.

cus has commented that "Fabrizio is hereby conferring his blessing on the marriage, handing down the mantle of familial property and prestige to Tancredi and Angelica and sanctioning this merging of the classes."[54]

The final touches to the ball scene take place during the banquet, where Don Fabrizio sits with Colonel Pallavicino and Princess Ponteleone. The dance with Angelica signifies Don Fabrizio's abrogation of dynastic power, and this scene marks his alienation from affairs of state. As the colonel waxes enthusiastic about Garibaldi as a man misled and betrayed by his own people, a man whose hand he has kissed in admiration, the prince wryly asks if this "was not going too far." The colonel responds that he was kissing a hand for the salvation of Italy, "a lady to whom we soldiers owe homage." Here Don Fabrizio is not only confronted with his irrelevance but with an image of his own complicity in "the salvation of Italy." This "salvation" will be exemplified by a shooting of Garibaldians at dawn.

Concetta learns from Tancredi that he supports this act in the name of "the new administration." He pompously tells her of the need for

"law and order" to defend against anarchy. The language of administration and of law and order at the barrel of a gun does not look backward in history, as the prince does, but forward, suggesting the language of fascism. In this scene Tancredi is revealed as the modern man,
the man of his time. Enraged, Concetta tells him that he has changed.
Condescendingly, Tancredi says of her as she sails away, "She's such a
darling when she's furious." His comment also reveals his unchecked
penchant for brutality and his indifference to critical reflection. Visconti called the Tancredi character "the kind of man who always
swims with the tide, betting on a certainty, like those who marched on
Rome or fought in Spain."[55]

No better than Tancredi, Angelica attributes Concetta's concern for
the doomed Garibaldians to personal motives, to the melodrama of
unrequited love. "She's still in love with you," she comments, and her
like-mindedness with Tancredi is sealed by their passionate kiss. The
new order is further sealed by yet another dance, this time with the
young people joined in a snake chain as they absorb Tancredi and Angelica into their ranks and move through the rooms, encircling the
older people still seated at their supper. By contrast, Don Fabrizio has
gone to the toilet. The waltz music suffuses this scene that has no dialogue. The music serves as melancholy commentary to Fabrizio's contemplation of his face in a mirror. The most ironic visual comment on
his mortality and on that of the guests occurs with his inspection of
numerous piss pots, the underside of this material splendor. As the ball
slowly winds down, with just a few couples on the floor and the guests
taking their leave of the Ponteleones (prefiguring the end of the film),
Don Fabrizio's earlier observation to Don Ciccio comes into ironic
focus: "This is a beginning, not an end."

The final episode of the film is another tableau. Don Fabrizio kneels
on the street as he sees a priest pass by, and he soliloquizes: "O star,
faithful star, when will you decide to give me an appointment less
ephemeral . . . in her own region of perennial certitude." His last
words are intercut with a shot of Don Calogero, Tancredi, and Angelica in the carriage as shots ring out, indicating the execution of the revolutionaries. The last words of the film are Don Calogero's: "Now
there is no more to worry about." The scene returns to Don Fabrizio,
as if in response to this comment. He rises, walks away from the camera, and the scene fades. Rota's musical theme then swells. The contrast between Don Fabrizio in his isolation and the group in the car-

riage serves to further highlight the effects of his actions: He had hoped to keep things the same, but he is responsible for this new order that infects every level of society. The marriage of aristocracy and money is complete, and the gunshots that reveal the death of the rebels mark not an end but the beginning of this threatening world that Don Fabrizio has helped to realize. The darkness of the night swallows up Don Fabrizio, but those in the carriage are seen in light. The visual leitmotiv of movement and stasis culminates in the contrast between the kneeling figure of the prince and the movement of the carriage, each going literally in different directions: The carriage moves toward the camera and the prince moves into the background.

## The Crystals of Time

In discussing the relation between opera and film and the problematic distinctions that critics want to make between them, Roy M. Prendergast writes: "If we equate the dialogue in film to the 'sung words' of opera, we can see there is little difference between opera and film."[56] The accompaniment of dialogue and action by the film's theme music provides words and events with an affective valence, distinguishing particular thematic investments. The leitmotivs of *The Leopard*, replete with ironies, are developed through image, language, and music. Though Don Fabrizio is committed to resisting change, he is a major instrument in producing change, a change that is designed to ensure sameness—with a difference. His perfidious role is instantiated through the incremental repetition of the music and of key words, phrases, and images. However, this repetition always functions with a difference, revealing varying stages in the prince's progression. The theme music moves in protean fashion to embrace others and finally to desert the protagonist. The uses of melodrama are well served by the operatic style, since the film is committed to obsessively dissecting the prince's motives and their effect on others. With the exception of the battle scene, the film enacts the paralysis of this passive revolution as a war of position, not of maneuver.

Pio Baldelli has argued that the film is a contemplative work as well as an autobiographical one.[57] Its contemplative cast is enhanced by its organization: The overture portrays the opulence of the house, the statuary, and grounds; the first act introduces the external threats that the Garibaldians present to family continuity; the second act at

Donnafugata dramatizes the efforts of the prince to obstruct change; the third act shows the rise to power of Don Calogero Sedara through the prince's planned union of Tancredi and Angelica and the failed romance of Concetta and Cavriaghi, staging the transfer of familial succession and property; the fourth act seals the victory of the new order and excludes Don Fabrizio; and the epilogue foreshadows his death. Like *La traviata*, whose music is so important to the film, the elegiac trajectory encompasses questions of class realignments, patriarchy, the production of the bourgeois family, loss, death, and recovery in a new vein—albeit ironically. The structuring absence in the film is Garibaldi. Though he is never seen, the effects of his role in the Risorgimento are constantly alluded to: in the image of the dead soldier in the garden, in the family's hysterical response to his name, in the Battle of Palermo, in the colonel's lengthy speech about Garibaldi, and in the shooting of the "rebels" at the end. His absence in *1860* serves to heighten his heroic and sacred character in relation to the myths of the Risorgimento that his name invokes. His absence in *The Leopard* serves also to preserve "his aura,"[58] but in the sense of his emblematic nature as representative of the Risorgimento and its failures rather than preserving him as a heroic savior. By taking the *failure* of the Risorgimento as its historical problematic, the film can better probe the ways in which class interests were compromised and can better examine Garibaldi as the sign under which these events transpired. This issue of historical betrayal (introduced in *Senso*) offers failure, not success, as a critical intervention in historical reconstruction.

The operatic in *The Leopard* inevitably comes into play in terms of the family melodrama, in which sexual politics are indissolubly linked to questions of nation and state. For the historical novel, as for opera, domestic issues are central, involving as they do questions of primogeniture, succession, inheritance, property, and power. The central conflict in *The Leopard*—from novel to film—is the relationship between the aristocratic and bourgeois family. Of the emergence of the bourgeois family, Gramsci comments:

> The revolution which the bourgeois class has brought into the conception of law, and hence into the function of the State, consists especially in the will to conform (hence ethicity of the law and of the State). The previous ruling classes were essentially conservative in the sense that they did not tend to construct an organic passage from the other

classes to their own, i.e. to enlarge their spheres "technically" and ideologically; their conception was that of a closed caste. The bourgeois class poses itself as an organism in continuous movement, capable of absorbing the entire society.[59]

In the aristocratic mode, the iron rule of the aristocratic patriarch, the necessity of arranged marriages, and the acceptance of familial duty rather than of romance are the rule. Hence Don Fabrizio must endure his wife's "Gesu Maria" when they have sex and seek sexual gratification outside conjugal bonds. By contrast, the bourgeois family that Tancredi and Angelica represent seeks to unite love and property through the semblance of choice in conjugal partners and the aura of reciprocity and common interests. The couple are the cynical harbingers of the new order of social class, the Italy that Chevalley seeks in idealistic terms to inaugurate as an instrument of change. While the prince wants no ties to the new nation-state, Angelica and Tancredi are fused with it. The couple's actions are exemplary of the fascist abuses of the state in the name of "law and order." Angelica and Tancredi are the new ruling elite. Whereas chivalric honor was the domain of the aristocracy, law and order are the province of the bourgeoisie. Angelica and Tancredi prefigure the emergence of civil society with its division between public and private spheres. While the new class appears to have greater freedom in its domestic affairs, it has in fact abrogated its prerogatives in the interests of a regulated society, the much vaunted law and order extolled by Tancredi as a stay against anarchy.[60]

Geoffrey Nowell-Smith has commented on the importance of Gramsci's writings to an understanding of the film, as has Millicent Marcus.[61] In his writings on Italian history and in his writings on the state and civil society, Gramsci speaks of the "crisis of hegemony, or general crisis of the state,"[62] characterized in this film by the defeat of the Garibaldians as well as by the expansion of the domination of the ruling class under the combined class forces of Sedara and Tancredi in the name of the monarchical state. The drama of this decapitation, this class collaboration, is also evident in the Visconti film in the domestic intrigue that makes this decapitation possible. The melodramatic affect resides in several related areas: in the portrayal of the aging and misguided prince, who is loath to renounce power; in the ambition of Don Calogero, who is determined to buy it; in the opportunism of Tancredi, who is willing to kill others for power; and in the figure of

Angelica, who is willing to romanticize and capitalize on this state of affairs for her own ends. Of all of the characters in the film, Don Fabrizio is the most complex as both betrayed and betrayer. He is the baritone to Tancredi's tenor. Though he is the villain, he is sympathetic and attractive by comparison to the others, perhaps because he appears to contemplate the terms of that betrayal.

According to Baldelli, the film was an opportunity to study this protagonist.[63] Like that of an opera protagonist, the role of Don Fabrizio is highly stylized and mannered. His character is largely conveyed through one-on-one interactions with other characters—Padre Pirrone, Don Ciccio, Tancredi, and to a lesser extent the princess. In these "duets" his rhetorical range is revealed. He appears to be always on stage, even in the moments when he is most isolated: observing others gathering for the election results, observing himself before the mirror, and praying on the street in his final brief soliloquy. His figure is especially linked to the ritualistic moments in the film—the initial scene of the family at prayer, the processional entrance to the church at Donnafugata, the church service, the stately dinner to entertain Don Calogero, and the ball scene. The use of language as sound to heighten the spectacle, to enhance the web of relations and themes rather than to produce any intrinsic or incremental meaning, is evident in the family scenes at prayer, at a group reading of a novel, and at the priest's chanting of prayers at the inn.

Marcus views the all-important use of mirror images as instrumental in underlining the nature of the prince's misrecognition, wherein he sees reflected back a delusory image of his wholeness and power. Fabrizio's melancholy gazing into the mirror at the ball reveals the fracturing of this self-image.[64] Gilles Deleuze, in his discussion of the time image in *Cinema 2,* has more to say on the nature of what he terms the "crystal image, a bit of time in the pure state." In his discussion of Max Ophuls's use of mirror images, Deleuze writes, in a vein relevant to the Visconti film: "[T]he mirrors are not content with reflecting the actual image, but constitute the prism, the lens where the split image constantly runs after itself to connect up with itself."[65] Moreover, in linking the spectacle of the circus with film itself, as Ophuls does in his film *Lola Montès* (1955), Deleuze writes:

> If we consider the relations between theatre and cinema in general, we no longer find ourselves in the classical situation where the two arts are

two different ways of actualizing the same virtual image, but neither do we find ourselves in the situation of a "montage of attraction." . . . The situation is quite different: the actual image and the virtual image coexist and crystallize, they enter into a circuit which brings us back constantly from one to the other.[66]

In *The Leopard*, as in *Senso*, there is an interpenetration of art forms, and as in Deleuze's description of *Lola Montès* and *The Earrings of Madame de* (1953), the operatic culmination of the film in the grand ball emphasizes that "life has become spectacle." Past and present, virtual and actual, and real life and spectacle blur. This "theatricality" divides everything; it makes everything a reflection and an object of reflection. In commenting on Visconti's films, Deleuze describes the treatment of time as "crystalline": "the aristocratic world of the rich, the artistocratic former-rich: this is what is crystalline, but like a synthetic crystal, because it is outside history and nature, outside divine creation."[67] Surrounded by art, the aristocrats "demand freedom but a freedom which they enjoy like an empty privilege."[68] Don Fabrizio lives in a decomposing world—a Götterdämmerung. History is important; it is "never scenery. It is caught obliquely in a low-angled perspective in a rising or setting ray, a kind of laser which comes and cuts into the crystal, disorganizes its substance, hastens its darkening and disperses its sides."[69]

The most important aspect of these crystals of time is "the revelation that something arrives too late."[70] The paintings, the use of the music of Bellini and Verdi, and operatic nature of the film contribute to this sense of decomposition and "too-lateness." Deleuze finds this most tellingly in the glance exchanged between Angelica and the prince at the ball. Similarly, the final moments of Verdi's *La traviata* dramatize the too-lateness of Alfredo's and Violetta's union: "Addio del passato" and "Gran dio, mori si giovane." Rodolfo's "Vi ravviso, o luoghi ameni . . . non trovo più," from *La sonnambula*, is another consummate articulation of the elegiac sense of opera that animates the film. Thus the use of the opera music in *The Leopard* is not a mere supplement to the action; it is the expressive vehicle through which the film's affective motifs are realized.

The operatic dimensions of *The Leopard* depend not only on Verdi and Bellini but also, though less directly, on Richard Wagner. The film fits the style of Wagner's operas: the "highly individual style," the symphonic form (Rota's theme music was derived from his own symphonic work), the relation between symphonic form and the episodic nature of the narrative, and above all the importance of the leitmotiv. In relation to the function of leitmotiv, Joseph Kerman comments that short, suggestive motifs are the necessary material from which Wagner constructs his dense symphonic web: "They are always present, always busy, reharmonized, rephrased, redeveloped."[71]

The variations in the theme music of The *Leopard*, the varying inflections in relation to different moments of the drama, heighten the internal dimensions of the political drama and enhance the nuances, variety, and the specificity of affect. Wagner's work, while ideologically different from Visconti's (even as Visconti's diverges from Verdi's), is significant for its linkage to melodrama in the portrayal of subjective experience. The aestheticism that characterizes the film, the focus on art, is also part of a tradition that links Visconti to Wagner as much as to Thomas Mann and the historical novel. Here, however, the film is cautious in its aestheticism, using artworks and music in ways suggested by Deleuze that undermine any clear notion of realism and representation. The self-conscious theatricality of Visconti's uses of the operatic in the service of history also links the two artists. For Wagner, the Middle Ages and the context of German and Norse mythology were the terrain of drama; for Visconti, the history of Italian unification and in particular the role of Sicily in that struggle.

Visconti ventures into a region explored by Gramsci, a region that has offered a perennial challenge to Italian writers and filmmakers and one that has been used for a variety of ideological purposes. *La terra trema (The Earth Trembles,* 1947) and *Rocco e i suoi fratelli (Rocco and His Brothers,* 1960) are Visconti's previous cinematic ventures into this region. The melodrama with which *The Leopard* invests the sense of Sicilian identity (in contrast to the northern Italian identity) is reminiscent of the tensions dramatized but then mediated by Blasetti's *1860.* At stake in *The Leopard* is the history of a region colonized by Austrians, Spaniards, and then Piedmontese, which continues to this day to pose a cultural, social, and economic problem in relation to the notion of Italy as a unified nation. This "southern question" addressed by Gramsci also involves the issue of the north as an "octopus which enriched itself at the expense of the South. . . . [I]ts economic-industrial increment was in direct proportion to the impoverishment of the economy and agriculture of the South."[72] The film is not silent on this issue. In the final visual image of the silent workers in the fields from which the scene shifts to the ball, the film takes note of economic differences. The alliance of the House of Salina with Don Calogero and with the House of Savoy constitutes another form of political and economic betrayal—of Sicily and of its subaltern classes as well as of Italian unity. The film takes note of the further colonization of Sicilians (which appears in Blasetti's films as a form of liberation) through a portrait of "the subordination and victimization of the native."[73] In a similar vein, Marcus comments that "[o]fficial histories presuppose that Italy was always an organic whole whose unity was suppressed by a series of foreign dominations until its popular liberation in 1870. Such a fiction conceals the reality of imperial conquest by the House of Savoy, which managed cleverly to identify its own dynastic interests with those of the mythic totality."[74] This is a view celebrated in Blasetti's film and critically dissected in Visconti's.

A final dimension of *The Leopard* involves cinema history. In histories of Italian cinema, Visconti is identified with the development of neorealism through his 1942 film *Ossessione* and his later *La terra trema*. Both films, as certain critics have noted,[75] are also dependent on the operatic. With *Senso,* Visconti moved to larger-scale production, utilizing U.S. funding and U.S. actors, a return to the historical spectacle with its expensive trappings and lavish costumes and settings and a return to a film form that the neorealists had so disparaged.[76] Yet *Senso* and *The Leopard* hardly qualify as monumental historical films. In their particular appropriations of opera, their resistance to binarism, mythology, and notions of progress, and their use of irony, they become a commentary on the kind of operatic historical film represented by Blasetti's *1860. The Leopard,* with its "essentially operatic spirit, dependent on large gestures, operatic design, and melodramatic movement,"[77] is able to exploit such features to offer a multifaceted and critical sense of history that mitigates the monumentalism characteristic of national discourses. The film is instead a critical historical reflection on the construct of the nation-state with its ties to family and property, an exercise in complicating and blurring the boundaries associated with official historicizing and its relation to opera and cinema. The film dissects the common-sensical character of popular representation on film and opera, which assumes a common fund of beliefs and goals and is mistrustful of analysis, intellect, and contemplation. In *The Leopard*, the self-conscious use of history in collusion with operatic themes and techniques contributes to a critical—not monumental or antiquarian—engagement with questions of politics and power, particularly with the failure of popular struggle.

# 4

## Sheets of the Past: Folklore, the Biopic, and *The Scarlet Empress*

D. W. Griffith's court of Belshazzar in *Intolerance* (1916) was, according to Kenneth Anger, a "portent of things to come." In this "New Babylon" of the 1920s, stars would provide audiences with "a new royalty, the Golden People."[1] Anger's evocation of Hollywood as Babylon and his linking of its stars to a legendary (and Orientalist) past reminds us of the conjunction of popular film with popular history. His words remind us of the dual historical role of the stars—as historical subjects of films and subjects as historical commodities—who helped to recreate and disseminate a folklore that provided divers versions of the past in relation to the present. Gore Vidal, in his *Screening History*, writes: "Movies changed our world forever. Henceforth history would be screened; first, in meeting houses known as movie houses; then at home through television."[2] The biographical film ("biopic") was a major source of historical representations. Feeding on a long tradition of biographical writing, the cinema, from the silent era to the present, communicated its sense of history through its reenactments of the lives of exemplary figures from past and present.[3] The television medium has not curtailed this form of historicizing; rather, it has in fact enabled it to proliferate. Not until recently has the genre received the attention it deserves, particularly in relation to an understanding of the importance of biography in the popular cinema.

Like any other genre, the biopic does not spring de novo from the minds of studios, directors, writers, and actors but is sensitive to and dependent on existing cultural lore, which in turn is dynamic, assimilating changing social conditions. As is characteristic of common sense as folklore, the biopic is not a seamless entity that fits into a hermetic classification of unique conventions and codes. Rather, it is a crude and stratified expression of motifs that are plundered from official history and memory as embedded in other literary forms, film genres, and artistic forms such as painting and music. Though the biopic has cer-

151

tain stable elements, the genre, like all genres, allows for differing perspectives on its historical subjects, revealing the requisite flexibility,
which inheres in popular culture (within social and political constraints). Just as the movie western feeds on fictional and historical
narratives that circulate in the culture in relation to the folklore of nation formation, such as foundational myths, biographies, and literary
fictions, the biopic cannibalizes existing forms of biography and a
folklore of individual agency. But how is it possible to understand the
writing of a life? What new factors does the medium of film introduce
into an understanding of biography as history that complicate the medium? What critical strategies are effective for understanding the constraints and possibilities of the genre? Discussing biography, Jacques
Derrida writes:

> [B]iographical novels or psychobiographies claim that, by following
> empirical procedures of the psychologistic—at times even psycho-
> analytic—historicist, or sociologistic type, one can give an account of
> the genesis of the philosophical system. We say no to this because a new
> problematic of the biographical in general and of the biography of
> philosophers in particular must mobilize other resources, including, at
> the very least, a new analysis of the proper name and the signature.[4]

The exploration of the proper name as signature is relevant to an examination of biography as a means of facilitating a critical interrogation of the social forces that get erased through the valorization of individual agency as a major determinant of history. "The very existence
of names," writes Christopher Norris, "is a sign that individuals are
subject to a social order within which they are no longer treated as au-
tonomous selves."[5] The rethinking of history via biography entails
analysis of how naming and classification facilitate the erasure and
forgetting of difference.

Though the biopic depends on an exceptional protagonist—on his
or her power for good or ill—too often the reading of agency becomes
preeminent, disarticulated from other more visual and auditory elements within the narrative: gesture, close-up, choreography, music,
landscape, and architecture. In relation to the narrative trajectory of
biography, the requisite conventional material relating to biology
and/or psychology can often be misleading, inviting causal explanations of the characters' roles in historical events rather than focusing
on the filmic conventions as fragments of cultural folklore. Spectacle—

often dependent in biopics on conventional images such as maps, paintings, sculptures, and buildings that seem to serve the ends of documentation—may not function in the interests of "authenticity." The mistrust of spectacle haunts reviewers' and critics' assessments of the uses of history, taking the form of measuring the images represented against existing scholarly documents. Yet these images provide clues to the types of history about to be unfolded, to the nature of the biopic's investments in the past, and especially to the figures that are its pre-texts for entertaining the past.

This chapter examines the multilayered uses of history that are embedded in the biopic. In contrast to George Custen's discussion of the biopic, my analysis is not primarily engaged in identifying the conventions and codes that are endemic to this genre. My major concern here is to challenge the commonsensical dimensions of history that are at the heart of the biopic as history. The initial premise of the chapter is that the notion of the biopic as mythic and hence as ahistorical needs to be translated into terms that reveal another form of history at work, not public history so much as popular history, not one history so much as sheets of history. As popular history, the films presume diverse rather than monolithic audiences and a multivalent treatment of their subjects. I discuss *The Scarlet Empress* as an exemplary text. It is significant for the ways in which it draws, intentionally and unintentionally, on many histories—existing popular beliefs about Catherine the Great, folkloric notions of Russia and Russian religious art, and star lore, especially as it relates to Marlene Dietrich, to narratives about her life, marriage, sexuality, and maternal behavior, and to her relationship with Josef von Sternberg. The film also draws on Hollywood folklore and by extension on commonsensical readings of the United States in the 1930s. The commercial and critical failure of the film may in fact have been due to its ambitious uses of history and may provide a basis for differentiating popular and mass culture. *The Scarlet Empress* encodes common sense as popular philosophy and as popular history. As such, one expects to find orchestrated in the film issues relating to class, gender, sexuality, and nation. Conceptions of history are filtered through the lens of melodrama and bear a similarity to history as shown in opera, especially Verdian opera, in which a wide range of exotic and spectacular historical settings are grafted onto the present in their treatment of the themes of power.

In Chapter 3, I examined two historical films—*1860* and *The Leop-*

*ard*—for the ways that operatic qua melodramatic strategies are revealing of differing investments in invoking the past. I suggested that their intertextuality and their treatment of image and sound called attention to a stylistic excess that frustrates conventional signification in ways charted by Kristin Thompson's close analysis of *Ivan the Terrible* with its implications for rethinking narrativity. The concept of excess as "counternarrative" and "counterunity" enables a rethinking of films and their reception. In both *Ivan the Terrible* and *The Scarlet Empress*, there are departures from the conventional uses of image and sound that have been generally identified with Hollywood films.[6] These departures, operatic and excessive in nature, are unsettling, suggesting a failure in familiar reading processes. The disjunctions violate expectations of narrative continuity and call attention to the fact that other, nondiegetic, elements must be accounted for. The excessive and disruptive nature of image and sound—the text's "broken rhythms of acting, its shifting space, and its heightening of stylistic devices"[7]— makes evident the need to draw on other sources of perception and cognition, involving different strata of information relating to past and present history. The biopic is polyphonic, drawing on the fragments that constitute commonsensical knowledge. Through its excessive style, *The Scarlet Empress* makes visible its engagement with heterogeneous discourses. In its studied and arch formulaic treatment of characters and events derived from cinematic conventions and clichés and from its embedded allusions to past and contemporary events, *The Scarlet Empress* violates the traditional bifurcation between past and present, public and private spheres, masculinity and femininity, truth and common sense, and realism and escapism, exposing the multivalent character of folklore and exposing its masquerade as history. However, the excess that signals heterogeneity and arbitrariness does not necessarily bespeak a new and radical reorientation to signification, forcing a critical examination of events: It may reconfirm the cleverness of common sense for anastomosing contradictory forms of knowledge, or as in the case of *The Scarlet Empress*, it may produce confusion, disgust, and a rejection of the film.

## The Folklore of the Biopic

In his terse definition of the biopic, Custen writes: "A biopic . . . from its earliest days is minimally composed of the life, or the portions of the life, of a real person whose name is used. Other than that, the definition of what constitutes a biopic—and with it—what counts as fame—shifts over with each generation."[8] The importance of this definition is that it enables a multifaceted reading of biopics, revealing the choices and possibilities in constructions of biography: their necessarily dynamic nature, their mutability from one time period to another, and their protean ability to entertain divergent points of view through the treatment of their subjects. Like other genres, the biopic has repeatedly suffered critiques that condemn it as anecdotal, unscholarly, and unrealistic, measuring its treatments of history against norms of facticity and documentation. These critiques are compounded by the long-standing animus against mass culture and its lack of "seriousness," an animus based on distinctions between traditional and popular forms of knowledge. The tendency to regard Hollywood as the dream factory, as a pernicious and invasive culture industry, has been tied to the assumption that genre films are ahistorical, leading critics to scavenge among psychoanalysis and myth theory to account for the construction and reception of the films. For example, Steven Bach, in his encyclopedic biography of Marlene Dietrich, finds that "[i]t is unlikely that Sternberg cared much about Catherine the Great, but he cared and knew about Marlene and sexual politics, which is the subject of the picture. No transaction occurs that is not motivated by sex or sexual jealousy, liberally laced with sadism. . . . There is a war going on in—Finland? Doesn't matter. Back to the real battlefield—the bedroom. Or the stable."[9] Bach's comments are symptomatic of a certain way of reading this film and by extension many biopics involving the so-called keyhole view of history. Bach recapitulates a psychosexual interpretation of biography, but as the subtitle (*Life and Legend*) to his voluminous biography of Dietrich indicates, there lingers the familiar bifurcation between "life and legend" as well as between public and private spheres, the bedroom and the world at large.

By contrast, Peter Baxter's discussion of *The Scarlet Empress* captures the complexity of the film's treatments of history:

> The "relentless incursion into style" that Sternberg later called *The Scarlet Empress* implies not just a deepening of Sternberg's alienation from the Hollywood cinema and the culture that it represented, but a shift into outright antagonism. . . . It is finally—for all its make-believe—nothing less than a nightmare version of the American dream as Sternberg had lived it, the dream quite literally of "upward mobility"

that overtakes its subjects, inflates them with limitless ambition, and gives them everything they want in return for everything they are.[10]

Though Baxter addresses *Blonde Venus* (1932) as an exemplary text, his reading of the Dietrich–von Sternberg film enables a better understanding of the contradictory but meaningful ways in which the style and substance of folklore are embedded in the biopic, enabling a different understanding of the film's designs on the past. Baxter's analysis is not a disavowal of history as dream or even as nightmare; rather, it is an expression of history in Gramsci's terms as common sense clothed in folklore.

A critical examination of history as folklore demands more in the way of information than do sociologically oriented analyses of the "public" or "domestic" sphere. Folklore, not as ethnography and not as exoticism but as a guide to nonofficial conceptions of the world, necessitates a recognition of the bits and pieces that make up its collage-like form. In his analysis of literary language and its relation to oral and recorded folklore and its relation to historicizing, Gramsci writes that the work of art "contains other 'historicist' elements besides its determinate emotional and cultural world. These elements are its language, understood not just as purely verbal expression which grammar can photograph in a given time, but a sum of images and modes of expression which fall outside grammar . . . [and] the expressive elements of the past, one can say of the entire past, are still alive in them."[11] Above all, I would argue that melodrama as an affectively "expressive element" serves as the adhesive for the shards of the past that are anastomosed to the present. Melodrama will address familial dramas that portray the abuse of paternal power, marital conflict, obstacles to maternal service, economic hardships that shatter the family, filial "ingratitude," and class misalliance—all of these situated within the discourses of psychology, which seek to account for success or failure. The melodramatic dependence on popular psychology and psychoanalysis tends to produce a semblance of causal explanation that favors individual agency and interiority, hallmarks of commonsensical thinking. Melodrama struggles to regulate the multivalent and overdetermined nature of power conflicts that involve the status of history and its problematic relation to questions of nation formation, sexuality, and familialism. Nonetheless, since the biopic entertains the confrontation with privilege, status, and justice as its major narrative and melodramatic trajectory, it will dramatize, directly or indirectly, the antagonisms that stand in the way of acquiring power. In the case of monarchy, these antagonisms will involve obstacles in the way of succession: wayward heirs, competing factions, a rupture between traditional ruling groups and the emergence of new interests and constituencies, and a tenacious adherence to the past and to tradition in the face of irreconcilable new challenges. In this way, the public and the private are related rather than disjoined. The perceived divisions between civil society and the state, between the public and the private domains, meet in the union of considerations of proper alliances that guarantee continuity, the distribution of property, and the stability of the state—all issues that are part and parcel of melodramatic representation. Melodrama as common sense and common sense as folklore articulate questions of legitimacy, ethical norms, justice, and the appropriate establishment and distribution of social roles. The sentiment so necessary to melodrama relies on the desire to reconcile personal and collective interests. The common sense of a culture serves to bring together a number of conventionally opposing elements, such as individual and collectivity, action and resignation, power and powerlessness, tradition and innovation, maintenance and change, antagonism and reconciliation.

In this context, a reading of the biography that is being dramatized through film cannot remain at the level of an analysis just of the film's text and of its auteur, singling out the personal whims, biography, and psychology of a director as the major determinant of critical assessment. This predilection for biographical attribution via textual analysis is exemplified by the following assertion: "The *Scarlet Empress* is either (depending on our view of von Sternberg's career at this stage) a bold experiment or the hyperbolic achievement of a director out of control."[12] However, the role of the auteur cannot be dismissed, if for no other reason than that authorship is an inevitable component of the folklore of the genre system produced by the film as social text. Concomitantly, the collaboration between certain stars, especially feminine stars, and their directors (in particular between Dietrich and von Sternberg), though not negligible, is insufficient to account for the multiple social texts that constitute popular history. An inordinate amount of text has been produced in commentary on the "Svengali–Trilby" relationship of von Sternberg and Dietrich, but that commentary needs to be considered within the larger context of the role this relationship plays in the production of the film as a social text.[13]

Just as a genre never exists in isolation but only in relation to the genre system, so too the star as a determinant never exists apart from the institution of stardom or outside the genre system.[14] The critical attention devoted in recent years to the phenomenon of stardom has challenged the folklore of the star as auteur and has examined the determinants of stardom from historical, industrial, and ethnographic perspectives.[15] In the case of stars and their reception, feminist studies such as those by Laura Mulvey and Gaylyn Studlar have also mobilized various versions of psychoanalytic discourse as a means of accounting for the positioning of the feminine star.[16]

While all of the elements that go into a film—genre, star, director, photographer, and costume designers, as well as the studio, technology, and publicity—are part of the folklore of the biopic among other film forms, these must be situated in relation to still other historical determinants. These determinants include the milieu in which these films are produced. As Pierre Sorlin has indicated: "The context is . . . the amount of previous knowledge which a given public invests into . . . images and it changes considerably according to the place and period in which the film is presented."[17] By introducing the question of the public and the role of audiences and of reception, Sorlin complicates further the question of historical representation, the different layers that are involved in identifying and understanding the pastiche of popular history. There is no end of attempts by media producers as well as critics to find empirical methods for identifying audience response. As an alternative to empiricism, the structuralist approach attempted to analyze the dissemination of cultural meanings through formalist analyses of texts. This analysis has yielded recently to an analysis of popular documents—fan magazines, tabloids, gossip columns—and of production data.[18] Moreover, the heavy emphasis on a monolithic ideological analysis has yielded to versions of cultural studies that stress the overdetermined and contradictory nature of popular and mass culture.

The kind of folklore, for example, that Gramsci proposed was not academic in scope and was not the province of the traditional intellectual. His notes on culture urged a rethinking of the nature of texts as social and political, emphasizing the circulation of texts in a given society. His notion of folklore was not ethnographic, arising from the impetus of a dominant culture to explore a subaltern culture and to have the subaltern culture explain itself to the dominant. As a multifaceted phenomenon, located in a number of places, and always only partial in terms of the knowledge it yields, common sense as folklore exceeds scientific measurement and codification. In his provocative notes on folklore, Gramsci wrote:

> Folklore should instead be studied as a "conception of the world and life" implicit to a large extent in determinate (in time and space) strata of society and in opposition (also for the most part implicit, mechanical and objective) to "official" conceptions of the world (or in a broader sense, the conceptions of the cultured parts of historically determinate societies) that have succeeded one another in the historical process (hence the strict relationship between folklore and "common sense," which is philosophical folklore).[19]

Furthermore, this conception of the world

> is not elaborated and systematic because by definition, the people (the sum total of the instrumental and subaltern classes of every form of society that has so far existed) cannot possess conceptions which are elaborated, systematic and politically organized and centralized in their albeit contradictory development. It is rather many-sided—not only because it includes different and juxtaposed elements, but also because it is stratified, from the more crude to the less crude—if, indeed, one should not speak of a confused agglomerate of fragments of all the conceptions of the world and of life that have succeeded one another in history. In fact, it is only in folklore, that one finds surviving evidence, adulterated and mutilated, of the majority of these conceptions.[20]

There is no systematic way in which to understand this folklore, to recover an authentic or unified sense of the thinking of a period. An approximation of this historical knowledge demands a multivariate analysis, bringing to light the various fragments that make up the layers of knowledge that are shared by various groups. The history that yields itself to investigation stands in opposition to official history, which presents itself as factual, unified, and universal. Common sense as folklore mandates a reading of every aspect of cultural representation and politics available in literary and popular narratives, songs, opera, rituals, proverbs, clichés, religion, education, journalism, architecture, family relations, dietary habits, and geography as these are articulated through national, gendered, sexual, and ethnic representation.

Gramsci's conception of folklore and common sense runs contrary to most conceptions of ideology. In his terms, ideology is not false consciousness, and it cannot presume to articulate subaltern knowledge. Folklore is historical, but it is necessarily partial and nontotalizing, the residue of forms of knowledge that are neither completely true nor completely false. As opposed to false consciousness, common sense contains a core of good sense, a rudimentary critical conception of the world. In its fragmentary, "decentralized," and "stratified" conceptions of life, common sense undermines the strict divisions that are normally made between state and civil society, just as it undermines other rigidly demarcated articulations of difference. Gramsci's observations bear directly on the question of biography and the biopic, in particular. The text of the biopic must be seen as a palimpsest. The history portrayed in the biopic, following Nietzsche's insistence that all history is of the present even when it speaks of the past, will have to be seen as a hybrid affair, grafting bits and pieces of the past onto the present and of the present onto the past. But this process is not transparent or even legible. Hence any of the prevailing notions of biography that seek to restrict the genre to voyeurism, to the fascination with the rich and famous, to an endorsement of wealth and power (or conversely a consolation for the lack thereof), to a paean to the unique and exceptional individual, or even to economic value as market value (selling itself as a product) obscure the fact that texts are an amalgam of cultural, political, and economic investments.

The constitution, circulation, and determination of the changing nature of value is not a mystical matter, nor is it a matter of pure measurement of commodities. Culture plays a material and interactive (rather than secondary) role in the determination of value: The problem is to identify the indirect yet material role that affective investment plays in the creation of social and cultural value. Fortunately, recent studies of melodrama have cleared a way to understanding the cultural and political value of affect, elevating melodrama from mere genre and situating its representations at the very heart of folklore. Rather than seeing melodrama as a debased discourse, Christine Gledhill has located it historically and dynamically in all forms of cultural expression, affecting and inflecting questions of nation, gender, and sexuality and their relations to the law and to the state.[21] In this context, the "excess" endemic to melodrama—and the sources of its disparagement—are associated with "hyperbolic emotions, extravagant gesture, high-flown sentiments, declamatory speech, spectacular settings and so on. Star personae produce similar excesses in the film realization of starring roles, in their high-living off-screen responses and in fans' and critics' responses."[22] Melodrama permeates all genres, percolating through all forms of media in the various life styles and narratives disseminated throughout the culture. A residue of earlier cultural forms in fairy tales, folk drama, theater, and opera, the affective valences of melodrama are inextricable from all forms of performance involving residual and emergent notions of gendered, familial, generational, class, legal, and power relations. What is important about melodrama in relation to folklore is that in its excessiveness it signals its role as a repository of common sense. Melodrama is obsessed with history, but its representations of time and space are, in Gramsci's terms, neither unified nor realistic; rather, they are "crude" and elliptical, a veritable repository of forms of knowledge that are contradictory and excessive. In relation to the excess it embodies, melodrama reveals that the emotions and behaviors it belabors are not excrescences but are intrinsically the carriers of value in relation to social phenomena.

The excessiveness of affect is surplus value that enables common sense to masquerade as truth and folklore as history, though, as evidenced by critical responses to it, this excess also produces a discomfort that must be identified on some level by audiences as a form of awareness of the fractures and artifices characteristic of commonsensical thinking. However, since all texts circulate knowingly in a capitalist economy in the commodity form as productive of exchange, the question of melodramatic affect cannot exist outside of economic considerations. This affect circulates in a number of ways to generate value: as economic product, as cultural repository, as validation for social institutions, as explanation for social and historical phenomena, and as evidence of the interdependence of cultural and economic value.

Thus my examination of *The Scarlet Empress* will draw on these many layers of history embedded in the film. The specific forms of folklore that are investigated in the discussion that follows include star lore, the folklore of Hollywood in the early 1930s and in the United States during that same period, the folklore relating to imperial Russia, the folklore surrounding the figure named von Sternberg, and the "legend" surrounding Dietrich. Other layers of folklore draw on film history—the studio system, the transition from silent cinema to sound, the uses of melodramatic representation with its dependence on familial, sexual, and national folklore, and the importance of architecture, statuary, costume, and music in the production of spectacle.

## Hollywood Folklore, Stars, Directors, and the Biopic

According to one rumor, Marlene Dietrich was brought to Hollywood in part to dethrone the reigning movie queen of Metro-Goldwyn-Mayer (M-G-M), Greta Garbo. Moreover this narrative has it that Dietrich was the creation of Josef von Sternberg, who singled her out to play the role of Lola Lola in *Der blaue Engel* (1930, make in English as *The Blue Angel*). He facilitated Dietrich's hiring at Paramount. At the time she came to Hollywood with von Sternberg, she was already married to Rudolf Sieber and the mother of Maria, a fact that she did not conceal and that was to become a factor in Dietrich's star lore. Heidede, renamed Maria, was a necessary appendage to the Dietrich entourage, and she accompanied her mother regularly to work at the studio. At the time of the Lindbergh kidnapping, the news carried the story that Dietrich had received threatening notes from kidnappers about her daughter. The news and movie magazines reported that Dietrich had installed all sorts of safety precautions at home and had hired bodyguards for the protection of her child, enhancing the image of Dietrich as a doting and concerned mother.[23]

From the time of her arrival in Hollywood, the publicity machines were set in motion, producing photographs of Dietrich in pants that were to figure in her sexually ambiguous offscreen persona as well as playing an important role in her films. Gertrud Koch claims that "Dietrich's discovery was not the secret sexuality of the mother figure, but an image of bisexuality which counter to all her assertions was part of her aura from Berlin of the 1920s."[24] Rebecca Bell-Metereau attributes a large share of the responsibility for Dietrich's "androgynous" persona to von Sternberg himself.[25] But the Garbo mystique had preceded Dietrich. Garbo's on screen and offscreen presence was also identified with androgyny, and she too shocked the Hollywood community by appearing in public sporting trousers.[26]

Other elements in the making of the Dietrich legend involved her marriage, which offered a facade of respectability with her husband. He in fact lived with another woman, a fact that was to remain discreetly in the background, as did the woman herself. Though Dietrich had her share of romantic liaisons, she stayed married to Rudi. Her relationships with women—Mercedes de Acosta and Elizabeth Allan—were shrouded in mystery.[27] And of course her relationship with von Sternberg was to remain a perennial source of speculation. Her image was also derived from her role in *The Blue Angel,* the film that established her as a star. The film, drawn from Heinrich Mann's novella *Professor Unrat,* played on a powerful image of femininity, drawing on the folklore of the fatal woman (e.g., the Lulu of Wedekind and Pabst), a variation on Carmen, the seductress who destroys men. Devoted to her pleasure and resistant to marriage, Dietrich is identified with cabaret culture and with lower-class life.

Lola Lola is represented as familiar yet exotic. She belongs to a long line of blonde sirens. Her persona is sexually ambiguous, and her seeming cruelty is mitigated by the fact that her victim is a pretentious, authoritarian and hypocritical professor. That Lola Lola lives on the fringes of the law, is an entertainer, and is a phenomenon of the urban environment marks her as being in opposition to the conventional morality of German bourgeois life. Moreover the character's androgyny coincides with the movements during the Weimar regime for liberalization of sexual mores. That *The Blue Angel* was made in both English and German and that Dietrich herself was able to make the transition from Germany to Hollywood on the basis of that film alone invites speculation about the protean characteristics of her image and especially about the way her image communicated a knowledge that crossed national boundaries, remaining foreign yet accessible and pleasing to Americans.

Among the many other elements that make up the ambiance of *The Blue Angel* and subsequent Dietrich films, a major element is her identification with the urban landscape and modernity. Dietrich is less at home in the rural environment, thriving in a more exotic milieu. Her frequent identification in the films as an entertainer stands in for less socially acceptable occupations. Her femininity and marginal class identifications, as presented on film and in information about her off-screen life, suggest her appeal across class lines, reinforced by her theatricality and foreignness. Her excessiveness of gesture, speech, and appearance enables a number of possible and contradictory readings of her star persona. Dietrich functions as an ever mobile site of opposing affects, capturing the contradictory positioning of national, class, and gender identification. That figures like Lola Lola convey militancy, insolence, cruelty, and cynicism as well as romanticism, thwarted maternity, and compassion testifies to the complex construction of the common sense that is, as Gramsci indicates, crude, fragmented, and above all contradictory.

Dietrich made seven pictures in six years with von Sternberg. The terms of their working relationship at Paramount were such that Dietrich was allowed to be handled exclusively by one director.[28] Their collaboration ended in 1935. This period coincides with the establishment of the Hays office and with the "lavish years" of Hollywood. Despite the Depression, Hollywood did not experience a financial crunch for several years. Peter Baxter has described in detail the conditions at Paramount under which the Dietrich–von Sternberg films were made. Unlike M-G-M, which was touted as the studio of the stars (though in reality authority emanated from above), Paramount "had a looser process of guiding individual projects."[29] According to Thomas Schatz, Paramount was a more market-driven company than was M-G-M.[30] Paramount had a "two-tiered market strategy." Known as a director's studio, one tier of its projects was identified with its major directors, among whom von Sternberg was counted. By 1932, the depression had finally hit Paramount, and the studio attempted to retrench in an effort to rationalize and contain its losses. It is very clear from both Baxter's and Schatz's descriptions that by that time the position of a director like von Sternberg had become precarious and was to become increasingly more problematic in the following years. Studio conflicts, the limitations of industrial production, censorship constraints, and the idiosyncrasies of men like B. P. Schulberg and Jesse Lasky, as well as von Sternberg's own personality quirks, were to make the situation increasingly difficult for von Sternberg, a man who had worked his way up the ladder of production to success. His disaffection was to make itself felt in the mode of production and in the content of his works.

Among the many anxieties that confronted studios and their personnel were dramatic changes taking place in the social, political, and economic climate of the United States. The Depression had exploded the bubble of capital speculation, exposing the tenuousness of untrammeled economic growth. Rising unemployment, breadlines, and the precariousness of survival that confronted workers did not portend well for confidence in existing economic structures. The threat of new immigrants did not sit well with a huge unemployed labor force, helping to bolster a rising isolationism that did not abate even as the threat of war drew closer. Those who were aware of events in Europe—Italian fascism and the rise of National Socialism—were not sanguine about the future and the possibility of "peace in their time." The images—published for the world to admire in magazines, newsreels, and newspapers of the lavish lifestyles led by the rich and famous and of Hollywood as a center of luxury and wealth—were starkly in contrast to the austere economic situation of the rest of the nation. However, in reading the star biographies of Dietrich and Garbo and of their careers in the 1930s, one is struck by the seeming remoteness of Hollywood from the exigencies of the Depression. The publicity mills that ground out the stories of the stars' day-to-day lives showed swimming pools, tennis courts, mansions, fancy automobiles, and premieres with stars dressed in the latest and most expensive designer fashions. But changes were taking place in the movie capital, changes that were already manifest in the transition from silence to sound and that were affecting the production, kinds of stars, types of genres, perceptions of audiences, and perceptions of national and international priorities.

At the time of Dietrich's arrival at Paramount, Hollywood was still in the heyday of its romance with Europe, a residual romance from the turn of the century that associated Europe with tradition and high culture and that still conceived of the United States as a frontier with a vulgar and unsophisticated population, a site of crude materialism. Moreover, in the realm of moviemaking, as Kristin Thompson has indicated, Hollywood entertained different conceptions of the medium of cinema from France, Italy, and the Soviet Union. The European and Soviet modes of production involved fewer intermediaries in the process of editing, had a less hierarchical and stratified division of labor, and accorded greater latitude to the director.[31] In fact some of the early tensions that certain foreign directors experienced in the Hollywood system may have been due in part to differing conceptions of production on the part of European directors and stars in relation to their U.S. counterparts. Baxter has, of course, pointed to von Sternberg's problems with studios, critics, and reviewers, as well as to his own thematic and stylistic predilections arising from his immigrant status. Other foreign directors did not fare as well as Josef von Sternberg, Ernst Lubitsch, or Rouben Mamoulian: Mauritz Stiller and Victor Sjöstrom were to return home to Sweden. But even those who stayed often experienced cultural disaffection. Along with émigré directors, Hollywood in the 1920s had also been a home to foreign stars such as Pola Negri and Greta Garbo, but the 1930s proved increasingly less hospitable. Negri's career went into decline, and Garbo was to make only a half dozen films after *Queen Christina* before her permanent retirement from the movies.

The settings of films ranged over the globe from the ocean to the deserts, from Europe to Asia. The images of foreignness may have been due to a number of factors: Hollywood's successful competition with other national film production, the mixed ethnic status of U.S. audiences, composed as they were of immigrants from western and eastern Europe, and the nature of filmmaking itself, which had been global from its inception, creating mobile workers for a mobile industry. As the success of Garbo and Dietrich indicates, in the early 1930s the foreign-sounding voice was not at all aversive, though within a few years—and for a number of reasons—a different version of national iconography would come to prevail that would make certain femmes fatales box office poison. In relation to the biopic, in particular, examining the biographical subjects that were undertaken in the 1930s reveals that there was a higher preponderance of British and European subjects in that decade than in the following years, which seemed to specialize more in Americana and also to focus less on royalty. Recollecting his early movie experiences, Gore Vidal has written that "[o]n our screens, in the thirties, it seemed as if the only country on earth was England and there were no great personages who were not English or impersonated by English actors. . . . England, and to a lesser extent, France, dominated our dreams."[32] Along with biopics featuring Elizabeth I and Queen Victoria, the 1930s witnessed films on Cleopatra, Marie Antoinette, Christina of Sweden, and Catherine the Great, among other royal subjects.[33]

The contentious biography of Catherine the Great that came to be titled *The Scarlet Empress* was described by von Sternberg as follows:

> I returned to the treadmill to make the last two of the seven films with her [Dietrich]. These last two, in which I completely subjugated my bird of paradise to my peculiar tendency to prove that a film might well be an art medium, were not bad, but audience and critics turned thumbs down. I took note of that with deep regret. *The Scarlet Empress*, the penultimate film, deserved to be successful by any standard then existing or now prevalent, but with few exceptions it was greeted as an attempt to assassinate a superb actress. The film was, of course, a relentless excursion into style, which, taken for granted in any work of art, is considered to be unpardonable in this medium.[34]

Allowing for von Sternberg's familiar battle cry against Hollywood as a place for lowbrows with no respect for great art, this quotation certainly provides evidence of his disaffection, a disaffection that was to work its way into the film.

In describing the projected biopic to Dietrich, he informed her that he had read Catherine's secret diaries and suggested that she look at the Garbo biopic, *Queen Christina,* as preparation for playing the role of Catherine. In England, Paul Czinner was directing *Catherine the Great* for Korda's London Films, starring his wife, Elisabeth Bergner, an acquaintance of Dietrich's from her years in Germany. The Czinner film was released in London at the time that Paramount began its filming of *The Scarlet Empress,* which, when it later premiered in England, received poor reviews. According to Steven Bach: "The film's catastrophic reception in England . . . prompted Paramount paralysis in America. Critics there in August were no less appalled; audiences fled from screens on which Marlene rode her horse in ecstasy."[35]

The fact is that Garbo's *Queen Christina* had also been less well received than had her earlier films. The lukewarm reception of these biopics was due to a number of factors that were to play a role in the future career of each of the stars. The remoteness of the settings and of the royal figures no doubt played as much of a role as did von Sternberg's baroque sensibility and Mamoulian's innovative uses of sound and image in his attempt to capitalize on the Garbo star persona. Both films may have marked the further turning away from the foreign and the exotic and toward more immediate, everyday issues associated with the U.S. milieu. In the case of Garbo, according to Frederic Sands and Sven Broman, *Queen Christina* "was a tremendous success with the critics, but not at the box office. The American public was escaping the Depression with Shirley Temple, not with Greta Garbo. During 1933 Garbo had ranked fourth in the popularity polls; a year later she was thirty-fourth."[36] And by 1937, she, along with Dietrich, was labeled box office poison. The increasingly tenuous attitudes toward the two stars can be seen in the popular film magazines of the time.[37] The predilection for more comedies, musicals, and women's films is an indication of a move toward rationalizing genre production and toward reinvigorating ailing audience attendance. The fixing of responsibility on von Sternberg for the commercial and critical failure of *The Scarlet Empress* is symptomatic of the search for a scapegoat to account for the failure (in fact, von Sternberg was only one source of the problem) and coincides with the martyr image that von Sternberg, along with many of his critics and admirers, constructed.

The negative reviews of *The Scarlet Empress* typically used such terms as "tedious," "foolish," "dull," and "pompous"; one critic described Dietrich as the unfortunate victim of von Sternberg's "idiotic affectation" and as a "hapless sort of automaton."[38] The film provoked other groups, in particular, the Roman Catholic Legion of Decency. In this case, it was not Dietrich alone who merited criticism but also Garbo and of course Mae West. It was hoped that by putting Dietrich (and Garbo) into historical garb, some of the criticism could be short-circuited. The objections were ostensibly directed at demeaning representations of women as prostitutes, as cabaret singers, and as sexually provocative and perhaps also sexually androgynous figures.[39]

Much was made too of von Sternberg's extravagance at a time when the watchword was economy.[40] In retrospect, *The Scarlet Empress* has gained critical appreciation as film scholars have come to recognize the formal, aesthetic, and cultural contributions of the film. In relation to the film's address of sexual representation, Andrea Weiss has commented on the ways in which biopics such as *Queen Christina*, *The Scarlet Empress*, and other 1930s films (featuring such stars as Katharine Hepburn) have provided historical access to alternative images of sexuality and gender. Weiss sees Dietrich and Garbo and the "ambiguous, androgynous qualities" they embody as finding "expression in the emerging gay subculture of the 1930s. Garbo and Dietrich were part of the aristocratic, international lesbian set which was this subculture's most visible and influential component."[41] Many biographies of both stars validate this international and aristocratic component, if not the issue of lesbianism, and particularly that many of the publicity shots of the women in magazines featured them in mannish clothing.[42]

As Richard Dyer suggests, female stars are an amalgam of the ordinary and the extraordinary, the familiar and the exotic. Their appeal appears calculated to cut across gender and sexual categories, to violate cultural binarism and prevailing images of heterosexuality. Hence with the coming of the censorship code, this androgyny does not disappear but takes on new and more subtle forms. In the case of the Paramount films that Dietrich made with von Sternberg, the violation of heterosexual norms, bourgeois taboos, and unduly saccharine notions of life and of power are not only characteristic of their work together but perhaps also of a view of life in the 1930s that gets anesthetized, becomes carefully coded, or goes underground in the next

Marlene Dietrich, in *The Scarlet Empress*. Courtesy of New York Museum of Modern Art, Film Stills Archive.

decade to reemerge more openly in the cycle of film noir. But *The Scarlet Empress* is an extraordinary compendium of common sense and folklore addressing the complicity of sexuality and power.

## *The Scarlet Empress* and Uses of the Past

The question of national identity plays a central, though subtle, role among the many ways in which the Dietrich star persona was constructed. Dietrich's Germanness (like that of the character Sophia Frederica of Prussia, whom Dietrich plays in *The Scarlet Empress*) is part of her star signature. She was German by origin but American by adoption, and she was outspoken in her criticism of the Nazis. Like many other stars, Dietrich offered her services to the United States government during World War II. Yet prior to the war, the question of her nationality was more indeterminate. Like Garbo in films such as *Queen Christina, Conquest,* and *Camille,* in which she plays European figures even though her nationality is amorphous, Dietrich's connections to a specific nation become blurred, and her gender and sexual identity is generally indistinct. The accents with which Dietrich and Garbo speak are sufficiently generalized so as to mark only their "foreignness" and not a particular nationality. This foreignness contributes to the overall sense of nonbelonging, or of transcending specific national or gender identification. Garbo and Dietrich had to be coached into modifying their accents so that they lost any distinguishing national characteristics (though a slight accent lingered on). The undifferentiated sense of their use of English is remarkable for the ways it reveals that the material of stardom, tied to the characters the stars play and the genres with which they are associated, often depends on capitalizing on the transgression of difference. Voice pitch is also important to the construction of the Dietrich star persona. Dietrich's deep voice evoked an undifferentiated aura of sexuality and femininity. The vagueness of the star's national origins and sexual predilections is the raw material out of which a number of contradictory values are crystallized, appealing to many different constituencies as well as calling critical attention to the theatrical and spectacular nature of femininity.

As an exemplary text for the folklore of stardom, *The Scarlet Empress* encodes the transformation of the star/character, in von Sternberg's words, "from a guileless young princess to a mocking and ruthless empress"[43] and constitutes a page from the transformation of Marlene von Losch/Sieber to Marlene Dietrich, the Hollywood star. In *The Scarlet Empress*, the specific stages in Catherine's conversion from ingenue to the "Messalina of the North" are visible in the costuming—in the light and frilly, tight-waisted dresses with their billowing skirts that she wears as a young girl, in the ornately beaded silver wedding dress and veil, in the opulent and weighty fur-trimmed dress with matching fur hat and muff that she wears to review the troops, and in the tight-legged and glittering white uniform with short cape and white hat that she wears at the end of the film. Dietrich's identification with veils, furs, and feathers, as well as with trousers, was already quite marked in *Blonde Venus*. The costumes for *The Scarlet Empress* were designed by Travis Banton in consultation with Dietrich. He had created the costuming for other Dietrich–von Sternberg films and was one of the inner circle of Marlene's trusted collaborators. The consistency of clothing styles from film to film highlights the protean nature of the star's femininity. The emphasis on opulence, spectacle, and inaccessibility are very much in evidence in this film.

Dietrich's clothing was designed to capitalize on specific features of the star's physical appearance. Her legs, though covered, were shown to advantage in the pants of the uniform she wears in the final scenes. Her lithe body is emphasized in her tight-waisted gowns. Her breasts, which (according to Dietrich's daughter) she believed were not among her major assets, were not exposed by low-cut dresses. Fur and ruffles detracted from cleavage. Even the hands (not always hers) when in close-up were often gloved or those of another person. The lighting of her films and the use of close-up were as consistent as the costuming. The photography of *The Scarlet Empress* was largely the work of von Sternberg,[44] though Bert Glennon, who had directed the photography for *Blonde Venus,* is credited. Lee Garmes was the director of photography for other Dietrich–von Sternberg films such as *Morocco* (1930), *Dishonoured* (1931), and *Shanghai Express* (1932), and he "laid claim to creating the classic Dietrich image," which depended on "the 'north lighting' he himself preferred . . . [which] brought out Dietrich's cheekbones and a fascinating dissonance between her heavy eyelids and the playfulness of those artificial eyebrows penciled in an inch above them."[45]

The ongoing attention to Dietrich's face is revealed by the consistent angles and lighting in the close-ups during the film.[46] Of the use of close-up in this film during the wedding scenes, Louis Audibert comments: "[T]his look, this face, this distracted character, yet weak and wounded, are captured here on canvas, every aspect of which is alight, and among which there reigns the silent image of power."[47] Barry Salt too, reviewing the use of close-up in *The Scarlet Empress* and comparing the shots in which people are looking at Dietrich with the shots where no one is looking at her in *Shanghai Express,* comments that "Sternberg's 'filtered feminine mystique' took a back seat in his films before the advent of Marlene Dietrich."[48] And Gilles Deleuze comments on the aspect of wonder and luminosity generated by the use of close-up in the film during the scenes of Catherine as a young girl.[49] The film thus capitalizes on the power of Dietrich's face to unite several elements: the theme of power, the centrality of femininity and its relation to that power, and the power of cinema to express the verbally inexpressible. In this biopic, Dietrich's costuming, the ways she is lit, and the intense uses of close-up graft the folklore of stardom onto the folklore of royalty. Through the film's style, the dual nature of monarchy—its mortal and immortal dimensions—is incorporated into the folklore of stardom.

The Dietrich–von Sternberg biopic went through a couple of titles—"Catherine II of Russia" (abandoned because of the London Films's production of *Catherine the Great*) and "Her Regiment of Lovers" (abandoned because of its risqué implications)—before becoming *The Scarlet Empress*. The Paramount film covers roughly the same events as the British film in its portrayal of Catherine's rise to power. The difference, of course, resides in the treatment. The British film stresses the helplessness of young Catherine at the hands of the Grand Duke Peter and his minions, making her a victim of royal machinations and depriving her of conjugal love and maternity. Gradually she is transformed into "The Little Mother," gaining the Russian people as her children. She has no romantic liaisons. Her virtue, altruism, and ethos of service are directed toward the patriotic ends of state formation, nationhood, and monarchy, a notion of aristocracy consonant with the British interwar lore of the 1930s (though Korda, the producer, and Czinner, the director, were of central European origin). Unlike von Sternberg, they sentimentalized aristocratic noblesse.

In Elisabeth Bergner's portrayal, Catherine's assimilation into the machinery of sovereignty at the expense of personal desire dramatizes a fusion of state and civil society in the interests of democratic rule. *Catherine the Great* is 180 degrees removed from *The Scarlet Empress* in the costuming, the architecture, the mode of characterization, and the uses of the star, which are more in keeping with the understated and restrained use of spectacle and sexuality characteristic of the British cinema of the 1930s. Korda's lavish biopic appears modest compared to von Sternberg's film. Not only differing cultural contexts but the strict British censorship of the time may certainly account for the difference between the restrained British portrait of royalty and the irreverent and sexually charged U.S. treatment,[50] but another factor that may account for differences is the drastically divergent uses of the star system in Britain and in Hollywood. In the case of the Paramount production, the narrative and spectacle function as a prism in developing the motifs of the film, as they splinter the various episodes and characters surrounding Catherine and even the character of Catherine herself. Cast as monumental history in a literal as well as a discursive sense, architecture, statuary, and iconography play a major role in refracting the film's themes. The actors merge with the iconography and statuary. *The Scarlet Empress* seems much closer to the silent cinema, inviting comparison with Gance's *Napoléon*. Both *The Scarlet Empress* and *Napoléon* experiment with visual and sound montage. Both rely on printed titles to provide information. And in both films, the acting is operatic and highly choreographed. *The Scarlet Empress*'s fusion of sexual and state politics and its obsession with power—particularly its ability to make the nature and effects of power concrete—are also characteristic of the Gance film.

In his discussion of affection-images, the expression of affect through the uses of the face in cinema, Deleuze explores how, despite their seemingly ahistorical appearance, these images express the "historical state of things, social roles, and individual or collective character, real connections between them."[51] Though in a film like *The Scarlet Empress* "the affect is independent of all determinate space-time . . . it is nonetheless created in a history which produces it as the expressed and the expression of a space or a time, of an epoch or a milieu (this is why the affect is the 'new' and new affects are ceaselessly created, notably by the work of art)."[52] The uses of the face, in particular, become a means for individuating characters, for linking the characters to their social roles, and also for producing a consonance between the individual character and the role that he or she is assigned to play. The affection-image, as "sensation, sentiment, emotion or impulse,"[53] is melodrama's instrument for providing expression of a possible past.

What are the common denominators in the recorded histories of the Russian monarch? That Catherine was a Prussian, that Prussia would be enhanced by a union with Russia, that Russia was an absolutist state, that the Orthodox religion played an important role in the consolidation of imperial power, and that there was a struggle for the throne between the grand duke and Catherine, which she won. The folkloric elements reside in the commonsensical attributions of motives, which make the royal world transposable to the world of the everyday. As the residue of "conditions [that] have been (or seem to be) modified or have given way to bizarre combinations,"[54] folklore thrives on connections with earlier social systems, but connections that are embellished by modern exigencies. The remoteness and power of the aristocratic world is reaffirmed but democratized through the equalizing character of affect. The sexual intrigue of the courtly world and its obsession with power and domination resonate as the common sense of the present. By thematizing familial and particularly sexual conflict as antagonistic to continuity and power—a theme that then cuts across class lines—the film can endow the alien events of Russian history with familiarity, even if not plausibility.

From its opening intertitles, the film offers evidence for its folkloric dimensions. Beginning with language reminiscent of the fairy tale, a title announces, "About two centuries ago, in a corner of the Kingdom of Prussia, lived a little princess—chosen by destiny to become the greatest monarch of her time—Tsarina of all the Russias—the ill-famed Messalina of the North." Before the viewer can fall under the impression that this is a fairy tale whose characters will live happily ever after, the reference to Messalina of the North, a figure identified with cruelty and excess, promises to complicate the fairy tale. Whether the audience is familiar with Messalina or not, the reference to "ill fame" produces another set of expectations more intriguing than those of conventional fairy tale lore. The proleptic tone of folklore fore-shadows a conflict between benign and malignant forces, a conflict that an audience aware of Dietrich's persona could anticipate. More-over the allusion to "ill fame" would, for those readers of popular film magazines, conjure up the naughty but enticing image of Dietrich in drag along with the exoticism promised by the biopic. Could there also be some allusion to the "ill fame" of the Hollywood Babylon of the 1920s and 1930s—the scandals, the opulence, and the reputed "or-gies"? Perhaps the narratives of star marriages to European royalty (as exemplified by Gloria Swanson's marriage to the Marquise de la Falaise) were also counted on to be familiar to audiences. Soap operas of the time, such as "Our Gal Sunday," were responsive to movies and to the society pages with their announcements of marriages between sweet young American girls and European nobility. The international, aristocratic set of lesbians referred to by Andrea Weiss, to which de Acosta, Garbo, Dietrich, and the Countess Dorothy di Frasso be-longed, might also be hinted at in the allusion to the "ill-famed Mes-salina." The publicity generated by the gossip columns and fan maga-zines about the relationship of the star to the director may also have entered into the resonating aspects of this allusion.

In a more general sense, the circulation of notions of aristocratic ex-cess were derived from silent epics, from Cecil B. de Mille and Eric von Stroheim in particular, but such notions have a longer history in Amer-ican and European popular literature in narratives about innocents abroad. The film taps into major melodramatic scenarios involving marital conflict and the tedium of bourgeois notions of marriage and reproduction, clothed in the distancing strategies of aristocratic garb, thus encoding the inevitable melodramatic conflict between romance and domesticity. Hence while von Sternberg and Dietrich may be considered as the auteurs or realizers of this film, it is clear that the biopic, intentionally or not, relies on existing popular lore. Perhaps the film touched too closely on the chords of social antagonisms to be successful at that time. Perhaps 1930s audiences understood the film only too well but were not ready for the annihilation of its folklore.

For a while, the trajectory of the narrative plays with the fairy tale of the intertitles by introducing "the little princess" played by Maria Sieber, Dietrich's daughter. In the introductory bedroom scene with its highlighting of the mother-child relationship through a focus on images of toys and instruments of torture, the narrative quickly positions the young Sophia Frederica as a victim of a pretentious and duplicitous mother and through superimposition links her to visions of cruelty. The film encodes a biographical parallel relating to the extradiegetic relationship between Dietrich and her daughter. Sophia Frederica, like Maria, was forcibly encased in braces for several years to straighten her posture. Sophia's mother, consulting with the physician, finally decides to remove her braces, as Maria's had been removed. The theme of toys also resonates on several levels throughout the narrative. On one level, it was known that Dietrich carried her "toys" with her wherever she traveled, and the doll that Sophia/Maria clutches belonged to Marlene. Sophia's mother's interdiction of toys for the child is also associated with the maternal discipline that the film plays out through both Sophia's mother and the Empress Elizabeth. Toys will become associated with the ruthlessness of Grand Duke Peter and with torture and execution. The image of toys and the theme of power are telescoped in the montage of executions, choppings, axings, and hangings that are superimposed on the child's image.

This initial scene materializes and orchestrates a number of images that provide a collage of power relations: physician/executioners, maternal despots, and Russian imperial despotism. That the initial scene takes place in the bedroom does not restrict the film's focus to the private sphere. Rather, the film's imagery of torture and its satiric treatment of usually benign maternal and physician figures suggests a blurring of boundaries between public and private power. In its indirect allusions to the star biography, the scene also merges Hollywood history with the film's historical subject. The style also foreshadows the film's consistent union between theatricality and the mundane. In overdetermined fashion, the film draws on various resources to produce a sensory overload, which the film will not only maintain but escalate.

The biopic often chooses to begin with the childhood of its subject, and the trajectory from childhood to maturity can serve a number of purposes. It can anticipate the destiny that the subject will realize. It can foreshadow the inevitable obstacles that stand in the way of that realization. And in the case of *The Scarlet Empress* in particular, it reinforces the importance of and the equation between power and cruelty. The transition of Sophia Frederica from a child to a young woman is accomplished through the superimposition of her image onto images of torture, thus hinting at her penchant for cruelty even as a child. This cruelty does not surface until her arrival at the court of Russia, and the way Dietrich plays the young Sophia makes the character seem quite innocent. Critics have complained of the awkwardness of the worldly Dietrich playing an innocent young woman. Yet the transition from innocence to disillusionment is central to the emergence of Catherine as the "ill-famed Messalina of the North" and to this biopic as a conversion drama. To a more sophisticated contemporary audience, Dietrich's rendition of the young Catherine appears like a parody of the U.S. portrayals of girlish innocence so prominent in the youthful images projected in many films of the 1930s.

Dietrich seems to be a parody of herself. The segments serve to dramatize the conflict between the star persona of Dietrich and what that persona is not. The episodes also serve as an ironic commentary on femininity and on its constraints: the banality of seductions, flirting, romanticism, submissiveness to elders, and virginal innocence. As a conversion drama, a strategy common to the biopic in its dramatization of the organic development of its subject, the film taps into the common sense of the melodrama of enlightenment, the emergence of forms of knowledge that construct the subject in relation to power. In particular Sophia's attraction to Count Alexei (John Lodge), the emissary from the imperial court, inscribes several important thematic considerations involving Dietrich folklore: her susceptibility to romance, her amenability to seduction, if not to sex, and her appreciation of physical attractiveness.

The mysteriousness with which Count Alexei handles her romantic questions about the character and physical appearance of the Grand Duke Peter is associated with the other innuendoes in the intertitles about the barbaric world that she is about to enter. For example, one reads: "Suddenly, like a swift storm appeared the Messenger of Russia—a vast empire that had built its foundations on ignorance, violence, fear, and oppression." Like those in a silent film, the titles are not innocent. They do not merely situate the spectator in relation to time and place; instead they "direct" the narration. Their very reductiveness also collides with the complexity of the images and scenes that are presented of the Prussian court and of the increasing disparity between Sophia's expectations and their realization. The titles place the spectator in a superior position to the protagonist at this point, though this relationship will be altered as the film progresses, and like the visual imagery, they will reinforce the multilayered ironies with which the biopic chooses to treat its subject.

Sophia's journey to Russia is noteworthy for the way in which the film uses Tchaikovsky's music to accompany the movement of the carriage. The vague images of natural landscape and the stops along the way with the images of people observing the retinue are not accompanied verbal dialogue; instead an intertitle, undercutting any sense of patriotism or high expectations the music and imagery might have generated, announces: "After weeks of hard riding, the Russian border was reached, where the populace hid behind shutters—out of the way of the fierce Cossacks, who with reckless fury protected their nobles from even a glance of the enslaved people." The unwholesome and unromantic image of imperial Russia conveyed in the film may be due to several factors. As a Jew, von Sternberg was no doubt aware of the Russian pogroms and the cruel treatment that befell Jews at the hands of anti-Semites, and this may have tempered his enthusiasm for Russian history. Though the film seems quite remote from the 1917 October Revolution and its articulated concern for the proletariat, it does not attempt to minimize the excesses of aristocratic rule that were common knowledge at the time (in part from such films as *Rasputin and the Empress*, 1932). The execution of the tsar and his family at the hands of the Bolsheviks was also common knowledge.

On Sophia's arrival in Russia, new images proliferate—especially of bells, churches, and Byzantine turrets with crosses—and the music is now mixed with the sound of ringing bells. The intertitles escalate in their irony, if not in their vampirish associations, as one announces that "new blood was being carried to the Kremlin to temper the madness of the Holy Russian dynasty." The ritualistic quality of the film becomes more pronounced as the procession of Alexei, Sophia, her aunt the Princess Johanna (Olive Tell), and the Cossacks ride through the palace gates to the sound of bells—another way in which the film plays with iteration. The sound of the bells will recur at different and momentous stages of the narrative, culminating in the final scene, in which Catherine assumes her imperial role. Once inside the court, the imagery changes drastically from that of the earlier scenes. As Carole Zucker describes the transformation:

> The stylistic departure of *The Scarlet Empress* is enunciated on a literal and figurative level, by the removal of Sophia Frederica from home in Prussia to the Russian court. Her childhood home is characterized by carved, gracefully curved wood furnishing, brocaded and embroidered upholstery, ornate writing tables, scalloped curtains and molded doors, pastoral tapestries, framed portraits, drop-crystal chandeliers, flocked wallpaper, and subdued but uniform lighting."[55]

By contrast, the first view of the Empress Elizabeth gives an indication of the ways in which Hans Dreier's artistic direction, in collaboration with von Sternberg, was designed to provide not a literal and "realistic image of the court" but a highly stylized and grotesque effect.[56] The empress (Louise Dresser) is seen first in long shot against her eagle throne, which, as Zucker says, "looks as if the eagle's wings arise from her body."[57] Throughout the remaining sections of the film, there will occur a fusion of characters and setting, especially with statuary and icons. The disjunction between the imperial splendor, with its large ornate throne, wood carvings, icons, and grotesque and leering statuary, and the banality of the empress's greeting, her hasty renaming of Sophia Frederica as Catherine, and the audacious medical examination as the physician peers under Catherine's raised skirts produces a moment of excess. The exaggerated and awkward acting, the bizarre decor, and the shifting perspectives in editing signal a moment when the present intrudes on the past. In the empress's peremptory behavior, in her emphasis on examining Catherine's physical condition, and in her providing her with an appropriate name, she seems like a Hollywood director examining a potential candidate for stardom. This episode, the prelude to Catherine's meeting with the Grand Duke Peter

(Sam Jaffe), also initiates the first steps of Catherine's conversion from innocence to knowledge as he appears, looking very much like the gargoyles that grace the palace and not at all like the romantic prince that she had envisioned.

The motif of toys, torture, and power is reiterated as Catherine is brought to Peter's room, where he treats her to a view of his toy soldiers. The intertitles mark the melodramatic excess characteristic of fairy tales as the protagonist moves into a new stage in her transformation: "With all of her ideas of romance outraged, Sophia Frederica was thrust into the Russian cauldron, her name altered, her religion changed, and pushed like a brood mare into the preparations for her marriage to a half-wit." Now the motif of maternity is reintroduced, and the mandate for Catherine to produce a royal heir comes to be linked with earlier images of maternal and child relations. Clothing comes into increasing prominence with the marriage ceremony, as Catherine appears in the ornate, finely embroidered silver dress and wearing a veil. The scene alternates between shots of sculpture, crosses, candles, and carvings and shots of Alexei, the empress, the Grand Duke Peter, and the Countess Elizabeth, but it carefully maintains the centrality of Catherine through the close-ups of Dietrich in contradistinction to the shots of others. The drone of the chanting accentuates the connections between religion, state power, and Catherine as the focal point of the intrigue.

Louis Audibert captures the complexity of Dietrich's image in this scene: "[T]he look of Catherine fills the screen, her eyes roll back and turn toward heaven while the candle flame shudders and lets us read the solitude and utter despair of one who has been bound over and betrayed."[58] Catherine's image fuses with the icons of religious martyrdom that liberally bedeck the palace. Her suffering is also connected to her gradual transformation into a figure of power, and an intertitle announces: "And thus Catherine took the first innocent step to become Russia's most powerful and sinister Empress, while the machine of the marriage went on." The wedding is the hinge between her suffering at the hands of others and her gradual immersion in power. Following the wedding, a number of contrasting scenes dramatize further stages in her enlightenment and conversion: a grotesque wedding feast and a procession to the nuptial chamber, where the bed is blessed by priests but where the religious imagery dissolves into an image of a skeleton.

Several scenes between Catherine and Empress Elizabeth as well as between Peter and the empress underscore the power of the Empress, complicating further the connection between maternity, power, and cruelty. Not only does the empress banish Princess Johanna, who had accompanied Catherine from Prussia, but she loudly and vulgarly chastises Catherine for her failure to produce an heir. Similarly, Elizabeth treats Grand Duke Peter as a footstool, kicking him aside as she reminds him of his royal duty to produce an heir.

The scene of Catherine in the stable with Alexei marks her own transformation from an ingenue to (in von Sternberg's words) a "mocking and ruthless" figure. Her transformed behavior is identified with an object, a piece of straw that she dangles from her mouth, offering the first inclination of the insolent way in which Catherine will now present herself to others. In familiar Dietrich style, chewing on the straw, she smiles enigmatically, teasing Alexei; but her playfulness is no longer innocent, and she is no longer curious or accessible. Studlar has noted that it is appropriate that the scene takes place in the stable. Alexei is, after all, the Master of the Hunt, and his association with horses is, like his treatment of Catherine, to be identified with power and eroticism. The horses will finally be associated with Catherine herself at the film's climax. In this scene, she toys with Alexei for his perfidiousness in withholding information about Peter prior to her arrival at court. Later she will punish him for his sexual involvement with the empress. When the empress orders Catherine to blow out the candles and escort a man through the secret doorway to her bedroom, that man turns out to be Alexei. The low-key lighting of this scene throws the grotesque statues and carvings into shadow, calling attention to their leering and sinister appearance. When Catherine descends the narrow stairway, the only light is that which reveals the person of Alexei, and as he leaves Catherine's face is thrown into relief through light and shadow.

As in Gothic melodramas, stairs play a key role in this film. From the initial shots of Catherine and Alexei standing together in the inn, observed from the stairs by Princess Johanna, stairs become assimilated into the film's play with control, dominance, and surveillance, culminating in Catherine's famous ride up the stairs to assume power. In the two sequences that parallel each other, Catherine's descent to find Alexei waiting to enter the empress's boudoir and later his descent down the same stairs to bring another man into Catherine's chamber, stairs are identified with the film's preoccupation with ascending and descending power.

Alexei comes to be identified with Catherine's conversion in yet another way. In rage after learning of his affair with the empress, Catherine throws a locket he had given her as a token of affection from the window, watching it descend from branch to branch. She runs below to retrieve it from where it had become snagged on a tree and is stopped by a guard who does not recognize her as the grand duchess. When she tries to identify herself, he does not believe her, saying: "I would not let you prowl like this if I were the Grand Duke." Rather than asserting her imperial prerogatives, she acquiesces to his misrecognition. In fact, the question of her identity is becoming increasingly ambiguous. She kisses the guard, and the camera in close-up focuses on the locket as it drops from her hands to the ground. Thus Catherine's career as Messalina is further advanced, and thus the film suggests the ambiguity of the identity of the imperial baby announced in the following scene.

The birth of the royal heir coincides with the illness of the empress, reintroducing maternal behavior in ways that violate sentimental and commonsensical notions of maternity as altruistic. Her illness is presented as another instance of her attempts to maintain her control; it also prefigures the limits of her power even as it prefigures Peter's death. While the empress asserts that she will not give her courtiers the satisfaction of dying, it is clear from her behavior and from the behavior of the courtiers that her end is near, thus bringing Catherine closer to the throne. But her last act of domination, her attempt to appropriate Catherine's baby, is connected to the initial scenes in which Sophia's mother imperiously orders the removal of the child's doll. An image of the empress on her sickbed fuses with one of Catherine in her bed as she receives a medal—not the child—as the reward for her maternal labor. Catherine dangles the medal like a toy as she had earlier dangled the locket given to her by Alexei, suggesting how she will now toy with him.[59] Images of cruelty escalate, fusing toys and torture in the encounters between Catherine, Empress Elizabeth, Grand Duke Peter, and Countess Elizabeth.

An intertitle alerts the audience to another turn in the narrative: "The second step forwarding a great career had begun. Firmly entrenched in her position by being the mother of a future Tsar, Catherine discarded her ideals and turned to the ambitious pursuit of power."

Yet her machinations merely involve playful scenes of seduction in the garden with her courtiers, scenes reminiscent of similar garden scenes of the carousing wealthy inhabitants in Fritz Lang's *Metropolis* (1926). However, Catherine is warned by the archimandrite that Peter intends to remove Catherine from the court after the empress's death and his ensuing assumption to the throne. When the archimandrite expresses the fear that she does not know Russia, she responds with familiar Dietrich irony, "I'm learning as fast as I can." The element of surveillance is a major element in the portrayal of the court, where not only people spy on each other, but the statues also seem to come to life as in a horror film and watch the people watching each other, and so the element of knowledge in relation to power assumes prominence. Each stage of Catherine's conversion is associated with increased knowledge of acts of cruelty and dissimulation—the levers that push her toward enlightenment and acquisition of the power to control others.

The film's divergence from conventional biopics is evident in the exercise of Peter's Hessian mercenaries. A scene that might merely function as ritual and spectacle turns into another instance of torture when Peter's men, marching about like toy soldiers under his orders, point their rifles aggressively at Catherine herself. When Peter subsequently invites her to his room to examine one of his toys, it turns out to be a miniature of her, which he beheads with a miniature instrument. Catherine's response is haughty as she matter-of-factly addresses him and his countess, recollecting the matter-of-fact way in which Empress Elizabeth herself dealt with subordinates. This interaction between Peter and Catherine and the image of decapitation also recapitulate the opening scenes of the film and the images of cruelty conjured up by the physician's telling Sophia of executions.

Whether this scene between Peter and Catherine is historically documentable is irrelevant. What is important is the way in which the film draws on its monumental images to mock versions of melodrama that work with binary notions of innocent, benign victim and malignant aggressor. In this world of intrigue and power, no one is spared complicity, and survival depends on the knowledge of threat and the ability to quickly counteract danger. The extent of the danger to Catherine is dramatized in the scene in which Peter stands gloating over the dead body of the empress. While the film had earlier made a great deal of the ritual of marriage, the empress's death does not become the occasion for a funeral ritual. The image of her unmourned dead body quickly dissolves into an orgy of cruelty initiated by Peter. A rhythmic montage of printed proclamations concerning financial extortion, of scenes of orgies, and of people being dragged from their beds dramatizes Peter's childlike and cruel game of power, a game in which he will be outsmarted by Catherine. His penchant for cruelty is identified with such obvious images of mutilation, implying castration, as the drill he uses to bore a hole through the eye of an icon and the ax that beheads Catherine's effigy. He shares his voyeurism with other members of the court. The film implicates the external audience too in looking, depriving spectatorship of its innocence, identifying looking with power and control. Like fairy tales that turn out to be not innocent stories after all but parables of cruelty and trials of torture, this film maintains its early promise of plumbing the cruelty that inheres in seemingly innocent folklore.

Catherine's public emergence as a figure of power is heralded by a visually opulent scene in which, dressed in furs from head to toe and holding a fur muff, she reviews her guard, whom, as a title announces, she had "added to the list of her conquests." Maria Riva, Dietrich's daughter, recollects that

> [t]his image of Dietrich inspecting her personal guard in tall mink Cossack hat, became the visual identity of *The Scarlet Empress*, just as the garter belt and white satin top hat is *The Blue Angel*'s. Only when I was much older did I realize that once again, she had superimposed her special brand of bisexual eroticism onto this scene. With her hair slicked back, hidden under that famous hat, she had the face of a beautiful young boy. The downward gaze then becomes an even greater accomplishment of silent acting.[60]

In these comments, Riva not only validates the importance of clothing to Dietrich's androgynous image, which links the star to her films but also confirms the film's affinities with silent cinema as historical residue.

Catherine's exercise of her power now involves her mocking relations with Alexei, who is forced to observe her as she playfully seduces others during her review of her guard. This scene is the prologue to her complete humiliation of Alexei. In the ensuing boudoir scene, which is a replay of her earlier scene with the empress, she forces Alexei to perform the same actions as she had performed prior to admitting him to the empress's presence. She tells him to blow out the candles, as he stands and awaits her invitation to the bed. She appears to undress but then stops, sitting on the bed behind a veil, forcing Alexei to gaze at her as she teases him, lifting the veil and then dropping it. He stands before a statue of a devil, and his image fuses with it as the horns on the statue appear to sprout from his own head. The image of the devil unites Catherine and Alexei as she utilizes her diabolic wiles to torture him, and in an ironic twist, Alexei, her former torturer, becomes the recipient of her cruelty. This scene undermines any sentimental sense of the woman as submissive and conveys most starkly the component of power that inflects sexual relationships. Furthermore, rather than segmenting private and public power, this scene welds public and private power in a mordant unity.

All that is left now is to consolidate her power over Peter. A banquet scene is the stage on which she and Peter confront each other. He humiliates her in front of the assembled guests, but she is unperturbed. As the archimandrite collects jewelry and valuables for the poor from the assembled guests at the table and as Catherine peels off layer after layer of jewelry, the film again embodies the struggle for power through objects—this time, jewelry. From the early scenes in which Alexei arrives in Prussia with gifts of furs and jewels, to the scenes of his giving the locket to her, to this scene in which she is weighted down with jewels that she casually discards, jewelry comes to function, as Carole Zucker indicates, as "a signifier of loss and deception."[61] Jewelry is associated with Catherine's former romantic dreams of life at the court of Russia. Later it comes to signify her betrayal by Alexei. Finally it comes to be associated with her cavalier attitude toward material objects compared to the greater rewards of power. In contrast to Catherine, Peter appears to believe in the power of material objects as the signs of power, thus exposing his impotence and vulnerability. The jewelry also has a particular association with Dietrich herself, who wore some of her own jewels in the film and whose extravagance in jewels and clothing for herself and for others was common knowledge.[62]

The climax of the film—the consolidation of Catherine's power and the death of Peter—is effected with minimal dialogue. The final image of Catherine in her white uniform, cape over her shoulder, white fur shako on her head, is as famous an image from the film as is her image in the mink outfit. The music is Wagnerian, appropriately from *Die Walküre,* as the troops gather to support Catherine in her assumption of power. The intertitle, the shortest in the film, announces the transfer of power: "Exit Peter III, Enter Catherine II." The spectacle involves the swearing of loyalty to the new empress, the sound of trumpets, and images of the various army contingents in procession. Intercut with the gathering of the troops is a scene of Peter, alone now in his room, ordering his black servant to bring Catherine to him only to learn from the servant that she is not in her room and is nowhere to be located. Thus his plans to kill her are thwarted.

Peter is murdered by Captain Orloff, whom he had sought to humiliate and demote. Orloff tells Peter before he kills him: "There is no Emperor, only an Empress." Then, to the music of Tchaikovsky and Wagner, the troops ride through the palace gates, and in one of the most unusual scenes in film history, the one that sent audiences "fleeing from the screen," Catherine rides her steed up the stairs that had witnessed her humiliation and from which so much surveillance had taken place. Here too is the culmination of the horse imagery, which, as Studlar has commented, has its roots in folklore concerning Catherine's reputed near-fatal attempt to have intercourse with a stallion.[63] The Wagnerian music then gives way to a rendition of the tsarist anthem. The last shot in the film is of the bell that Catherine has rung to announce the beginning of her reign and is a culmination of the other images of bells throughout the film, images that announced her arrival, the birth of the child, and the death of the empress. The use of the bells themselves are surrounded by lore about conflicts between Dietrich and von Sternberg and about his imperiousness toward her as he forced her to ring the bells over and over again in the final episodes until he was satisfied with the results, despite her raw and bleeding hands. The bells, like other repeated images throughout the film, underscore the film's immersion in a view of history as reiteration. The sound of the bells also serves as an aversive jarring sound, a corollary to the aversive world that the film enacts.

## Reflections on History

The film's means of realizing its historical investments depends as much as anything on its lighting, the valences of light and dark, which serve to signify the conflictual psychosocial dimensions of power that seem to be the film's main interest. Not surprisingly, for a director that had worked at Universum Film Aktiengesellschaft (UFA), the film has many resonances of the German style of the silent era, particularly in its use of lighting and of mise-en-scène. This form of lighting, succinctly analyzed by Deleuze, depends less on the reflective play of light and shadow and derives more from a sense of refraction. The whiteness of the clothing, of the sheets, and of the face of young Catherine herself seem finally to be more a "rivalry" with rather than a parody of expressionism.[64] The effects of such a technique seem to lie in the ways that the film, in contrast to *Blonde Venus,* seeks to renounce "the values of intimacy."[65] The world presented, therefore, is neither one of choice nor one of melodramatic alternatives between ethical choices. The court is an environment in which one seems immersed in a desperate struggle over control and survival. As shown in Dietrich's cavalier attitudes toward jewelry throughout, the film veers away from the crass materialism of objects and toward the materiality of power.

Several critics have commented that the characters seem to be automata, a feature that again bears on expressionist representation and particularly on the mechanics of horror that are its distinguishing feature. Central to the film is the way in which the human becomes non-human or mechanical and the mechanical or inert seems to resemble the human. The mode of historicizing, the monumentalism (in Nietzsche's sense of the monumental) on which the film draws, does not therefore seem to exalt the great figures and events of the past so much as to acknowledge cruelty and torture as inevitable components of power. History becomes like a puppet theater, with its marionettes, religious artifacts, costuming, statuary, and various other artifacts bordering on the horrible and the grotesque. The spectacle in this form of monumentalism relies on antagonisms, but they are not Manichaean. Rather, the characters are the effect of blurring distinctions. The use of dissolves, the synesthesia commented upon by Studlar, the constant fusion of characters, events, and objects—all undermine ethical considerations between good and evil, falling on the side of negativity.

Unlike Soviet cinema's use of history in its representations of the masses, the portrayal of the people in *The Scarlet Empress* is as flat as the iconography itself. Though the intertitles will speak for them and the proclamations to them and the sense of their oppression is recorded, they too exist only as puppets. The importance of the body—in movement, in stillness, of the individual, and of the group—suggests that in this negative view of power, the body serves as the major instrument of that power. The emphasis on the face in the film, especially as derived from the close-ups of Dietrich's face, serves to identify the particular sense of time that the film entertains. "Real" time and place are tenuous, but through character they assume materiality through the affective valence of power and domination. As the vehicle for the affect, the star—in her face and body, in her use of gesture, and in her relation to objects—is the incarnation of this power.

*The Scarlet Empress* is not invested with documentation—maps, paintings, letters, facsimiles of buildings, and events. Its investment is in the imaginative reconstruction of history through statues, icons, and painted backdrops of church turrets to create the spiritual drama necessary to convey its view of power relations. Even the protagonist is less individuated than depersonalized as an icon of power, thus enhancing Catherine's folkloric dimensions. The issue of truth or verisimilitude in representation in a narrow and litigious manner becomes irrelevant. This Paramount film, produced by a studio described by Peter Baxter as in "corporate disarray" with its "collegial system of production controls" no longer intact, encodes an allegory of "the corrupting effect of power on even the most personal of relations."[66] From the portrait of Catherine to those of the other characters, we are given a view of history that reeks of intrigue, competition, betrayal, and revenge without mitigation. Once Catherine is cured of her naiveté, the world is made safe for intrigue and counterintrigue, power and countervailing power. This is a cruel fairy tale that ends with the triumph of the good witch, who is only a more attractive version of the bad witch. The film is no "Cinderella": it is closer to "Beauty and the Beast," though beauty is the beast.

The film's apparent aspiration to resemble a benign fairy tale should have made it accessible to audiences. Instead *The Scarlet Empress*'s use of folklore serves as an exposé of a society built on competitiveness and indifference, a society in which brutal power rather than benevolence and justice triumph. There are many levels of the exposure that indicate that the film, for all of its period aspirations, seeks to find its target in contemporary history: its use of Dietrich, which overflows the frames of its narrative, its constructed parallels between stars and royalty, its portrait of the hypocrisies of familial relations, its links between sexual power and other forms of social power, its insistence on connections between looking and power and looking and profit, its obsession with surveillance as a form of personal and social control, and its version of historicizing as an act of theatricality and performance.

In its uses of common sense and folklore, the film violates the consolatory dimensions of common sense. Through the film's use of

Catherine's biography, we are witness not merely to the psychologiz-ing of the biopic but to a form of psychologizing that weds psychic phenomena to social events. Commentaries on the film have variously read the characters as being engaged in sadism, in sadomasochism, or in the Deleuzian conception of masochism. The last view, in Gaylyn Studlar's critical work, has the merit of complicating the study of power and sexuality in ways charted by Deleuze. Instead of seeing the film in traditional Freudian terms as a reiteration of oedipal conflict with the paternal figure as pivotal, Studlar, following Deleuze, empha-sizes the maternal figure as primary to pleasure and power.[67] Much as Michel Foucault sought to complicate notions of power, seeing power as disseminated throughout the culture rather than emanating from above, Deleuze's conceptions of power relations are less hierarchical and binary than are many melodramatic versions of power. Seen in this light, the film counteracts reductive notions of power, not only re-versing traditional oppositions between masculinity and femininity and between dominance and submission but confounding their rela-tion to representations of history in cinema and in cinema.

The portrayal of sexuality and power in the film acknowledges the common sense of religion as a major conduit for conceptions of agency, power, and ethical norms. On the one hand, Catherine's power seems to be aligned with and consolidated by the religious figures in the film. But, for all of the icons painted on walls and doors, for all the statues of Christ, Madonna and child, and the devil, and for all of the religious chanting, by no stretch of the imagination is the film a conventional religious film. In the Gramscian exploration of the pres-ence of common sense in folklore, religion is tied to morality, serving either to fortify "official morality" or to reinforce "forms or condi-tions of life which are in the process of developing and which are in contradiction to or simply different from the morality of the governing strata."[68] Here too the film departs from commonsensical views of Christianity, preferring to use religion as a further index to the materi-alism and power that the film investigates. The icons of Christ and his martyrdom augment and complicate the film's explorations of torture, cruelty, suffering, and power rather than stressing their cathartic ef-fects. Catherine, like the empress, like her own mother, and like a god-dess, has the power to chastise and to punish, and this she does.

The use of sound in the film has the same valence as the imagery and monuments: It does not serve as historical documentation (e.g., the music of Wagner and Tchaikovsky was composed much later than Catherine's reign) but, rather, provides critical resonance in the ways these compositions are associated with historical intrigue and with power. The music, especially Tchaikovsky's, merely creates the aura of a Russian connection similar to the film's "painterly" uses of Russian architecture. The bells serve as punctuation of the various rituals and events that mark Catherine's transformation and rise to power. The use of close-up also contributes to the film's sense of history. It serves to link Catherine to religion, religion to the state, and the state to power. During the wedding ritual (and also in the bedroom scene with Alexei), the tight close-up of Catherine threatens to decompose her image through the intensity of the scrutiny it invites. The camera both materializes and threatens to dematerialize that image that serves by extension to call attention to the constructed nature of the image and to Catherine as a creation of the film, or more particularly, the creation of Dietrich. At times, the star image threatens to overwhelm the historical figure, who serves not as a negative effect in the film but as a way of linking past and present, theater and history, star persona and royal personage. Several times in the film we see Dietrich/Catherine in the act of being dressed, and her robing and disrobing serve the ends of historical representation as masquerade in the interests of exposing simplistic and sentimental interpretations of biography as history.

In its cavalier treatment of documentation, the film undermines official history: It is certainly not an overt or covert polemic about nation formation, a drama of the transition from autocracy or despotism to democracy or of the amelioration of poverty, injustice, or inequality. It is indifferent to liberal humanist conceptions of progress, but it draws visible parallels between monarchy and entrepreneurism 1930s style. By using the court of imperial Russia, the film can bypass the direct portrayal of middle-class values while at the same time offering itself as an implied critique of them. Thus *The Scarlet Empress* reveals the porousness of the biopic, its potential for engaging critical points of view. It also reveals how dependent the biopic is on folklore, not as exoticism, as a static portrait of a bygone society, or as a reductive moral parable but as a means for dramatizing what Gramsci described as a "conception of the world and life,"[69] one that is in no way trivial or dismissive of history. While the film does not adopt or speak from the position of subaltern classes—it makes its critique from above—it does flout official history, offering instead its pastiche of the common sense of power. This dramatization of power grafts past conceptions of history onto the present. The film traffics in repetition, clichés, and even historical formulas and rituals, but they are presented in ways that are opposed to the legitimation of conventional liberal and populist panegyrics. The use of the fairy tale format, the stylization of character and setting, and the equally stylized use of ritual and music serve to dramatize commonsensical conceptions of power but in such a way as to call them into question. Particularly, in its implied parallels between the folklore of Dietrich the star and that of Catherine the Great and between Hollywood and imperial Russia, the film reveals the plasticity of the biopic as a form and its ability to draw on the past in ways that are meaningful to the present. In fact the film as history is a form of antimelodrama, exposing a complicity between gender, sexuality, and social power for those inclined to be critical of familial sentiment, romance, patriotism, and progress.

# 5

## "You Remember Diana Dors, Don't You?": History, Femininity, and the Law in 1950s and 1980s British Cinema

In describing her "love" for the film *Berserk* (1967), Candy Darling (who was sometimes referred to by friends in Greenwich Village as "Diana Doorways") comments: "Diana Dors was in it and she was sawed in half. You remember Diana Dors, don't you? She was England's answer to Jayne Mansfield. Oh you remember a real cheap looking tomatoe [sic] with a tremendous bust, platinumized hair, big lips on a hard trashy face."[1] Allowing for Candy's reconstruction and interpretation of this image, what is significant about this description is its singling out of the star's physical measurements and especially her platinum blonde hair, features rarely associated with British cinema, conjuring up other star images: Jayne Mansfield, Marilyn Monroe, Mamie Van Doren, and before them Jean Harlow and Mae West. One way of disturbing official history and of capturing elusive conceptions of popular memory is by rethinking the historicality of such images and how they resonate and circulate throughout the culture. Candy's comments also invoke the phenomenon of stardom as embedded in a dynamic appropriation of popular history. The interfaces between stardom and value production are located in the heterogeneous, seemingly dissimilar ways in which images as products circulate throughout the culture at many levels and at great speed, revealing the protean, mobile, affective, and effective nature of capital through the forms of its cultural commodities.

Gayatri Spivak has lamented the persistent binary opposition between the economic and the cultural, an opposition

> so deeply entrenched that the full implications of the question of value posed in terms of the "materialist" predication of the subject are difficult to conceptualize. . . . The best that one can envision is the persistent undoing of the opposition, taking into account that fact that, first, the complicity between cultural and economic value-systems is acted out in almost every decision we make; and, secondly, that economic reduction-

191

ism is, indeed, a very real danger. It is a paradox that capitalist human-
ism does indeed tacitly make its plans by the "materialist" predication
of Value, even as its official ideology disavows the discourse of human-
ism as such.[2]

In tracing this complicity between economic and cultural phenomena,
questions of subjectivity and affect shed light on the creation, perpetuation, and transformation of value that cannot be measured solely in
terms of a cash nexus. Cultural discourses are saturated with affect,
circulating seemingly independent of the marketplace. Affective representation is closely tied to social representations that circulate knowledge involving sexuality, gender, and national identity.

The star is a major current in the circuitry of the creation, assignment, and perpetuation of value. The income produced by stars, producers, theater owners, distributors, and exhibitors is the most visible
manifestation of the cultural value of economic production. Accounting for the complex character of cultural artifacts as commodities has
always been elusive, for as Marx reminds us: "At first glance, a commodity seems a commonplace sort of thing, one easily understood.
Analysis shows, however, that it is a very queer thing indeed, full of
metaphysical subtleties and theological whimsies."[3] "Subtleties" and
"theological whimsies" inhere in the ways value is assigned to the
commodity, since "[v]alue does not wear an explanatory label. Far
from it, value changes all labour products into social hieroglyphs. Subsequently, people try to decipher these hieroglyphs to solve the riddle
of their own social product—for the specification of a useful object as
a value is just as much a social product as language is."[4] Thus the commodity form functions to occlude the nature of social relations, focusing attention on the concreteness of the commodity itself and concealing the conceptual quality of the creation and perpetuation of value.
The "magic of money" is the general measure of value, but the money
form of commodities "is distinct from their palpable or real bodily
form. It is . . . only an ideal or imaginary form."[5] Marx's concept of
fetishism is crucial for an unraveling of the mystery attached to commodity relations. The relation to the commodity is a form of enchantment whereby objects are divorced from social relations and from history, appearing to be part of the natural order of things, sundering
mental from physical labor and underestimating and misrepresenting
the affective work involved in the construction and maintenance of the
value. Marx's concept of fetishism thus provides clues to the indirect

and subjective, not merely quantitative and objective, ways in which value functions historically.

Following Marx, Gramsci asks, "How, in the system of social relations, will one be able to distinguish the element 'technique,' 'work,' 'class,' etc., understood in an historical and not in a metaphysical sense?"[6] Gramsci is at pains to locate the affective investment in social and political phenomena, and in so doing he offers clues about the character of affect in his discussion of common sense, art, and intellectuals. In revising historical materialism, Gramsci valorizes "a certain level of culture, by which we mean a complex of intellectual acts and as a product and consequence of these, a certain complex of overriding passion and feelings, overriding in the sense that they have the power to lead men on to action 'at any price.'"[7] Gramsci's uniting of intellect and feeling suggests that he is aware that affect plays a role not as an excrescence but as a fundamental factor in commodity production. His conception of common sense as folklore signals the intricate ways that affect can be regarded as a commodity that circulates and as a basis for ensuring the "fetishistic character of commodity production."

The affective (and historical) dimensions of sexuality and femininity in relation to the family, gender, property, and the law are inextricable from more complex considerations of the law and the state than the traditional notions of relations between base and superstructure, quantified labor and surplus value. The importance of historicizing remains fundamental to this process insofar as an understanding of the dynamics of change helps to track the various ways in which the production of value is constantly on the move but everywhere discernible.

The dependence of melodrama on binarism—femininity versus masculinity, victimization versus domination—and on a scenario of anticipated justice, with its confidence in the law and its obsession with the reproduction of the family, is inextricable from the question of feminine sexuality, and feminine sexuality is inextricable from the personifications of the forces involved in the struggle to sentimentalize "ethics. . . . in the working out of poetic justice."[8] Working through the medium of melodrama, the star/diva personality is an embodiment of economic forces *and* of social forces and the carrier of an all-important affect that serves to guarantee the materiality, legitimacy, and credibility of the represented conflicts. In situating discussions of stardom within the context of melodrama's role in cultural commodification and value construction, it becomes clear that the univalent statement that stardom is the top-down creation of demonic and unscrupulous industry executives is inadequate to account for its popularity. Stardom is a complex mode of production and reception. Like production generally, the creation of this commodity entails manufacture, distribution, consumption, reproduction, and recycling, all of which are dependent on a close affiliation with prevailing hegemonic discourses, especially in relation to affective value's role in the process not as excrescence or superstructure but as the heart of cultural creations. The importance of affect in the determination of value construction lies in its revealing the interested and constitutive, rather than innocent and essential, character of subjectivity. As a person in drag, Candy Darling offers an incisive insight into the multivalent aspects of economics, gender, and sexuality, into their asymmetrical relations to each other, and into the forms of historicizing in the interpellation of subjectivity. Darling writes: "I am not a genuine woman but I am not interested in genuineness. I'm interested in the product of being a woman and how qualified I am. The product of the system is important. If the product fails, then the system is no good. . . . The main thing is will I benefit from it."[9] This passage could have been written by a "genuine" woman, but its importance lies in exposing genuineness, in linking sexuality and gender to production, and in highlighting the complex nature of the value associated with this production.

This chapter examines the case of Ruth Ellis, the last woman to be executed in England, who was put to death in 1955 for the murder of her lover, David Blakely. This case—the subject of several books, numerous newspaper articles, and a 1985 film, *Dance with a Stranger*—orchestrates questions relating to the power and the circulation and appropriation of star images to questions of femininity, sexuality, and social class. The particular problem raised in this type of investigation involves a reading of popular history that integrates rather than disjoins the workings of history and modes of popular representation, especially in relation to femininity. The star is not the reflection of externalized social forces, nor is subjectivity the determinant of representations. Representations are the subject and object of history.

In tracing the forms of melodrama, their expression through particular stars, and their specific connection to the case of Ruth Ellis, I concentrate on the star persona of Diana Dors. A British film and television star, Diana Dors was the incarnation of a familiar and popular version of what has been variously called the "blonde sexpot," "blonde Venus," and "blonde sinner." The role she played in the social problem film *Yield to the Night* (1956), which was identified both with Ruth Ellis's plight and with Dors's narrative of her own rise to stardom, sheds light on the direct and indirect bonds between stars and their audiences. I discuss the brief "stardom" of Ruth Ellis, her reincarnation in the press and in the cinema, its connections to the Dors persona, its representation in *Yield to the Night,* and its recreation in *Dance with a Stranger.* I also examine the social problem film as a conduit through which melodramatic affect flows, generating value in cultural and economic terms in the post–World War II era. Further, I examine the social problem film as a new medium for melodrama and stardom and the relation of both to emerging social discourses that address criminal transgression and juridical discourses central to an understanding of the circulation of affective value through femininity.

## Remembering Diana Dors

Photos of Ruth Ellis reveal an image very like the one of Diana Dors described by Candy Darling:

> The star of the show, Ruth Ellis, was brought from the cells. All eyes turned to the wooden dock as she entered. Many of the public were surprised at what they saw. Instead of a dejected young woman, tired-looking, sombre, and about to stand trial for her life, she looked like she was attending a West End show. She was dressed in a two-piece suit with an astrakhan collar, and a white blouse. Her hair was immaculate and dazzling blonde. . . . That her hair looked brassy in its platinum sheen certainly was a mistake as far as the defence was concerned. Jean Harlow and other film stars had equated ultra-blonde hair with a leaning toward "tartiness." . . . So now all eyes were on this woman. This blonde tart, as somebody in the public gallery whispered too loudly, focused around the "theatre." This was to be her stage, and nobody was going to take that away from her.[10]

Allowing for the authors' assumptions about the intentions of Harlow and other film stars, what is striking about their description and about the course of the Ruth Ellis story is the importance of hair color, fashion, versions of Americanness, sexuality, legality, and popular memory.

At the time in the 1950s when Ruth Ellis was consolidating her position as a dance hall hostess, Diana Dors (born Diana Fluck) was at the height of her popularity. A brief examination of Dors's recollec-tions of her life and career reveal convergences with Ellis's story. In her autobiography, *Dors by Diana*, Dors describes her family class affilia-tions as a "climb from working class to *upper* middle class."[11] Reflect-ing on her aspirations as a child, she says: "I wrote in an essay entitled 'What I would like to be when "grown-up"' that 'I was going to be a film star with a cream telephone and a swimming pool.'"[12] She was wearing make-up at the age of twelve, wore nylons, adored dancing, had elocution lessons, went to dances with American GIs, and won beauty contests ("looking as much like Betty Grable as possible").[13] Of her hair, she comments that it "was now long and fairly honey-coloured—with the help of some lightener."[14] And of blondeness, she adds: "[M]y best friend, Christine . . . sported natural platinum-blonde hair, whereas mine was merely mousy. Somewhere, in the re-cesses of the mind . . . was born the dream of becoming a blonde, al-luring film star, a woman who enchanted men and lived a life of glamour and fame."[15] In a comment that will bear directly on Ruth Ellis's obsession with a glamorous appearance, Dors says that "specta-cles were the bane of my life, although I only wore them for reading and at the cinema. My vanity, encouraged by my mother, was preva-lent even then and I was terrified of anyone, particularly a boy, seeing me wearing the wretched things."[16] The identification of glasses with an undesirable appearance is a commonplace of feminine representa-tion. For example, in *Now, Voyager* (1942), Bette Davis's "undesirable appearance" is marked by the fact that she wears glasses.[17]

At the age of sixteen, Dors won a scholarship to study at the Lon-don Academy of Art, the springboard to her work in first theater and then film. In early films such as *Holiday Camp* (1947), *Here Come the Huggetts* (1948), *Good Time Girl* (1950), *The Weak and the Wicked* (1953), and *A Kid for Two Farthings* (1955), she was primarily cast as a precocious and socially threatening sex symbol. Overall she made sixty-five films, some of them in Hollywood. She also appeared on U.S. and British television. Of her major film, *Yield to the Night* (distrib-uted in the United States as *Blonde Sinner*), which she and the critics considered her finest piece of acting, she writes: "At the time everyone thought the film moguls were cashing in on the unfortunate story of the tragic murderess, Ruth Ellis, the last woman to be hanged in Eng-land, but strangely enough the story had been written two years earlier by authoress Joan Henry with *me* in mind for the leading role."[18]

Dors was married three times, to men with whom she had violent and financially exploitative relations, all of which were frequently and luridly recounted in the scandal sheets. She became known for her encounters with the law, revenue officers, and morally upright clergy. Of her later career, she writes: "The years went by and my career went steadily down and down, until by the middle sixties, I was forced to leave my children in Hollywood where we had all been living, and come home to England in order to make money by trading on a screen name that had once been big."[19] Her brush with the law, she claims, "did not damage my career. On the contrary it helped to make me a household name, and the public were extremely sympathetic."[20] What is crucial about the shape of her career and relevant in particular for the reconstruction of the Ruth Ellis case is the equation that she, her admirers, and her detractors make between blondeness, tartiness, and self-destructive behavior. The blonde sinner is also associated with the "dumb blonde" as characterized by Marilyn Monroe, Jayne Mansfield, and Judy Holiday; however, this seeming obtuseness turns out in the final analysis to be a form of shrewdness.

Christine Gerahty identifies Dors's star image as a contradictory icon of "vulnerability and knowingness."[21] The qualities with which Dors (along with Brigitte Bardot and Marilyn Monroe) is associated are bodies on display, an "emphasis on experience and sensuality," and a reputation for selecting and being surrounded by incompetent and inadequate men.[22] Gerahty also cites the stormy "often destructive life of the sex symbol . . . as a sign of excessive female sexuality, bankruptcy, [and] decline."[23] Nonetheless, Dors is a survivor and Gerahty attributes this survival to the fact that Dors's image was popular among all social classes. In the construction of Dors's persona, both in her social life and in her films, her identification with working-class experience was an important source of her appeal. This identification was to continue during the period when she became a television personality. David Lusted, who has written about Dors's effect on television audiences, says: "Established initially as a sex symbol . . . [as] she aged, she pushed at the connotations of a variant type known as 'the good time girl,' retaining its characteristic self-regulating search for pleasure, but denying its characterisation as sin."[24] Dors's image makes "connections with women of all ages in a comparable variety of social roles," as well as with "men troubled by conventional models of male-regulated heterosexual relationships."[25]

An examination of Dors's persona reveals how the star is tied to a range of cultural and social positions identified by Richard Dyer: artifice and authenticity, the everyday and the exceptional, the individual and the collective, the private and the public, the accessible and the remote. Most conspicuous in the configuration of the blonde bombshell is the slippery relationship between transgressiveness and conventionality, success and anticipated failure. The narrative that best exemplifies a convergence between Dors's physical appearance, personality, and her reception as a sex symbol is *Yield to the Night*.

## Stars, Star Texts, and Cultural Discourses: The Case of *Yield to the Night*

The common sense of melodrama, which provides a sense of naturalness and legitimacy if not rationality, relies on familiar images, sounds, clichés, and popular wisdom, functioning as a collage by bringing together bits and pieces of past and present that create the aura of credibility. In this sense, the social problem films of the late 1940s and 1950s are commonsensical texts. The form of the social problem film is a collage, absorbing elements from pre–World War II melodrama in its various genre guises: women's films, action pictures, film noir, historical films, and biopics. Sensitive to changes in the culture and in the industry, the social problem film is also a distant relative of neorealism and of docudrama. Its amalgam of crime detection, police drama, and melodrama has connections to television as well as to the emergent tabloid culture.

The social problem film emerged in Great Britain during a time of working-class pacification, Keynesianism, growing affluence, consumerism, a rising youth culture, an increasingly overt racism, and concerns over sexual permissiveness (expressed in the Wolfenden Commission, which addressed the status of the family, prostitution, and homosexuality), as well as concerns in the film industry for its health and viability.[26] These issues are tied to the increased international role of U.S. economic and cultural interests in the immediate post–World War II era in Great Britain.[27]

The social problem film was particularly sensitive to the "news of the day" and to immediate social issues that were identified with journalism, social science research, and legislative–political developments. Particularly associated with social problem films were directors and writers such as Basil Dearden, Jack Lee Thompson, Michael Relph, and the Boulting brothers. The scripts were often based on contemporary novels, biographies, or exposés as exemplified by the writings of Joan Henry. The narratives focused on threats to the family, criminality, prostitution, same-sex sexuality, juvenile delinquency, and to a much lesser extent racial tensions. Such films as *Sapphire* (1959) dramatized the social problem of race, while *Victim* (1960) addressed the social problem of homosexuality. The hybrid, generic nature of the films, the new faces associated with them, their emphasis on youth, their timeliness, and their greater investment in sexuality addressed several audiences simultaneously: the liberal audience that saw itself as sympathetic to the plight of disenfranchised social groups, another audience that saw itself as sympathetic to the containment of rapidly spreading noxious social practices, a youthful audience that was no longer interested in the traditional offerings of British cinema, and yet another audience that might connect to the more audacious aspects of the subject matter without any ostensible or articulated investment in its politics.

The actors in these films enhanced the sense that there was a changing climate of representation in Britain, and this was certainly true if one contrasts them to earlier British stars. As with Diana Dors and Dirk Bogarde, their physical appearance revealed strong links to Hollywood iconography. The newer actors who played key roles included, among many others, Diana Dors, Yvonne Mitchell, Glynis Johns, Jack Warner, and Dirk Bogarde, though older actors such as John Mills, Laurence Olivier, and even Michael Redgrave made appearances. According to Richard Dyer, the function of bit players differed from its function in conventional genre roles: they now appeared to lend "a certain form of 'realism'" to the role.[28] If there is evidence for the noncomplacent, contradictory nature of class, gender, and sexual antagonisms in the post–World War II era, such antagonisms can certainly be read in the British social problem films of the 1950s as well as in the dramatic works and polemics of the "Angry Young Men." Pieces of an affective collage involving class and gender (and to a much lesser extent race) are embedded in Dirk Bogarde's portrait of a lawyer in *Victim* and in James Mason's portrayal of a schoolteacher in Hollywood's *Bigger Than Life* (1956). Both films portray threats to a respectable middle-class lifestyle arising from over- or underadherence to prevailing notions of masculinity. But the problematic nature of femininity is writ large in the social problem film. In accounting for its importance, however, Dyer errs in adhering to a basic opposition that "places man inside history and women as ahistoric and eternal."[29] Though I agree that women play a prominent role in the films as characters and as actresses, I challenge this binary distinction between active and passive, inside and outside, historical and ahistorical as reductive. The pastiche quality of the social problem film disturbs a monolithic sense of history, a reductive sense of power, and a binary sense of victim and aggressor in relation to gender. As an analysis of Diana Dors demonstrates, the image that emerges of her star persona is far more complex than that of a passive, ahistorical, and excluded victim. Her own narratives, the roles she played, and audience reception of her persona run counter to the notions of center and margin embedded in Dyer's statement. Dyer's taxonomy of social problem films, which situates them between those that address youth and those that address deviance, seems to be too narrative-driven to identify the contradictions posed by these works, especially the complex ways in which they all address issues pertaining to juridical discourses and the state, and their relation to questions of gender, race, and forms of sexuality.

The representation of the blonde sinner as conveyed by Diana Dors in *Yield to the Night* has multiple connections to complex and unexamined, though widely enacted, notions of feminine sexuality circulating in the culture, notions that are inseparable from questions of legality. The film participates in the discursive dimensions of the blonde bombshell through a set of affects relating to physical wantonness, criminality, and anticipated punishment, especially the attribution of being a "bad lot" or the prophecy of "coming to a bad end." Dors herself describes being "probably written off as a thoroughly bad lot from childhood."[30] Later she was denounced from the pulpit "as a wanton hussy." But, she adds, "this was of course before Christine Keeler overthrew the Conservative government."[31] That Dors's "story" and her screen roles parallel those of other young women of the 1950s and particularly that of Ruth Ellis, a convicted murderess, is material worthy in itself of historical inquiry. Dors's comment that Joan Henry's book (on which the script of *Yield to the Night* is based and which accounts for Henry's own brushes with the law) was written before Ellis's execution emphasizes the fact that the problems raised by the life and death of Ellis are endemic to the culture and to its common sense of itself. The narrative confirms that to understand what hap-

The "blonde sinner" (Diana Dors), in *Yield to the Night*. Courtesy New York Museum of Modern Art, Film Stills Archive, and by permission of Lumiere Pictures, Ltd., London.

pened to Ellis one must go beyond the individual facts of her case and situate those events within a specific cultural milieu.

*Yield to the Night* was identified with the movement to eradicate capital punishment. In summarizing the film, Leslie Halliwell describes it as a "[g]loomy prison melodrama vaguely based on the Ruth Ellis case and making an emotional plea against capital punishment."[32] Halliwell's designation of the film as a prison melodrama is another reminder of how the social problem film absorbs earlier (Hollywood) antecedents, helping to account for the style of the film and for its use of certain types of character and situation. Though *Yield to the Night*

makes claims to realism in its apparently liberal humanistic orientation and in its timeliness in relation to immediate social questions, the
film form is more revealing for the contradictions it exposes concerning gender, sex, and class. Like other social problem films, *Yield to the
Night* uses location settings and draws from a familiar pool of social
problem actors (e.g., Dors, Michael Craig, Yvonne Mitchell, Liam
Redmond, and Athene Seyler). The focus on legality and on state intervention are integral to the melodramatic treatment of the central
character.

The protagonist is a victim, to use a designation that might apply to
the protagonists of social problem films generally, but she is also an
aggressor, a murderess who expresses little remorse for her actions.
That *Yield to the Night*, like many social problem films, has a woman
as its protagonist is a testimony to the complex discursive links between femininity and law. Significantly, the other "victim" in this film
is also a female, a rival for the affections of the male protagonist, as
we learn through a series of flashbacks. Mary Hilton (Dors), married
and working as a clerk in a department store, meets and falls in love
with a middle-class man, Jim Lancaster (Michael Craig), who is in love
with another woman of his own class. For a while he carries on a relationship with Mary, but his own career failures and his rebuff by the
other woman, Lucy, drive him to commit suicide. Distraught over his
death, Mary seeks vengeance on Lucy, kills her, and is condemned to
death. The highly stylized opening of the film builds shot by shot from
body parts (legs, hands, and torso, with no facial shot) of an as-yet-
unidentified woman who shoots another woman; these shots are intercut with shots of a city street. The full form of the first woman, the
murderer, is only shown after the murder has been committed. In this
fashion, we are made aware of the enigmatic connection between the
feminine body and transgression. The images of the second woman,
the murdered woman, are also fragmented, revealing her legs and her
lifeless braceleted hand as if amputated. This emphasis on female body
parts is retained throughout the film.

The film hinges on a number of contrasts. Mary's stripped appearance in prison, without makeup, wearing drab clothing, and subject to
the harsh uncovered light bulb in her cell, is contrasted to her appearance in the flashbacks, heavily made-up, wearing clothes—tight
dresses, close-fitting two-piece suits, and low cut sheaths—that accen-
tuate her voluptuous body. Mary's face, in the full-face image after the

murder, is not heavily made-up, which contrasts with her appearance in the flashbacks that reconstruct the events leading to the murder. The claustrophobia of her prison cell is contrasted to the sights and sounds of life associated with the nightclub. The contrasts between past and present highlight the differences between her expectations of a better life and the failure of her hopes as she contemplates death. The film also underscores the difference between her own passion for pleasure and the cynical, bureaucratic, or pious attitudes toward sexuality exemplified by the representatives of the law—prison guards, governor, chaplain, and social philanthropists. Her overly feminine image is juxtaposed to that of her masculinized guards. The middle-class portrait of her lover differs from that of her working-class family just as her own appearance differs from that of Jim and from what is shown of the woman she murders.

Significantly, the images of her past in relation to her family, to Jim, and to her work fuse with the images of the prison cell. In spatial and temporal terms, the use of flashback creates a confusion between inside and outside, between society and prison, and in which came first, the crime or the punishment. Similarly, the initial fragmented shots of her body anticipate the later shots in the cell in the ways that the camera and editing focus on shots of her feet, legs, torso, hands, and eyes as if dismembering Mary before the actual execution, reiterating a familiar animus against femininity. In reconstructing Mary in the flashbacks, the text configures her as a familiar 1950s figure of femininity, inextricably associated with social disapprobation, condemnation, and punishment. Despite her identification with biological femaleness and her appearance of superfemininity, Mary as the blonde sinner transgresses by making herself the stalker rather than the stalked and by identifying herself with action rather than reaction, with activity rather than passivity, with recalcitrance rather than submission. As Mary Hilton, Dors is hardly devious and simpering; rather, she is direct (if vulnerable). Like Diana Dors, the character of Mary Hilton is associated with dancing, jazz, popular music, and an interest in fashion.

That notions of femininity are at stake is evident not only in Mary's highly eroticized persona but in the severe, sexually neuter, even masculinized women who are her jailers. The difference between Mary and the most sympathetic of the prison guards, Mac (Yvonne Mitchell), is most striking, highlighting the disjunction between Mary's blatant femininity (even without makeup and in prison uniform) and Mac's plain appearance and restrained behavior. The appearance of the prison governor (Marie Ney) is severe: She is completely covered up, tightly encased in her suits, and rigid in movement. The portrait of the prison guards and the governor connects, perhaps unwittingly, to another aspect of cultural lore relating to women, making the unattractive equation between women in authority and masculinity and raising the specter of lesbianism. In the film's trajectory of feminine types, a contrast is evident between Mary and Lucy, the murder victim. Mary's striking blondeness and buxom nature are set off against the brief glimpse that we have of Lucy as a dark-haired woman dressed stylishly and expensively but conservatively. The differences between Mary and her mother are marked too, the mother belonging to a familiar representation of older British working-class women (the Huggett mother of *Holiday Camp* and *Here Come the Huggetts,* among others): dumpy, indifferent to style, thoughtless, and speaking in a style of speech identified with "lower classes." Mary's speech is indicative of a movement toward "cleansed" pronunciation, and her sensibilities, particularly in relation to familial issues, are clearly superior to the older woman's. Finally, Miss Bligh (Athene Seyler), the prison reformer who seeks to alleviate the pain of Mary's last moments, is a familiar figure to British moviegoers, one largely identified with comic portraits often played by Margaret Rutherford: a de-eroticized, upper-class image that, like the portraits of the prison guards, captures the neutralized and androgynous sense of aging femininity.

The film's representation of masculinity in the figure of Jim Lancaster seems to be particularly at home in the 1950s social problem film. His troubled masculinity is endemic to the genre. He is another instance of transgression against predictable forms of masculinity in ways that are intimately tied to conventional notions of femininity. First of all he is not a sportsman but a pianist. He reads poetry. He had wanted to be a professional pianist but presumably was not successful. His stance is introspective, depressive, morose, pensive, and passive. He is from a middle-class background, and his use of language reveals that he is well educated. Mary describes him in her recollection as "moody." His physical appearance too is 180 degrees removed from that of British actors of the period, such as Jack Hawkins, Stewart Granger, and Jack Warner, who are associated with physicality and virility. His national origins—his mother is Irish and his father, Canadian—also distinguish him from the other masculine characters. His vulnerable masculinity is further underscored by his inability to successfully negotiate a relationship with a woman of his own class. Even his suicide over unrequited love unsettles conventional notions of masculinity. His obsession with Lucy provokes Mary's knowing remark "What's the good of that kind of love?" Moreover he is unwilling to establish a relationship with Mary, attempting to pawn her off on others. His differences from Mary combined with his social failures are suggestive of his inability to come to terms with social (especially sexual and class) expectations.

An important aspect of the portrait of the blonde sinner resides in her inevitable mismatch with the men in her life. The social problem film follows the melodramatic paradigm of denied gratification that Fassbinder once described in relation to Lauren Bacall's role in Douglas Sirk's *Written on the Wind* (1956): "She picks the one with whom things can't possibly work out in the long run."[33] Mary loves Jim who loves Lucy who loves someone else, and this formula for frustrated desire generates obsessional behavior and its attendant aggression. Similarly, one is reminded of the other ungratifying, exploitative, and violent relations that are part of Dors's own narrative. This scenario suggests a malaise with heterosexual cultural expectations packaged in the form of class and gender expectations and often expressed in aggression. The film plants psychological clues, stemming mainly from Mary's lack of accommodation to her own class affiliations, her unsatisfactory marriage to her husband Fred, and her vain attachment to Jim. In fact, her relationship with Jim is developed not so much through an erotic attachment to him as through her fascination for the way he speaks, for his books of poetry, and for his contrast to the working-class image of masculinity offered by her husband and the other men of her own class that she meets. Rather than being exceptional, the ultimately lethal nature of her attachment to him, which culminates in her murder of Lucy, seems to be intrinsic to the scenario of the "blonde sinner," the fulfillment of the often stated prophecy that she will "come to a bad end."

Much like Dors's description in her autobiographies of her youth, Mary's desire to escape the confines of her family life, her desire to be exceptional, and her attention to her physical appearance suggest that Mary identifies such aspirations with a life different from the constrained life of her family and social class. While not a "nightclub queen" (her words) like Dors or for that matter Ruth Ellis, Mary is portrayed as desperately in search of alternatives to the constraints of her life. Of her murder of Lucy she says that she was "sick with hate" and that she planned to kill Lucy in cold blood. This assertion hardly accounts for her act of violence. The film provides no further motive. The flashbacks that take place while Mary is on her bed or walking in the prison yard take on the quality of a dream that offers for analysis only fragments of the relationship between the feminine body, feminine desire, and the pre-scripted scenario of coming to a "bad end."

This bad end is a punishment reserved for those who violate class, gender, sexual, and national expectations. The notion of punishment beyond the ultimate end of hanging by the state is visualized in terms of bodily images and spatial images of constraint. As the flashbacks cease and the execution draws closer, space begins to close in on Mary until she is confined to her bed. The film blurs the temporal sequences, so that it appears that the punishment precedes the crime or rather, that the punishment is not so much for the act of murder as the fulfillment of a prophecy for flaunting and acting on her femininity, revealing Mary as transgressing even before she legally transgresses. When the guard tells her, "If you accept your punishment, not fight it, you will find it easier to bear," the comment carries a dual significance: Though it applies to Mary's facing her execution with equanimity, it applies even more to "punishment" for being feminine.

The absence of a courtroom scene in *Yield to the Night*—replete with expert witnesses, cross-examination of the protagonist, a recounting of the events leading to the murder, and suspense over the verdict of guilt or innocence—has a bearing on the text's investment in the question of punishment: Who is being punished, and for what? The exclusive focus on the prison drama, on the last moments of the protagonist's life, and on whether a reprieve will come at the last moment underscores the film's investment in the question of the ethics of capital punishment. But in the text's visual and narrative obsession with the protagonist's physical appearance, her relations to the men in her life and to her family, culminating in the act of murder, suggest that the punishment precedes and exceeds the crime as a life and death sentence for the sin of femininity and its effects on society. Furthermore, this punishment serves as a reminder that femininity is inseparable from considerations of the family and of the family's ties to other civil, state, medical, juridical, and educational institutions. Elaborating on representations of familial relations within melodrama, Jackie

Byars has found that underpinning conflict is a gap left by the family, "a structuring absence expressed through a loss of family." The "function of the female character in these social problem films is to maintain the integrity of the family."[34] Conversely, one might expect that the absence of a character who serves as a guarantor of familial integrity would signify trouble in the text. Mary Hilton's crime incorporates her transgression against the integrity of the family and not merely her criminal act of murder. Through Mary's flashbacks and the scenes of the family visits to the prison, *Yield to the Night* provides a portrait of a disintegrating working-class family. Mary's transgression dooms two families: her parental family and her conjugal family. Her "sin" arises from the conflict between her pursuit of pleasure and the familial obligations that she disregards. The film's dramatization of a disintegrating marital environment includes the prison guard Mac's mentally ill mother who dies shortly before Mary's execution is to take place. The "mixed" marriage—Irish and Canadian—with which Jim is identified is perhaps another indicator of problematic familial relations. One of the last acts of reconciliation that the narrative seeks to effect is familial, between Mary and her mother. Mary repeatedly refuses to see her mother, berating her among other things for bringing her younger brother to see her in prison. Ultimately, with the encouragement of the chaplain, Mac, and others, Mary agrees to make peace with her mother and to allow her to visit.

Prior to any act of criminal transgression that engages public attention through the law, the profoundly disruptive character of the blonde sinner has already blurred the boundaries between home and the world. Her public spectacle is familiar: peroxide blonde hair, usually long and loose, large breasts, a swinging-hips walk, tight-fitting clothing with low backs and necklines that call attention to the body, an availability for play and pleasure, a love of dancing, and a disregard for the opinions of others. Along with such qualities, the blonde sinner is identified with love attachments that are fatal, leading to the demise of herself, of the love attachment, or of both. All this marks her as fundamentally out of step with bourgeois values yet makes her absolutely essential to their representation and maintenance. This figure, so much a part of the cultural landscape of the movies, popular novels, and music, reveals itself not as marginal or exceptional (though it is regarded as unique). Like discourses of sexuality generally, this representation of femininity embodies threatened and thwarted feminine sexuality. In her blatant presentation, the blonde sinner calls attention to the unsuccessful containment of sexuality within the heterosexual family. This publicized form of femininity, because it generates so much interest, is never disjoined from its economically productive dimensions nor can its productive dimensions be concealed: Its affect proclaims its presence. In its obvious exposure of its produced (and disruptive) nature, the blonde sinner threatens to expose the constructed, unnatural dimensions of social cum sexual expectations. It is not surprising that Sir Oswald Mosley compared Dors to "only one other woman of any importance at all, namely, Margaret Thatcher."[35] In the context of reconfiguring the cultural uses of femininity, Mosley's comments are instructive. Mary's character emerges as more than a passive victim of the social order. She is also an "iron lady," a figure of power and threat. From both sides of the law, femininity comes to take on a more complex appearance. *Yield to the Night* and the much-praised acting of Diana Dors—like Dors's own escapades—seem to touch a number of raw nerves of 1950s culture involving social antagonisms that foreground gender, class, and sexuality and reveal their inextricability from considerations of the role of the state and its juridical apparatuses. Furthermore, Mosley's conjunction of Dors and Margaret Thatcher provides clues to the resurrection of Ellis's story in the 1980s and its relation to contemporary antagonisms involving the history of gendered and sexual representation.

## Re-Membering Ruth Ellis

The execution of Ruth Ellis in 1955 was an event that was slow in taking hold of the public imagination but that has now become an important fixture in British popular memory. The effects of that event reverberate and, as these effects show up in movies like *Yield to the Night,* continue to express the continuing and perhaps even increased profitability of woman-centered scandal, especially scandal involved with sexual transgression and class conflict. Peroxide blonde Ruth Ellis, like Marilyn Monroe and Diana Dors, lived in the fast lane. From her teen years, she was keen on dancing, meeting men (especially U.S. servicemen with money to burn), having fun, and escaping the conflicts and dreariness of her family environment, especially the oppressive presence of a father who tyrannized her mother and was dependent on the women in the house. During World War II, she was involved with

Another "blonde sinner": Ruth Ellis (Miranda Richardson), in *Dance with a Stranger* (stills photographer, Diana Newell; director, Mike Newell; producer, Roger Randall-Cutler). Courtesy of New York Museum of Modern Art, Film Stills Archive, The First Film Company, London, and Sam Goldwyn Company, copyright MCMLXXXIV National Trust Co. Ltd. All rights reserved.

a Canadian soldier who promised marriage to her. Unaware that he had a wife at home and pregnant with his child, Ruth learned, too late for an abortion, that he had betrayed her. She delivered the child, Andy, and received support from the father, who had been sent back to Canada, but the support dried up after a year and she no longer heard from him.

A popular figure with men, she moved to London, where she became acquainted with an underworld figure, Morris Conley, who owned clubs where men, mainly professional and upper-class men, would go to get drinks, entertainment, and sex. The women, like Ruth, thought of themselves not as engaging in prostitution but as granting social favors: Sex was part of the job of entertaining the clientele. Ruth's reputation spread, she was much sought after by men at the club as a woman who was great at sex, and she rose to be manager of the Little Club, owned by Conley. It was there she met George Ellis, a dentist who was an alcoholic and could not hold down a job. She married him, left the club, and had a child, Georgina. George tried to stay on the wagon for a while but could not resist the lure of drink, and eventually he not only lost his work but became brutal and abusive toward her. Because of his heavy drinking and his abusiveness, she left him and returned to her work at the club.

It was also at the Little Club that she met David Blakely, also a man of a higher social class (she boasted of the pedigrees of the men who came to the club) and the man whom she would ultimately murder. Blakely, like George Ellis, was another of those men unable to hold down a job, but he was passionately interested in car racing and was supported in this activity by his stepfather. Blakely would come to the club, drink prodigiously, and spend the night with her in the upstairs apartment that she shared with her son, Andy.

At first the relationship was affectionate, but it became physically and verbally abusive. He was engaged to a woman of his own class but assured Ruth that he had broken off the relationship. He invited her to racing events, where she came in contact with his friends the Findlaters and with Desmond Cussen, another man who was to play an important role in her life and death. Blakely was more interested in his racing than in her, and their interactions became characterized by Blakely's indifference to her needs coupled with his unwillingness to let her go.

Public displays of violence between them became familiar to the people who saw them at the club. Ruth was later to claim that the Findlaters were a major cause of the trouble between her and David. They found Ruth, not of their social class, too loud and vulgar. At the same time Ruth was also seeing Cussen. Also of a higher social class, Cussen was described by some of Ruth's acquaintances as sullen and withdrawn. He was in the tobacco business and was generous to her and to her son. After too many violent scenes in which Blakely destroyed property at the club and with the attendant decline in business, Ruth was fired by Conley and forced to leave her upstairs apartment at the Little Club. Cussen, who was paying her son's fees at school, took her to stay at his lodgings, where Andy would also stay during holidays. She continued her relationship with Blakely, a relationship that was becoming even more physically abusive. He and she both carried physical scars from their violent and aggressive interactions. Cussen would tend her wounds after such squabbles. Blakely was also strapped for funds, since he had undertaken the enormous expense of building his own racing car with the aid of his friend, Ant Findlater.

At this time Ellis became pregnant. It is not clear whether she had an abortion or whether, in another of their physically aggressive encounters, Blakely was responsible for the loss of the baby. He had promised to marry her, but he reneged on the promise. She took to chasing him at his various haunts—his apartment, the Findlater's home, and the garage where he and Findlater were working on the racing car. Cussen would chauffeur her as she desperately sought to make contact with Blakely, who had taken to avoiding her. She telephoned incessantly. As a consequence the phone at his apartment and at the Findlaters' was kept off the hook. At one point Ruth broke the windows in his car, and when the police came she claimed that the car was partially financed by her money. She was not arrested, nor was any effort made to restrain her activities. Finally, after Blakely had promised to take Andy out one afternoon but then did not show up, Ellis, filled with liquor and tranquilizers, took a gun that Cussen owned and had taught her to use. On the fatal day, she waited outside Blakely's house until he came out to go to the pub and shot him several times.

Her trial took place during a newspaper strike. It was a brief trial without much attendant notoriety for what gave all the appearances of an open-and-shut case. She did nothing to save herself, and the defense was not aggressive in her behalf. She claimed that she wanted to die. The jury was only out twenty-three minutes, an outstandingly short time considering that a woman's life hung in the balance. According to Laurence Marks and Tony Van Den Bergh, who interviewed one of the jury members many years after Ellis's death: "A member of the jury explained to the authors what went on during the twenty-three minutes they were out. . . . 'The thing that sticks out in my mind was that the others were going backwards and forwards to the toilet. I reckon that of the twenty-three minutes we were out only about thirteen were actually spent discussing the case.'"[36] Public responses, however, were more engaged. Marks and Van Den Bergh describe the case as polarizing the public: "To many people . . . she was . . . a foul-mouthed club hostess who whored on the side. . . . To others, David Blakely was the villain of the tragedy. . . . A third group . . . believed that Desmond Cussen was really responsible for the murder. . . . What sort of man was this who, even though inflamed by jealousy, could provoke a drunken, half-crazed woman whilst he stood watching safely on the sidelines?"[37]

The details of this affair are hardly tucked away in the archives. Rather, it is very much in the public eye almost four decades later, as attested to by the various books, newspaper articles, and scholarly articles that continue to appear and by the 1985 film *Dance with a Stranger*.[38] This brief synopsis of the events leading to the death of David Blakely and the trial and execution of Ruth Ellis reveals a full-blown melodramatic scenario with all the ingredients of a film comparable to *The Weak and the Wicked* (1953), *Yield to the Night*, and of course Hollywood's 1958 prison melodrama about a woman sentenced to be executed, *I Want to Live*, starring Susan Hayward in her Academy Award–winning performance. The ingredients of the Ellis case are familiar by now: a promiscuous blonde, a mother of questionable fitness, the manipulation of the "sinner" at the hands of her lovers, associations with the underworld, scorn and stigmatization for her working-class credentials, indifference on the part of "respectable" institutional representatives until the major crime occurs, the climactic brush with law.

The urban milieu is major actor in this drama of the underside of respectability—club life, cabarets, gambling, and extortion, along with the selling of sexual favors. While the women's prison dramas usually include a spectrum of female social outcasts—young, first-time offenders as well as recidivist women offenders, women of all ages, classes, and occupations representative of various antisocial acts—in films that focus on a woman facing capital punishment, the narratives tend to isolate the woman, focusing on her struggle to survive and on the psychological effects of her confronting her death, as in *I Want to Live* and *Yield to the Night*. The fascination with the woman's punishment and the step-by-step involvement in her approach to death seems to parallel the interest in the representation of other forms of violence enacted on women, whether by serial killers or lovers.

## Re-Constructing Ellis: *Dance with a Stranger*

*Dance with a Stranger* returns to the 1950s and to the familiar details of the Ellis case. The names are the same, as is the sequence of events. What is different is the deliberate absence of either a trial scene or a scene of the women in prison. Like *Yield to the Night* and the later *Scandal, Dance with a Stranger* is not a glossy, expensive film. A product of Goldcrest Films, a company that is identified with such expensive films as *Chariots of Fire,* this film was budgeted at far less money, and the principals involved in its production were not big money makers. *Dance with a Stranger* was the first feature film for Randall-Cutler, the film's producer. The director, Mike Newell, had limited film experience, though he had television work to his credit.[39] Shelagh Delaney, known for her role in writing *A Taste of Honey* and *Charlie Bubbles* for the New Cinema of the 1960s, had not done a script since then and was reluctant to undertake the project. According to James Park, she declared that "[s]he didn't want to write about real people," but Roger Randall-Cutler, the producer, "pleaded that the film would be a fictional account of a love affair with the facts of the case functioning as a springboard for imaginative interpretation."[40] The agreement on the parts of the producer, writer, and director was that this was not to be a "political" film but a "tale of people caught in the dead-end of extreme emotion."[41] In short, it was to be a melodrama. The filmmakers did not acknowledge this but it was also to be a biopic (although hardly a heroic one). The film, in fact, constitutes a transgressive use of the biopic model, which is usually associated with a hagiographic treatment of its subject, as characterized, for example, by Richard Attenborough's *Gandhi.*

Another important dimension of the Ellis story was to be "its hold on the public consciousness." Commenting on the "press write-ups from the period [which] revealed that the Ruth Ellis saga had opened a window into British society that many wanted to keep shut,"[42] the filmmakers sought to provide a set of visual images, through the clothing and makeup—tweed suits, evening dresses, peroxide hair—that could serve as aids to popular recollection. While the film was not considered to be political, the filmmakers were concerned with the public drama and in particular with the "speed with which Ellis had passed through the judicial system [which] suggested that society had been taking its revenge on her for living a fast lifestyle." In its social problem zeal, *Yield to the Night* had also "opened a window onto British society" by addressing antagonisms among social class, gender, sexuality, and national identity through its adoption of the prison drama format and its tentative explorations of the implications of this "fast lifestyle" and its consequences.

Neither the 1956 film nor the 1985 film *directly* address the ways in which the responses to a woman's execution "indicated that the law was out of touch with the public mood in attempting to dam up transformations in social mores that could no longer be held back."[43] Both films, in different ways, are concerned with exposing the profound social disjunctions that are best conveyed through the women's melodrama. In ways that exceed authorial intentionality, *Dance with a Stranger* resurrects that mid-1950s world through a 1980s investment in sexual "scandal" and in the centrality of gender and sexuality as a political phenomenon. Re-creating the club life of the period and the ambiance of a world in which people do not conform to the traditional expectations of public service and familial ideals, focusing on a protagonist who enacts the worst fears of working-class promiscuity and violence, and linking the events of her life to images of film and television through her appearance and through the self-reflexive uses of media throughout, the film links the 1950s to the 1980s and to the conflicts generated by Thatcherite social and economic policies. Thus, contrary to official history, this film offers a multivalent reading that, beyond familiar narrative plotting, is able to mingle the assorted elements of past and present (star images, fashion, music, dance, dialogue, automobiles, and home appliances), focusing on the historic significance of Ruth Ellis as the carrier of otherness. Rather than isolating a specific problem—juvenile delinquency, prostitution, same-sex relations, racial tensions—the film, through its pastiche of elements of 1950s life, appears to offer itself to audiences as an object of reflection and retrospection. There is no guarantee of a unified reading; rather, it offers a number of contradictory readings. The hybrid way in which *Dance with a Stranger,* like the social problem film, draws on other genres but reconfigures and recycles its borrowings is a further index to the ways in which affect as value production must circulate: remaining the same yet containing difference through combining perennially and erotically charged images with new and threatening dimensions of legal transgression. Gone are the 1950s social agents who are incarnations of the law, the state, and the discourses of social responsibility against social chaos: the social workers, psychiatrists, clergy, and reformers. Still present are the transgressive and disruptive figures of sexual excess who inhabit the melodramatic landscape, particularly the femme fatale of film noir. The problematic urban world remains, no longer under or outside the world of respectability but at its center.

Like film noir, with its disturbed and violent milieu, its sense of fatality and disaffection, and its ambiguous representation of the law, *Dance with a Stranger* evokes the darkly lit streets, "lonely places," claustrophobic environments, and sense of toughness of the urban, American-like environment, where its inhabitants are mired in cruel, sadistic, and vain struggles to achieve personal and social objectives. This resurgence of film noir in *Dance with a Stranger* supports Mike Davis's claim to the creation of "an elaborate counter-history."[44] From Barbara Stanwyck in *Double Indemnity* (1949), Gloria Grahame in *In a Lonely Place* (1950),[45] Marilyn Monroe in *The Asphalt Jungle* (1950), Susan Hayward in *I Want To Live,* and Dors in *Passport to Shame* (1958) to Miranda Richardson in *The Crying Game* (1992) and in *Dance with a Stranger,* we are confronted with figures of femininity who are victimized but that are also capable of victimizing. Knowing but vulnerable disaffected housewives, prostitutes, movie stars, and political activists inhabit this world where relations with the same sex and with the opposite sex are never transparent or predictable. Others are drawn to this figure in fear, loathing, violence, and inexplicable dependency and fascination. Moreover many of these feminine figures in quest of romance are either destroyed or left destitute. The melodramatic elements follow the course, described by David Rodowick, of the 1950s melodramas: They force the "equation of sexuality and violence," a violence that involves feminine sexuality that is "in excess of the social system that seeks to contain it."[46] (This paradigm also applies to instances in which femininity is not identified with biological women, as represented in such films as *Prick Up Your Ears,* 1987.)

*Dance with a Stranger* is tied to its protagonist; all of the other characters are satellites, and all scenes involve her. Significantly, critics did not know what to make of her role (or, for that matter, of the other characters, especially Blakely). For example, Vincent Canby, working on the model of "new" and "positive" images of women, describes the characterization of Ellis (among other 1980s women's roles) as "active forces in the environments that contain them. They aren't passive little creatures who accept their fate without question. They play roles more often associated with men. They do things." However, he then complains that "they do these things at a certain cost to dramatic coherence. In not one of these films does the woman protagonist have a relationship of any importance with a man who comes up to her collar bone."[47] His qualifying comments reduce gender and sexuality to the naturalized binarism of activity and passivity, to biological conceptions of man and woman, which characterize essentialist address of representation. Moreover old/new/progressive/regressive formulations do not address the complexity of the social antagonisms that Critical Theory has been trying to explore, particularly at the moment when the critique of subject construction has addressed the pitfalls of historicism, especially its linearity, teleology, and reductionism. The heterosexist assumptions about the need for appropriately matched men and women flies in the face of the darker and slipperier aspects in the representation of gendered and sexual relationships that critical investigation has begun to name and describe. The politics of the films, particularly the British films, of the 1980s concentrate "on the everyday lives and memories of 'ordinary people,' and in many cases push female characters to the fore, offering a different range of narrative pleasures and identifications."[48]

One other, perhaps parallel, critical comment about *Dance with a Stranger* deserves attention. A critic from *Variety*, while sympathetic to the film, singles out Rupert Everett as Blakely and complains of the actor's "inability to convey more about David Blakely than that he's set to fail consistently in work and life." This complaint is matched by praise for Ian Holm for his success as "the well-meaning Desmond Cussen whose human decency cannot satisfy Ruth's deeper longings."[49] This reading of the character reproduces the usual strategy of asking for "realist" acting and its corresponding "pop psych" exploration of motivation. For example, the reading of Cussen's character as "well-meaning" does not in any way correspond to the ambiguity of his representation. This characterization seems to spring from the pervasive realist assumption that characters must still be "well-rounded" and transparent. The willful misreading of cultural signs resurrects conventional notions of gender and sexuality. The comments reveal the implicit assumption that masculine figures need to come up to (if perhaps not compete with) their feminine protagonists by equal time in the narrative. Such comments neglect the ways in which contemporary British films are engaged in historicizing "in a manner that maintains a complex, bifurcated perspective shifting between past and present."[50]

An examination of Miranda Richardson's re-creation of the blonde sinner reveals its imbrication in a number of historically specific events. Her appearance and her gestures are a calculated simulacrum of Ellis, as can be seen if one looks at the photographs of Ellis and reads descriptions about her makeup, clothing, and mode of speaking. This emphasis on her appearance—on its calculated nature—throws the spectator into the cultural terrain of the 1950s, where the film's questions about history are generated. The spectacle of Ellis further evokes the visual memories of 1950s Hollywood stars that are associated with Marilyn Monroe (whom Ellis seems to resemble most, to judge by photographs). Ellis's image evokes Diana Dors as an icon of the period, and it evokes connections to the consumer culture of femininity. Much of *Dance with a Stranger* presents images of Ellis before a mirror, primping her peroxide blonde hair, adjusting her false eyelashes, and fixing her maquillage. In one scene with Cussen, the dialogue explicitly addresses her appearance. He asks her, "Why don't you let your hair go back to its natural color?" And she answers, "I'm a blonde now." Unrelenting, he then says, "I didn't know you wore false eyelashes," and she quips, "I'll wear anything that improves on nature." She offers to put false eyelashes on him and to shave his mustache, thus calling attention not only to her construction of femininity but to the tenuousness of "natural" masculinity as well.

From the first moments of the film, the camera clings to her face and body, reminiscent of the shots of Dors in *Yield to the Night*. Her dresses are a reproduction of 1950s feminine attire and especially of 1950s movie attire: tight-fitting, low-cut, sometimes flared from the waist, rustling, and off the shoulder—like the gown she wears to the ball with Cussen. Her attire offers a striking contrast to that of Carole Findlater (Jane Bertish), Ellis's upper-class detractor, who wears the requisite 1950s middle-class uniform, which is sporty, even dowdy. Similarly the upper-class women at the dance with Ruth are more conservatively clad than she is.

Close-ups of the Ellis character reveal the mask-like spectacle of her face, framed by the platinum hair. Rather than conveying great expressivity, this face seems frozen in its make-up as if we are forbidden to see what, if anything, is being covered up. Though she wears glasses (and this becomes an important element in the unfolding of the drama), she only wears them at the cinema, when she is called upon to read a business document, and in the final murder scene. In the first scene at the car races, she is told in hostile fashion by Carole Findlater that she could see the event better if she would only put on her glasses, and predictably she responds in the commonsensical vein: "Men never make passes at girls who wear glasses." The question of looking and of being looked at assumes a central place in the film through the emphasis on glasses, on mirror shots, and on chiaroscuro noir scenes as a metaphor for perception and misperception by Ellis, by others in the film who look at her, and also by the external audience.

Of her peroxide hair, Marks and Van Den Bergh comment that as Ellis got older, her hair got darker, "and she resorted to the peroxide bottle to remedy this. For the rest of her life she was to be inordinately fond of her peroxide blonde hair. She believed the popular saying that 'Gentlemen prefer blondes.' It would not be an exaggeration to say that her fixation to remain blonde was a contributing factor to the poor impression she made when giving evidence at her trial."[51] Putting aside the ways in which Marks and Van Den Bergh presume to "explain" her character and events—though from a sympathetic perspective—what remains from their discussion is the consonance between their descriptions of Ellis, the image of Dors as Mary Hilton in *Yield to the Night*, the image Dors constructs of herself in her autobiography, and Miranda Richardson's enactment of the character of Ellis.

In this context, another conjunctural aspect raised by the film has to do with the way in which Richardson as Ellis adopts upper-class speech patterns and intonations, managing at the same time to make them seem stilted and affected. Her dialogue is a compendium of clichés, but she is also capable of witty one-liners. In response to one of Blakely's manipulative and insincere pleas for her to marry him, she snaps, "Why? Are you pregnant?" At work in the Little Club, she liberally bestows the appellation "darling" on the various men. Her risqué comments are evident when she is with Cussen, who seems to be more of a prude than the other men in her life. Dangling a banana and taunting Cussen, she says, "Terrible things, aren't they?" She laughs loudly at a pissing dog in Cussen's presence. Marks and Van Den Bergh comment that Ellis was reputed to have been fond of four-letter epithets and used them to shock her auditors (which the film tones down somewhat). In one scene, Ellis rages at David, "I don't give a fuck for your social standing."

As hostess in the club, Richardson plays Ellis as businesslike and competent, ever on the lookout to improve the standing of the club. She manages her boss as well as the other workers to get what she wants. Things only begin to deteriorate when her relationship with Blakely begins to unravel. (The film does not develop her relationship to George Ellis.) She dances gaily with the men and occasionally entertains them with ballads from the time (in fact, she sings the title song, "Dance with a Stranger," in 1950s ballad style). Of the use of music in the film, Richard Combs has said that the "subject—the theme which seems to come through the refrain of the songs—is the social conditioning which shapes this romance."[52] More than a "theme" and "social conditioning" come across through the ballads and dance music. The milieu in which the songs are sung and the lyrics themselves are carriers of the film's invocations on past history.

The image that Richardson/Ellis projects in her speech, dress, and behavior is reminiscent of Gerahty's description of Dors's dual qualities of vulnerability and knowingness. As a character who is able to handle her business affairs and produce and use herself as a commodity in this environment, Richardson/Ellis appears to be a tough survivor. Her assessment of events and of the people in her life is, like Dors's, not at all sentimentalized; rather, it recognizes failed expectations and contradictions. Her relationship with Cussen seems to capture her ability to cope and to get what she wants. On the other hand, her relationship with Blakely reveals her vulnerability. As the enigma at the film's center, her character raises questions about femininity but neither reduces their complexity nor explains them. As her scenes with both Cussen and Blakely dramatize, neither Ellis nor the two male characters adhere to dominant cultural expectations of masculinity and femininity. I have commented that in *Yield to the Night* the character of Jim Lancaster violates accepted notions of masculinity in a manner characteristic of social problem films. This is also the case with Cussen and Blakely. Cussen, as played by Holm and as derived from the literature surrounding the Ellis case, is a sexually ambiguous figure. He is soft-spoken and slow of speech. He retreats from the sporty world associated with Blakely. His positioning as a spectator of events (especially of Ruth's affairs) is his most marked characteristic. He is attached to her in a seemingly inexplicable fashion, follows her every movement, chauffeurs her everywhere, takes care of her son, and offers her cash and lodgings with little hope of gratification. His rivalry with Blakely for the attention and affection of Ruth's son and his curiosity about the sexual relations between Blakely and Ruth are emphasized in the film. The two men are united in their curiosity about the other's sexual activity. The film subtly hints at rather than dispelling the possibility of Cussen's complicity in the murder of Blakely, a possible complicity that did not come out until Ellis was already awaiting execution. Friends convinced her that for the sake of her children, if not for herself, she should seek a stay of execution. Persuaded, Ellis did finally request a stay, only to be denied. It was not until later, as others began to forage about in the facts of the trial, that the information about Cussen's possession of a gun, his teaching Ellis how to use it, and his accompanying her (actually driving her), to the scene of the shooting without ever dissuading her from the act came to be known. In addition, she was under the influence of liquor and tranquilizers at the time of the murder. Holm's clothing, his body movements, his stilted gestures, and his placement in the background as a spectator testify to the text's cognizance of his ambiguous persona and role. His mask of gentility is allowed to drop a few times—once when he is castigating her for leaving her child alone, another time when in rage he forces sex upon her, though she is drugged and indifferent to his demands. His investment in a relationship with Ruth's son is complex. At times, he appears to use that relationship to gain an entry into her affections; at other times he appears to be competing with her for the maternal role as well as with Blakely, using Andy as a wedge to incite Ruth against Blakely. Though rivals, both Cussen and Blakely agree in their assessment and accusation of Ruth as a bad mother.

By contrast to Cussen, Blakely has minimal pretensions to a relationship with Ellis's son, though the boy seems to prefer him to Cussen. Blakely invites the boy to the races and gives him goggles but breaks his promise to take the boy to a fair at Hampstead Heath. Ellis later attributes her final murderous rage to this broken promise. Blakely's conflicts emerge through his ambivalent connection to his class, his equally ambivalent attachment to his mother and stepfather, his failure at a career and as a racing driver—all expressed in his tempestuous and violent relationship with Ruth Ellis. The forms that his relationship with Ruth takes are as complex as Cussen's. At times, she appeals to him as the idealized mother whom he cannot do without; at other times he is attracted by her tartiness. His behavior alternates in oedipal terms between being her lover, her son, and her scourge. He seeks to rid himself of her, and yet he cannot. Physical violence is built into their interactions and is closely tied to the "fighting and fucking" paradigm. He scorns the way she "rears a child in a knocking shop." He humiliates her in public and is the major cause of her losing whatever economic independence she had. Through Ruth's relationship with him, the film builds inexorably to the anticipated climax of violence, beginning with their passion, moving on to their verbal violence, escalating to the physical violence, and culminating in the fatal shooting.

The film's abandonment of the docudrama style often attributed to social problem films is most evident in the ways in which it handles these encounters between Blakely and Ellis. At one point in the narrative, as the violence escalates, they meet on a foggy street at night in a scene reminiscent of Jack the Ripper movies or Hammer horror films. Ruth asks him how he got there, and he quips, "I followed your scent." Taunting him, she asks whether he would like to hit her again and he responds with the familiar "You ask for it."

The camera singles out a cross that she is wearing around her neck (an object not previously seen on her), and when Blakely comments that she is wearing a good luck charm, she retorts, "It's to protect me against devils and vampires." He then drags Ellis into the alley and forces her against a wall, where they engage in violent sex. In the context of the film, this scene has the effect of making an affective transition, providing an appropriate language to account for the escalation to the violence of the murder.

In using Ruth Ellis as protagonist, in creating a sense of a 1950s landscape, the film announces an investment in the past, or rather, in "popular consciousness," as Randall-Cutler has termed this history. Yet how can one assess this interest and investment in the past? The film can be read as part of a familiar commonsensical scenario, as a parable of social disintegration. The resurrection of the blonde sinner—the conventional home wrecker, an enemy, even against her will, of the family—acknowledges the much decried contemporary threat to family values that is being widely circulated through media such as films, soap operas, talk shows, political speeches, and courtroom reportage. In the context of British society, *Dance with a Stranger* recapitulates the usual British fascination and horror with class misalliance. *Dance with a Stranger* also has similarities to films of the

1980s like *Prick Up Your Ears* and *Another Country*, films that are more directly critical of heterosexual familial values and that explore same-sex relations within the context of a critique of traditional British class, national, and sexual values. *Dance with a Stranger* seems to participate in the recycling of images of violence as a rampant and mobile threat that invades and infects respectable sectors of society. The images of media in the film help to link social concerns of the 1950s to those of the 1980s, making the spectator conscious of the ubiquity of media: in the image of Ruth Ellis and in her conjuring up of certain female stars, or conversely, stars who are created in the image of Ruth Ellis, in the newsreel footage of the race at Le Mans with Zsa Zsa Gabor and Porfirio Rubirosa in the spectator box, and in the television shows that Ruth and her son watch. To put it in terms of Antonio Negri's conception of postmodernism, is the film an exercise in nostalgia, a portrait of the social antagonisms of the post-Keynesian world, or a harbinger of the creation of new subjectivities that are no longer docile?

The film invites a comparison with the numerous works that now are identified with some form of feminism or postfeminism. By using Ellis and reinforcing her relationship to a particular version of femininity, the film inevitably participates in this discourse through its focus on women's position in relation to social structures of power, on physical violence toward women, on women's representation in the media, on women's role within the family, and on women's relations to the law. The letter that Ellis writes to Blakely's mother captures a number of the familial and juridical issues in the film. It provides information about the punishment meted out to her after the shooting. Since the film does not include a trial, it makes the last spoken dialogue in the film that of Ruth Ellis rather than the courts, which serves to problematize in a nonjudgmental fashion the values she articulated and acted on. It focuses on the maternal theme, recapitulating the film's flirtation with her role as a mother and others' perceptions of this role in the final scenario. The film problematizes femininity by entertaining its constructed rather than essential nature, but it also problematizes maternity. The letter Ellis leaves Blakely's mother is given as follows:

> Dear Mrs. Cook, No doubt these last few days have been a shock to you. Please try to believe me when I say how very sorry I am to have caused you this unpleasantness. . . . The two people I blame for David's death and my own are the Findlaters. No doubt you will not understand

this but before I hang . . . . I implore you to forgive David for living with me, but we were very much in love with one another. Unfortunately, David was not satisfied with one woman in his life. I have forgiven David. I only wish I had it in my heart to forgive him while he was alive. Once again, I say I am very sorry to have caused you this misery and heartache. I shall die loving your son and you should feel that his death has been repaid. Good-bye.

This letter has the same stilted and affected quality that characterizes Ellis's appearance and way of speaking. In the context of the events in the film, especially in the context of the contradictory character of Ellis, the letter portrays her as not merely a victim of femininity but as actively furthering a prescribed scenario. The letter reinforces her commitment to commonsensical notions of romantic love, maternity, crime, and retribution. Her allusions to her death as repayment for David's reinforce the sense given throughout the film that she has few illusions about her situation or about the inevitability and appropriateness of her punishment. Her plea for forgiveness from and identification with David's mother and her justification of her actions in the name of love are the staple of melodrama, revealing its basis in conventional values. This letter is not the defiant statement of an exploited woman. The only complaint expressed by Ellis involves David's friends, the Findlaters, and her only lament is David's inability to be satisfied by one woman.

Given such sentiments, the portrait of Ruth Ellis in this film raises disturbing questions about the constitution of femininity. Jacqueline Rose explores these questions in her seemingly strange juxtaposition of Ruth Ellis and Margaret Thatcher, which reverberates beyond the mere comparison of two historical female figures. Rose writes:

> In one sense there is no common point or even dialogue between these two women: from different historical moments and opposite ends of the social spectrum; they stand respectively for criminality and the law. . . . Yet Margaret Thatcher and Ruth Ellis were brought together at this historical moment in a scenario whose imaginary basis may well be what constitutes its importance and force. "Victim" and "executioner," they meet at the point of violence where the ordering of the social reveals something of the paradox on which it is based. . . . Drawing attention to themselves precisely as women, they can serve to gloss over that paradoxical and double location of violence—the perversion of the state in relation to violence can be transposed on to the perversity of the woman."[53]

*Dance with a Stranger* and *Yield to the Night* extend their narratives far beyond the legal question of capital punishment. In their separate ways, the films move into the more tangled web of social and psychological discourses that are embedded in gender and sexual politics. The historical pastiche that emerges from these discourses links gender and sexuality in nonessentialist terms to such social and cultural activities as social production, reproduction, work, leisure, and ethnic and national identity.

## The Blonde: Violence and Value

The trajectory of the blonde bombshell is neither merely the excluded underside or binary opposite of the Angel in the House nor the negative of conformity; instead it is far more powerful as the sine qua non, as one of the very bases, of constructing social values. Ruth Ellis's line in the film, that she is in favor of "improving on nature," refers to more than her appearance. It is an index to the unnatural dimensions of life, which, in her commonsensical adherence to social values, she sees only dimly. She and the things she does are therefore "unnatural constructions" that produce social value in a number of ways and in a number of sectors. The affective value of these constructions of feminine sexuality depends heavily on their representability in a commodity form that allows them to circulate. The persistence of the transgressive blonde is as necessary as prostitution to the social construction of restraints, to the maintenance of social constraints on gender and sexuality, and to the melodramatic discourses that establish the problematic and contradictory nature of her image. Vulnerability and knowingness, centrality and marginality are integral to the production of this form of femininity, if perhaps not to femininity generally.

Society's punishment by execution of Ruth Ellis and the affective conflicts surrounding her life and death are part of a familiar and also indispensable scenario that serves to define, legitimize, and devalue femininity at the same time that it sets it up as a necessary value. Ellis's value, like Diana Dors's value and like the value of Richardson's re-enactment of Ellis, resides not in hiding her "value" but in exposing the cultural and economic relations that inhere in femininity and in making Ellis's image available for circulation in affectively economic terms by linking it to other commodities. The blonde as a source of entertainment is a commodity that begets other commodities not only in the realm of sexuality but also in the arena of entertainment, exposing connections between property, money, sexuality, and class relations. Her image produces a set of affects, clothed in common sense, that are necessary in order for this commodity to be experienced as valuable and therefore for it to exist and circulate.

Of the affects embedded in the melodramatic medium, the most striking involves the "publishing" or "advertising" of this commodity through the courts, the newspapers, the tabloids, films, star discourses, television, biographies, and even scholarly articles. The figure circulates through the culture at large. Because of its ubiquity, familiarity, and attractiveness but also because of the critical scrutiny it receives, a campy appropriation of the image or even the slightest second look will expose its representation as manufacture. In this ever present possibility of exposure lies the threat to any belief in natural qualities. The persona exists as a counterclaim to realism and to essentialism as well as to strictly binary forms of differentiation. Even the scenario of disaster that dogs the blonde sexpot has to be understood as constituted in the interests of the social value and not as a measure of fate or destiny. This intuition, this anticipation of disaster, of the "bad end"— and its realization as well—is part of the calculated scenario and is as much narratively constructed as the physical appearance of the persona is constructed. Similarly the aura of individuality and uniqueness identified with one or another attribute—breasts, hair, joie de vivre— is itself belied by comparisons, by the attributes' association with the blonde bombshell: Marilyn Monroe, Jayne Mansfield, Diana Dors, Ruth Ellis, and even Madonna.

Figures who, like Ellis, brush directly with the law are not represented as conventional victims, as lambs going submissively to the slaughter. Their threat goes far beyond the narrow retributive sense and beyond conceptions of common morality. Figures like Ellis are threatening because they endanger the very common sense they seem to embody and espouse. Despite their often articulated adherence to conventional notions of family, religion, monogamy, and maternal behavior, everything about the figures contradicts such notions. Ellis's refusal to stay within the family milieu, her frequent abortions, her work for underworld figures, her sexual promiscuity, her indifference about caring for her offspring devotedly and to the exclusion of her own pleasure, her involvement in violent sexual practices, and above all her taking revenge on her tormentors—these all become acts that expose antagonisms between sexuality and morality, education, and the state.

No wonder that one woman at the time of Ruth Ellis's trial wanted Ellis hanged so that she could sleep better at night. Moreover the woman urged, "Let us remain a law-abiding country where citizens can walk abroad in peace and safety."[54] Ellis's admission of having paid with her life for Blakely's death reinforces this sense of the culturally necessary dimensions not only of her death but also of her transgressive life. The particular nature of the blonde sinner's role as victim and later as aggressor reinforces the sense in which the landscape of gender and sexuality involves violence, not as an excrescence but as a fundamental requirement. In affective terms, then, the element of rage as the affect that generates vengeance and violence needs further investigation, and the women's prison melodramas, specifically those dramas that address the issue of the state and capital punishment for the crime of murder, are especially sensitive to this dimension.

Thus the issue of the involvement of femininity in violence and of the perpetuation of violence against femininity by others assumes a more complicated configuration. Not only is it part of the coercive fabric attached by the culture to femininity, but it also serves to help clarify the frequent warning of coming to a bad end as a self-fulfilling prophecy that inserts the state into the civil sphere. If the law itself, as in Ruth Ellis's case, involves the state in retributive justice, that justice presupposes not merely the experience of transgression but its necessity. Ellis satisfies society's expectations and confirms its fears: that she is threatening and violent but entertaining. And since she is a member of the working class, her history doubly confirms the fear of her as feminine as well as working class. In both roles she contains the potential to challenge law and order. Both acquiescent and transgressive femininity share the same relation to the law. While the former supports the violence of the state in the name of law and order, the latter is expected to run afoul of the law and so reinforce the law. In the construction of value, what makes for the affective investment in and profitability of modes of production that seem to be valueless is that they are profoundly allied to forms of coercion that are not immediately manifest.

Like the other star narratives and films discussed above, Ruth Ellis's history is a melodrama—but not in the sense that the affect serves to conceal connections among gender, class, and sexuality and to render them depoliticized. Rather, the melodrama functions to expose how affect provides its "visible fictions." The narratives are neither escapist nor fantastic. The characters are exemplary of how antagonisms are acted out through the conjunction of media and other cultural institutions. The union of melodrama with common sense (in the Gramscian sense of residual knowledge, knowledge belonging to an earlier time that is anastomosed to present ways of thinking and behavior) is neither false consciousness nor mere ideology. It is a form of history—the history of subaltern groups—and aids reading into that history and understanding its position both as a conduit of value and as an antagonist to it. The film's uses of the past require yet another look into certain images of femininity as circulated through biography, of biography as circulated through melodrama, of melodrama as common sense, and of common sense as popular history.

The figures represented through the star biographies and the films discussed here are not static: We witness an image of femininity that, though appearing "mythic," is nonetheless closely tied to cinematic and social history (if the two can even be considered to be separate from each other). On the route from Mae West to Madonna through Diana Dors can be found the necessarily varying shapes, voices, images, and personalities, as well as the intensities relating to their pleasurable and dangerous dimensions. In discussing the particular configurations of Mae West's persona, Ramona Curry has argued that "West's role as prostitute in her films up to and including *Klondike Annie* cast her doubly as consumer object; as character within the narrative; and as fetishized star within the movie."[55] Curry argues that West's star image presented "multiple threats to the dominant order upheld by both the reform movement and the industry, which first exploited then attempted to contain and repudiate it as a powerful embodiment of transgressive female sexuality."[56] These comments apply to Dors's star image and to Ruth Ellis: "[I]t was not West's characterization of prostitute that constituted the primary threat . . . but rather her success as star and character in the ironic and pleasurable exploitation of her own body, along with her power in herself representing a transgressive consumer of sexuality."[57]

The "successful" impersonation of femininity is dependent—to return to Candy Darling's description yet again—not only on the movie moguls and the reformers but on a more broadly shared cultural consensus that circulates among producers and consumers. The scenario of pleasure is not extricable from retribution; rather, it is built into the very characterization, if not prescription, of "transgressive" femininity, thereby producing and enhancing its value. The blonde tart is not exceptional in her "transgressiveness"; transgressiveness is a necessary attribute of femininity and inheres in the constitution of the affective value of this image as character, fetishized star, and carrier of the commonsensical lore of culture that helps to circulate such values. Ruth Ellis's story is not an isolated chapter in a "social history" of passive feminine victimage but a significant and productive locus and carrier of history.[58] The Ellis case, like the films devoted to it, like the reiteration of blondeness and transgression, exposes how femininity as affective value requires its visible fictions and how the British cinema is haunted by these fictions.

# Historical Capital: Mourning, Melodrama, and Nazism

*Schindler's List* is a reminder of the obsession with and dissension over history that has been pronounced in the last decades of the twentieth century. In contention is whether we are witnessing an end to history or the end to "a certain *concept* of history" as narratives and arguments over the nature and efficacy of historicizing proliferate.[1] A case in point is the constantly growing and divergent critical analyses addressing representations of Nazism and the Holocaust in books and journals across academic disciplines—history, sociology, philosophy, and religious studies—and the growth of programs specializing in Holocaust studies.

The preoccupation with Nazism and the Holocaust is not confined to academic history and cultural analysis. Film and television productions, with their predilection for historical narratives, are a major, perhaps even *the* major, circulating source for images of that past. Historiography "may well be playing a secondary role to film and television."[2] Central to the narrativization of Nazism and the Holocaust is the question of the relationship of official history to popular memory. Written commentary, visual representations, and museums (a growth industry) dedicated to the recollection of the Holocaust invite critical reflection on the political investments in historical and biographical texts. Has this past become part of the common sense of folklore, assimilated into the familiar pedagogical notions that "those who do not know history are doomed to repeat it" or that "the act of remembering is an act of resistance, dissent, and challenge"?[3] Has the past been subjected to the excesses of monumental history, in which deeds of villainy and heroism are uncritically commemorated and enshrined? Or has the past been assimilated into the discursive modes of popularized psychoanalysis, with its corresponding melodramatic commonsensical uses of memory?[4]

In the common sense of folklore, the past is not eradicated so much

229

as it is circulated in familiar and affective images. Andreas Huyssen, in discussing the U.S. television series *Holocaust*, writes of "the needs of audiences for emotional identification with specific human characters, their problems, and their contradictions."[5] Affirmative responses to the impact of *Holocaust*, as well as reactions to the German television series *Heimat*, have stressed the positive effects of the intense emotional responses generated by the texts, regarding them as instrumental in generating debate about the Nazi past. This position explicitly or implicitly redresses the long-standing antipathy toward mass cultural forms as anti-intellectual and melodramatic and challenges the valorization of avant-garde practices as intellectual and analytic.

In the representations of history discussed in this chapter, I examine the commonsensical nature of the therapeutic and melodramatic discourses on which representations of Nazism and the Holocaust rely. Among the seminal notions that appear to constitute commonsensical attitudes toward National Socialism is the notion that "the postwar generations have not inherited guilt so much as denial of guilt."[6] This observation is central to many evaluations of the postwar German psyche, revealing the centrality of psychoanalysis (especially its conceptions of repression and denial) to cultural and political analysis. Equally important is the paradigm of mourning, with its emphasis on the importance of replaying the past, of confronting loss, and of acknowledging guilt and responsibility. The concept of mourning is rooted in a traditional Western notion of history that is associated with the elegiac tradition, a form that enacts the mourning process, "conjuring up the past, confronting . . . guilt about surviving," and hence reaffirming beliefs about providence.[7] Mourning has also come to represent the requirement to experience "remorse, and the need to make amends."[8] The paradigm of mourning assumes the character of common sense in the form of folklore, where the uses of the past are pragmatically tied to narratives that convey a desire for the amelioration of existing conceptions of nation, community, family, and the psychic integrity of the individual. The mourning process, as a form of historical excess, is saturated with affect connected to the memory of loss, "seeking consolation through remembering."[9] Implied in the valorization of mourning is an uncritical attachment to experience, a melodramatic desire for justice and restitution, and a faith in the possibility of redemption. Finally, there is something profoundly ahistorical and repetitive about the attachment to loss, guilt, and recovery.

The emphasis on the therapeutic importance of mourning has been central to the work of Alexander and Margarete Mitscherlich that addresses as a national imperative—the need to confront the specters that are presumed to haunt German culture and society: "Where there is guilt, we expect remorse and the need to make amends. Where loss has been suffered, mourning follows, and where an ideal has been tarnished, where face has been lost, the natural consequence is shame."[10] The concept of mourning, transposed from the individual to the nation, draws on familiar discourses of psychic health and disease to account for social behaviors and their deviations. Embedded in psychoanalytic discourses are commonsensical notions of salvation that rely on familiar melodramatic binarisms concerning victimization and oppression. But instead of presenting a distinct and clear-cut notion of the aggressors as evil, these discourses describe them as flawed, decentered, melancholic, lacking in stable oedipal identification, and mired in denial. According to the Mitscherlichs, "[t]he difference between political science and psychoanalysis is not so great as might seem at first sight. The question of whether a social phenomenon, a role stereotype, a social communication, is 'healthy' or 'sick,' normal or pathological, is of concern not only to the physician but also to the diagnostician of political systems."[11]

Though the impetus for such a comparison derives from the urgency of understanding political behavior, the recourse to notions of collective pathology presents glaring problems, the most crucial of which is the notion that collective guilt is efficacious for characterizing the different and multivalent expressions of "political behavior." The conception of collective guilt also rests on a totalizing assumption about what constitutes history, the nation, and the identity and character of its inhabitants. Nor does it distinguish between forms of coercion and consent. By failing to make such distinctions, the concept of collective guilt precludes the possibility of understanding the complexity of power and the different constituencies and interests involved in the creation and maintenance of hegemony. The psychiatrization of politics is offered unproblematically as being exempt from discursivity, concealing its own disciplinary investments in explanation and prescription. The importance of confession and the imperative to acknowledge guilt and to atone for transgressions are deeply embedded in the folklore of the West, assuming new form in the discourses of psychoanalysis.

Is it possible that in the psychiatrization of politics, a new form of power is established as a means of disciplining the putative "pathological" nation? Does the thesis of collective guilt and pathology merely invert the relation between victim and aggressor, creating a technology of power rather than an analysis of the ways in which power is constituted and sustained? Does the oedipal paradigm and its emphasis on parental and gender identification exist as an effect of a social formation rather than its cause, "at the end, not at the beginning?"[12] And does the emphasis on mourning partake of a fascination with death as "kitsch" as described by Saul Friedlander, arising from the desire to rehearse and memorialize, in the name of "working through?"[13] Despite its insistence on the didactic and transformative nature of confrontation with loss, the mourning paradigm monumentalizes, schematizes, melodramatizes, and hence oversimplifies the dynamic nature of the past and the role that the past plays in the present. The language of trauma, loss, and awaited restitution lends itself to universalizing tendencies as a meditation on mortality that tends, in Saul Friedlander's words, "not only to dehistoricize . . . [but to] flatten out and homogenize . . . complex differences."[14] This language also lends itself to pop psychology and essentialist animadversions on identity, tied to discourses of castration, imaginary constructions of self and other, and conceptions of subjectivity and subjection.

Similarly the proliferation of material monuments serves to freeze and increasingly to commodify the past. The creation of monuments as a perpetual reminder of suffering and as an expression of the need for restitution is addressed both to the perpetrators and their heirs and to the handful of survivors and their offspring. The injunction to remember, the coupling of recollection to the motto "Never again," the insistence on the healing effects of memory, and the need to provide appropriate cultural instruments to enhance this "work" are articulated for German as well as for Jew, Gypsy, and homosexual, and perhaps for all modern humanity. The specter of the Holocaust—memories of the Nazi terror, its totalitarian state, specifically as identified with the concentration camps and genocide—serves as a master signifier governing certain representations of the Vietnam War and of AIDS.[15] The events of the Holocaust have also been transposed and applied to contemporary politics governing ethnic, racial, gendered, and sexual politics. Such comparisons rely on an affective, monumental, and totalizing treatment, inviting anger and judgment rather than critical consideration. The loss of specificity represses the ability to analyze and understand either differences or similarities. The uses to which the representations have been put have become remote from Primo Levi's conception of the uses of memory: "[P]recisely because the Lager was a great machine to reduce us to beasts, we must not become beasts; . . . even in this place one can survive, and therefore one must want to survive, to tell the story, to bear witness."[16] This statement is not monumental; it particularizes rather than universalizes; it offers a dynamic sense of the importance of memory tied to notions of survival rather than death.

With the passing of time, "the sheer multitude of specialized studies on the minutest aspects of this epoch tends to erase the sharp outlines of certain central issues, be they conceptual or ethical. Therefore, whether one wishes it or not, the very momentum of historiography may serve to neutralize the past."[17] The neutralization of the past may also result from the multitude of monuments and melodramas that are assimilated into folklore, rituals, and monuments dedicated to "this epoch." In the recourse to univalent attempts to account for the nature and effects of National Socialism, emphasis has been laid on its homogenizing and totalizing tendencies, particularly as they have been conveyed through the monumental imagery of mediated spectacle, which Susan Sontag has described as "fascinating fascism." This absorbing spectacle involves "the ideal of life as art, the cult of beauty, the fetishism of courage, the dissolution of alienation in ecstatic feelings of community; the repudiation of the intellect; the family of man (under the parenthood of Leaders)."[18] Sontag's identification of the monumental dimensions of fascist art is a reminder of one aspect of the aesthetics of fascism, depending on representations of the body as classically sculpted, a choreography identified with sublime images of physical power, suppleness in movement, and purity.

*Triumph of the Will* (1936), Leni Riefenstahl's documentary of the 1934 Nuremberg Rally, with its mass choreography, its worship of the charismatic hero, and its funerary ceremonials to its martyrs, offers dramatic testimony to the ritualistic side of National Socialism, a view of National Socialism that continues to circulate. Beyond the notion of a nation bewitched by spectacle stand more complicated historical questions. In writing about the multiplicitous and contradictory strands that constitute the National Socialist past, Detlev J. K. Peukert writes:

Historical concepts are always more metaphorical than definitional, because they bring together, in interpretative cast, specific bodies of fact from a complex, contradictory past reality which is irrecoverable in tangible form and which can be constructed only on the basis of fragmentary surviving sources, for the purpose of building bridges between the present and the past. Ambiguity and vagueness are therefore inescapable ingredients of historical conceptualisation, since it is these very features (as in all literary metaphor) that allow the partners in historical dialogue to make their own intellectual connexions with ideas that are under discussion in the interest of creating a more richly nuanced "picture" of the past and a wider range of possible contemporary interpretations.[19]

Peukert's views on history offer the possibility of a critical understanding of an epoch that has become economically and culturally valuable through the production, circulation, and consumption of remembrance commodities. His emphasis on the need to identify the everyday, contradictory, coercive, and consensual strategies of life under National Socialism challenges the monumentalizing tendencies in many critical essays, books, and films and in the museum culture devoted to the Holocaust. Without disregarding or minimizing the role of state apparatuses but paying attention to everyday life in the formation and maintenance of consensus, Peukert invites an examination of the nature of both coercion and consensus, thus offering by implication a critique of the totalizing dimensions of mourning discourses ("*Trauerarbeit*"). In looking at a selection of Nazi feature films and documentaries, I seek to identify their melodramatic strategies to see how they participate in a familiar and parasitic cultural discourse concerning uses of the past that govern and animate contemporary representations of Nazism, its "character," and its lingering effects.

## Nazi Uses of the Past

German films of the Nazi era were not all built on the scale of *Triumph of the Will* and *Olympia* (1936) with their aestheticization of the body, their use of mass choreography as spectacle, and their fascination with monumentality. Other productions of the time, particularly those that emerged from the commercial cinema, include a range of disturbing but instructive uses of historical images. Veit Harlan's *Jud Süss* (1940) and *Der ewige Jude* (1940) associate the "true" character of "the Jew" with Orientalism, with ritual killing of animals, with inordinate sexuality, with a symbiotic attachment to the leisure classes, with a penchant for Christian women, and with a fetishized attachment to money.[20] The film uses history to situate the "Jewish problem" as a long-standing problem, providing it with a genealogy through the animated diagrams of the Diaspora and an accompanying explication in the voice-over narration.[21] These characteristics are also evident in *Die Rothschilds* (1940), which recounts the rise to prominence of the Rothschild family from its humble beginnings in Germany to an international power through the efforts of its patriarch and his sons. The films reveal that representations of "the Jew" are a compendium of racialist strategies:

> The image of "the Jew" as the root of all evil, "pulling strings" behind the scenes, was an ideological synthesis of diffused anxieties about civilisation and separate, self-contradictory racialist notions all focused onto a political target. The very diversity of actual modern Jewish experience was taken to point to the existence of the mythical hate-figure of the essential "Jew" lurking behind the most disparate surface appearances. The intellectual, culturally assimilated Jew stood for detestable modernity; the religious Orthodox Jew matched the traditional hate-image of Christian anti-Semitism; the economically successful Jew stood for "money-grubbing capital" and liberalism; the Jewish socialist represented abhorrent "Bolshevism" and "Marxism"; the "Eastern Jew" from the alien culture of the ghettos was a suitable target for the aggression and arrogance of the civilising and colonist missions of the imperialist era. Unlike traditional anti-semitism of a religious or nationalist cast, the anti-semitism of the NSDAP was thus directed not against selected characteristics of the Jews, but against an abstract object, the "Jew" as such: an artificial racialist construct.[22]

*Jud Süss* and *Der ewige Jude* create a pastiche of distinct and contradictory qualities in relation to Jews: intellectualism, artistic avant-gardism, socialism and communism, undeserved wealth, warranted poverty, orthodoxy, urbanity, and provincialism. The characteristics seem to correspond to many of the determining and contradictory dimensions of the Nazi platform involving modernity, tradition, leadership, sexuality, capitalism, and socialism, among others.

*Jud Süss*, a biopic, orchestrates its thematic concerns through the codes of melodrama, drawing eclectically on the experiential character of common sense to provide the affective elements to fuse its thematic fragments. The narrative involves the attempts of Süss Oppenheimer (Ferdinand Marian) and the Jewish community to gain legal recognition for himself and his community and to assimilate into the city life of Stuttgart. The historical setting of *Jud Süss* also highlights the uneasy relationship between modernity and tradition represented by "the Jew"—modernity represented by Süss's iconoclasm and tradition represented by Dorothea, her father, Sturm, and her husband Christian Faber. The visual representation of the Jews as signifiers of modernity is graphically presented in Süss's physical transformation (similar to the dissolves of the bearded Jews into clean-faced counterparts in *Der ewige Jude*) from a traditional ghetto Jew into a cosmopolitan figure in the court. In the film, Süss, like his assistant Levi, becomes an entrepreneur, a reincarnation of the vilified Rothschild father and sons in *Die Rothschilds*. *Die Rothschilds* identifies "the Jew" with cynical imperialism, in alliance with the British, desirous of world conquest but without any conscience about the consequent suffering and losses of others.

Süss is seen as guilty of encouraging the duke's penchant for sensuality, for art, and for "liberal" attitudes toward the assimilation of the Jews. Unlike the 1934 British melodrama *Jew Süss,* the German film denies the Jews' claim to citizenship, attempting to expose their fraudulence by dramatizing the pernicious effects on the community of granting Jews citizenship. Süss (particularly in his desire for legitimacy) is portrayed as a diabolic figure who bedazzles the duke with jewels, money, and women and derides the Christian church, the rites of marriage, the respect for conjugal sex, and the morals of the bourgeois community. The melodrama accumulates grievances against him, making Süss responsible for all of the ills of the community. In images reminiscent of *The Birth of a Nation*, the core of *Jud Süss* involves the familiar melodramatic trope of the rape of an innocent young woman, thus identifying Süss with the barbaric racial defiler who violates the purity of womanhood. Portrayed as both virginal and maternal, devoted to her family and also to the community, Dorothea (Kristina Söderbaum) is the incarnation of what Klaus Theweleit describes as "a split figure," gentle and harsh, loving and aggressive, capable of heroism especially in defense of family. "It is striking," writes Theweleit, that "no one lifts a finger to ease their [women's] suffering. Suffering is not only taken for granted, it's expressly admired."[23] As the object of Süss's desire, Dorothea becomes the consummate figure of suffering, a martyr in her refusal to defile her body and her family, fending off the threat of miscegenation through self-destruction.

Faber, Dorothea's husband, retrieves her body from the water and carries it through the town in a sequence similar to scenes in *The Bride of Frankenstein* (1935), directed by James Whale, in which the body of a young female child victimized by Frankenstein's monster is carried through the town in the arms of her father as an angry crowd gathers. In *Jud Süss,* this image, like the image of the greedy and exploitative Levi, who forces the townspeople to pay tolls for crossing a bridge, turns the Jews into figures of horror. They are continually identified, literally in the case of Süss, with the rapacious image of the "Jewish" capitalist. The martyred feminine figure becomes instrumental in maintaining society—the family, the domestic hearth, and the community—against the corroding and disunifying effects of the outsider. In defiling Dorothea, Süss has attacked the pure body of woman, the surrogate for the body politic. The gravity of Süss's crimes of rape and exploitation are articulated as the basis for his trial and punishment, signaling, as the judge intones, that Christian justice rather than the vengeful code of "An eye for an eye" is enacted by his death. The image of Süss, being encased in an iron cage as he is lifted to the gallows (reproduced from *Jew Süss* but to different effect), visually reinforces connections between otherness and animality, so prominent in representations of "the Jew" in the Nazi era.

The film does not conceal its designs against Süss; rather, it uses him as the consummate signifier of social destabilization. Ironically this also makes Süss the agent responsible for creating the unified community visible at the film's end. United over Dorothea's martyrdom, the community is fused by a common desire to try and execute Süss. The remote historical context reduces the threatening implications of the narrative that pertain to contemporary anti-Semitic designs. The melodrama functions further as a means of valorizing the aggressive designs against the Jews that the film inflames. Playing with images of inside and outside—home and court, ghetto and town, belonging and exclusion—the film expands on the Orientalist elements that are also central to *Der ewige Jude,* which is constructed like a catalogue, itemizing and elaborating on street life, domestic scenes of squalor presented as signs of Jewish bestiality, images of "decadent" sexuality, connections between Jews and plague, bargaining and haggling as a major dimension of Jewish life and culture, and scenes in the synagogue with the men in their prayer shawls and skull caps, swaying rhythmically and chanting. The film capitalizes on voyeurism in its intrusive uses of close-up, with its probing of marginalized individuals and its focus on the strange and exotic nature of their clothing, behavior, and language. *Jud Süss* too creates a collage of cultural anxieties out of existing folklore. Both films cloak their prejudices in conventional melodramatic images: the fear of disorganization, the threat of abnormality, defilement, contagion, and death. Also inherent in this collage is the seemingly benign and domestic metaphor of dirt and of the need for housecleaning. What emerges from an examination of the films is their insistence on suffering and loss, their search for the causes of that suffering, and their insistence that "the Jew" is the instigator of social unrest and corruption. From the perspective of *Der ewige Jude* and *Jud Süss*, the victims of history are not the Jews but the Germans, who are in need of salvation. The melodrama is constructed on a simulacrum of the edifice of mourning in its obsession with martyrdom, loss of national identity, and the quest for resurrection, for a new life through individual and collective domination over the sacrificial victims that have been invented in order to be destroyed.

The motif of deprivation, loss, and anticipated redemption is also evident in *Ohm Krüger* (1941), a biopic. Emil Jannings produced the film and played the part of Paul Krüger, leader of the Boers, founder of the Transvaal Republic, and a prominent figure in South African politics until the turn of the nineteenth century.[24] An actor familiar to German audiences of the pre-Nazi cinema, Jannings was particularly identified with the role of the doorman in *Der letzte Mann* (*The Last Laugh*, 1924) and that of Dr. Unrat in *Der blaue Engel*. In the Nazi period, he directed and starred in many of the films that heroized figures from German history such as Bismarck in *Die Entlassung* (The dismissal, 1942) or as the factory owner, a threatened figure of masculinity, who is ultimately victorious over family and society in *Der Herrscher* (The master, 1937). *Ohm Krüger* is a cinematic memorial to its historical subject, focusing on the drama of nation building through the melodramatic career of Krüger. Beginning with the image of an aging, blind, and isolated leader, the film returns in flashback to narrate his struggles on behalf of the Boer people. Shots of Boers as they undergo the hardships of founding a new land to escape the English alternate with shots of the British "imperialists": Cecil Rhodes, his assistants, and missionaries who distribute guns while singing Christian hymns. Commerce differentiates Rhodes and the British generally from Krüger's altruism and devotion to his people. This anticapitalist theme reinforces connections between anti-British sentiment and anti-Semitism.

Krüger is portrayed as being devoted both to his immediate family and to his extended family of Boers, virulent in his disapproval of and anger toward those who do not share his mistrust and hatred of the British. At great personal cost, he chastises and constrains errant Boers who are willing to profit commercially through an alliance with the British. Closer to home, he resists his son Jan, who has returned with his family from England, where he has studied international law, because Jan advocates cooperation with the British. Characteristic of masculine oedipal melodramas, the film features conflict between father and son, resolved when Jan finally recognizes the barbaric behavior of the English. The film portrays Krüger's encounters with the British through melodramatic contrasts. The high-minded and socially committed Boers are contrasted to the perfidious British: Queen Victoria is wily, crass, and intemperate; the imperialist Rhodes is devoid of patriotism and single-mindedly concerned with gaining wealth, and Chamberlain is a rogue. Because of British aggrandizement and gratuitous cruelty, the beleaguered and innocent Boers are driven to defend their homeland, presented in scenes of impassioned mobilization and heroic battle, visualized in lengthy sequences of singing men marching with banners. The Boer's slogan is "We know our cause is right. We fight for freedom and Fatherland." After initial victories, the Boers are defeated and placed in concentration camps where their women and children contract diseases and die. Major Winston Churchill, another target of the film, is portrayed as a sadistic camp commander who feeds his dogs food from his table while he starves the Boers and who has no compunction about shooting the helpless inmates. The famous scene of the maggoty food from Eisenstein's *The Battleship Potemkin* (1925) is quoted in the film's climactic concentration camp episode. When the women complain about the rotten food, they are told by the doctor that it is edible.

The film's martyr turns out to be Jan, who is hanged by the British. Before his death he cries out, "I die for you, our people, our Fatherland." The film closes with a montage of the dead Jan, a live child with her dead mother, and a superimposed image of Krüger as Janning's voice intones that "a day of revenge will come. Blood cannot have flowed in vain." The identification of the Boers with the Germans is not lost on the viewer. Both have lost a war, and both are shown as needing to revenge themselves against their enemies. The implied connection extends to the expectation of vindication for humiliation and suffering. Similar to the rhetoric of *Die Rothschilds*, the film's rhetoric relies on an anti-imperialist and anticapitalist critique to mobilize sympathy for the protagonists as the victims of a massive international conspiracy. Krüger's blindness is used metaphorically to indicate that though he cannot physically see, he is endowed with insight and prophecy. By contrast, Jan can see but is temporarily blinded to his duty. Krüger's blindness also serves the melodramatic function of isolating the protagonist, making him appear vulnerable to the treachery of others, a martyr to a heroic cause, and thus reinforcing the case for his vindication. The emphasis on blindness also has contemporary currency as an allusion to Hitler's blinding in World War I.[25] The melodrama of the Boers as surrogates for the German nation is elegiac, dwelling on defeat and on the unrelenting need for sacrifice in the name of the nation. Consonant with the affective valence of melodrama, the nation "has nothing in the first instance to do with national borders, forms of government, or so-called nationality. The concept refers to a quite specific form of male community, one that is 'yearned for' for many a long year, that arises from the 'call of the blood.' Like sexual characteristics, its essential features are incapable of being 'learned' or 'forgotten.' The nation is a community of soldiers."[26] The community of soldiers, as exemplified by Krüger, is united in war where they exorcise the shame of defeat and "regenerate both the nation and the soldier male himself."[27]

The epic and monumental portrait of the suffering nation is complemented by more immediate domestic and personal conflicts, involving generational difference between fathers and sons and its threat to unity. The melodramatic narrative of conversion into familial and national responsibility also neutralizes the more blatant aspects of the film's monumentalism, providing access to historically remote events. The bifurcated emphasis in the film on conflicts within the family and within ethnic and national groupings is reminiscent of Peukert's descriptions of everyday life under National Socialism as "split into a multiplicity of opposing groups and individuals with competing privileges (or apparent privileges)" who could be united "only in meaningless rituals and mass organizations."[28] The destabilizing effects of National Socialism have their counterpart in the film's dual emphasis on physical force and the threat of isolation and psychic disorganization.

*Ohm Krüger* reiterates the commonsensical notion of the ultimately productive nature of loss and adversity in creating community solidarity and in the realization of justice. The film seems to exemplify Josef Goebbels's statement: "It must be our ambition to set an example today on which later generations can model themselves in similar crises and times of stress just as today we must take our cues from the past heroes of history."[29] Goebbels's invocation of the cues afforded by past history invite further exploration of the nature of the historical sensibility afforded by such prompting. This sensibility has to be tied to daily existence, those "mute forms of knowledge in the sense that their precepts do not lend themselves to being either formalized or spoken."[30] This form of knowledge, associated with the "mute" language of melodrama, is commonsensical experience buttressed by folklore that passes as official history. In the films discussed above, it is not the factual knowledge of the past events, images, and issues portrayed that produces sympathy but the connection of the past events to the affective language of daily life. This common sense relies on strategies of survival conveyed through the melodramatic and elegiac language of immediate suffering, with its expression of a longing for justice and an anticipation of redemption.

Writing on National Socialism's uses of the past, Carlo Ginzburg, in an essay on Georges Dumezils's *Mythes et dieux des Germains*, picks out the following sentence from Dumezils's text as crucial: "It is this sort of preestablished congruence between past and present, more than the instances of conscious imitation of the past, that constitutes the originality of the current German experience."[31] Ginzburg confirms that the "spontaneous congruence between past and present" was central to National Socialism, which "drew a powerful element of ideological legitimacy from this repeatedly-flaunted continuity."[32] Because of this congruence between past and present, the past is not remote but ever present, and even if not verifiable scientifically, it is verifiable by experience through "instinct" and "intuition." Clichés, formulas, axioms, proverbial insights, and prophecies take on legitimacy, attached as they are to a core of truth derived from the past and anastomosed onto the present. "In all of fascism," George Mosse writes, "we find this combination of looking backwards to the national mystique (in Germany and Austria, to the racial mystique)— and at the same time forward to the war, to the new race of heroes which came from the war."[33] Consonant with strategies of popular historicizing, the Nazi films especially the commercial narratives, directly or obliquely orchestrate conceptions of nation, family, race, sexuality, and gender. The representations of national unity are constructed on notions of specialness, purity, and physiological difference. At the end of *Der ewige Jude* in particular, the imagery of masculine youth, of male bonding, and of their links with past societies (*Männerbunde*) assumes an importance as an elaboration on the distinction between degenerate sexuality and health. The linking of a concept of modern nation formation to the folklore of "male groups in the films is presented as an essential stage on the path towards the formation of an authoritarian, hierarchical and warlike society."[34]

The excesses of history in the Nazi films discussed above are thus not antiquarian but monumental in the Nietzschean sense. The images from the past are designed to serve the immediate interests of creating a sense of immediacy and legitimacy, reinforcing images of the power of the autocratic, dictatorial state. The congruence between past and present is evident in clear-cut distinctions between the "elect" and the "damned." Differences between election and damnation are clothed in the contradictory common sense of folklore of gender and sexuality. For example, homoerotic desire is aestheticized for the elect and evident in the monumental images of heroic, masculine, Aryan figures. For those who are not of the elect, same-sex desire is a sign of degeneracy and deserving of damnation, as in *Jud Süss* and *Der ewige Jude*.

Similarly, despite the injunction on women to reproduce in the interests of the state, only racially sanctioned relationships are legal. Thus tradition and modernity, science and folklore, promiscuity and conjugal rectitude, same-sex desire and heterosexuality are fluid categories, serving to underscore distinctions between the privileged and the outcast and capable of producing and maintaining disequilibrium over membership. The Nazi films capitalize on the consequences of tolerating undesirable difference, of threats to personal and economic survival, and of the disabling effects of social disorganization, most importantly a sense of loss of identity and a desire for restitution. Their uses of history reveal the importance of melodrama as a commonsensical strategy for endowing past events with affective significance and experiential validity. The Nazi films share with many anti-Nazi representations a psychological orientation, an obsession with settling a past injury, the imagery of health and disease and purity and corruption, a voyeuristic fascination with the forbidden other, a binary mode of thought that precludes complexity and hybridity, and an obsession with legality and judgment.

## From History to Memory

The appearance of the U.S. television series *Holocaust* in 1979 awakened debates, particularly in Germany, about popular history and the uses of the past.[35] What is most important about the debates is the way in which they sought to gauge the consequences of filmmaking about the Holocaust. Discussions have detailed the massive pre-and-post publicity about the program and the political problems involved in its airing on television. The size of the audience has been measured. Audience responses to the film have been analyzed, and the positive and negative effects of the program have been assessed. Reviewing the commentaries, Siegfried Zielinski comments: "Since the telecast of "Holocaust," the question of its *effect* has been asked *ad nauseam* and has remained unanswered just as often. I personally feel it is a moot point for theoretical reasons and also for practical considerations which are linked to cultural processes."[36] Though one can agree with the need to contextualize media representations, the nature of the theoretical and practical considerations posed by their analysis—especially of the cultural and political processes in which representations are imbricated—remains difficult to assess. The existence of problems in relation to historical texts such as *Holocaust* and their reception is testimony to difficulties in representing Nazism and the Holocaust.

Generally, the negative assessments of the television program focus on the "aesthetic issues of the film," criticizing film's inability to "portray a subject of such magnitude as the Holocaust," or they decry the use of effects and media gimmicks to portray a tragic event that only victims and survivors can understand, whereas the positive assessments focus on "the film's *political* implications and *pedagogical* dimensions."[37] The negative assessments raised familiar objections to mass media, its soap opera quality, its commercial context, its trivialization of events, its melodrama, and its connection to the reigning political party. The positive evaluations focused on *Holocaust* as a means for reaching a mass audience, stressing its importance for "understanding the past."[38] For some critics, the film's ability to facilitate this understanding of the past resides in its power to produce for the audience "emotional identification with the individual members of a family . . . with the Jews as Jews—like themselves members of a family, united by and conflicting in their emotions, their outlook, their everyday concerns."[39]

Like the thesis of collective mourning, this valorization of identification and collective catharsis presumes the existence of guilt, denial, and suppression, the pedagogical and psychological value of replaying the past, the importance of identity formation, and the unproblematic aspects of melodramatization. Recent critical work on melodrama has focused attention on the need for complex reading practices that are neither positive nor negative but that are capable of revealing long-standing cultural contradictions.[40] An emphasis on the therapeutic nature of identification in popular representations raises the unresolved question of the nature of the reception of popular works. This stress on the positive nature of affective responses reinforces a commonsensical perspective on history—the familiar, the experiential, and the affective; in short, the melodramatic.

*Holocaust* was cast in the mold of grafting melodrama and history. In its strategies of blending documentary footage and fictional narration, in its focus on the falling fortunes of the Weiss family and the rising fortunes of the Dorf family, in its distinction between aggressors and victims, and in its relentless cataloguing of the events leading to the Final Solution, does the film domesticate, even if it does not neutralize, the horrendous character of the Holocaust and minimize the complex theoretical issues associated with that past event? If the uses of history are inextricably fused with the present, and if melodrama provides the affective glue to make those events palpable, then, in Zielinski's terms, what are the "cultural processes" at work that identify *Holocaust*'s investments in history?

*Holocaust*'s family melodrama captures the preoccupation with the survival of the family and local community in line with 1980s concerns. Gender issues are placed at the forefront. Berta Weiss (Rosemary Harris), at first unwilling to grasp the seriousness of events and resistant to taking any action, gains in wisdom and heroic stature through suffering, though Marta Dorf (Deborah Norton) is vilified for her unregenerate maternal role. The film also highlights the importance of youth. Rudi (Joseph Bottoms), the survivor, will find a new life in Palestine. As is typical of the melodramatic scenario, the criminals (the Nazis in this case) are punished for their crimes. Running through the episodes are the repeated lamentations: "What did we do to them?" and "What crime have we done to you?" The program addresses long-standing stereotypes associated with middle-class Jews. The use of classical piano music, annoying to some critics, heightens the sense of the cosmopolitan and educated nature of the upper-class Jews. The casting of the Weiss family—Berta Weiss, in particular—appears to counteract stereotypes of Jewishness. Like the Nazi Eric Dorf (Michael Moriarty) and his wife, Marta, Berta is also blonde. In terms of physical appearance, Jews and Germans are indistinguishable so as to visually counteract Nazi stereotypes concerning physical differences between Germans and Jews.

The domestic drama of *Holocaust* addresses the commonsensical imperative of compromise and survival in familiar, middle-class representations of marriage, romance, monogamy, physical health, and economic security. As a program designed for a mass audience, the drama is subject to direct and indirect censorship governing what can and cannot be shown to a television audience. Therefore the family melodrama provides a familiar format in which to embed the gruesome events of the Holocaust. The elegiac aspects of the narrative and its memorialization of Holocaust victims in the persons of the Weiss family make possible a formally benign medium in which to present that event. However, the affective appeal of the elegiac nature of melodrama, with its emphasis on the threat of death and the need for justice and restitution, is ambiguous. This ambiguity arises from the universalizing tendencies of elegy. The generalizing character of the threats to be overcome are such that they are easily transposed from one set of historical conflicts to another, antithetical, set and from one group of protagonists to another, opposing, group. What might be gained in creating an affective relation to events may also be lost in the neutralizing of the specificity of past events.

Another television series, alternately celebrated and criticized, the German production *Heimat* also presents a mixture of melodrama and history. The German series, in contrast to *Holocaust*, brings the audience into contact with contemporary events. Spanning the years from 1919 to 1982, this family melodrama functions elegiacally. *Heimat* reconstructs a past image of rural life. In almost sixteen hours of viewing time, the audience is introduced to this world through a variety of characters who inhabit the Hunsrück, specifically through their familial and generational conflicts.

*Holocaust* recapitulated the officially recorded events of the Holocaust, but *Heimat* stubbornly refuses to present a parallel history. Commenting on the response by Edgar Reitz (the director of the series) to the U.S. television series, Thomas Elsaesser writes that "Reitz himself wrote a furious article against the series at the time, pillorying as hypocrites the German critics who seemed to applaud the sensationalist, melodramatic thriller." In melodramatic terms Reitz declared, "With *Holocaust,* the Americans have taken away our history."[41] Reitz's fighting words are indicative of the identity politics that are embedded in the current conflict over the nature and uses of history writing. Among the other complex responses to *Heimat* is the question of who owns history. This question raises yet another: Is history national property?

*Heimat* focuses on the Simon family through several generations, using the characters to highlight motifs that concern the nature of memory and popular history. Reitz's treatment of German history calls attention to the interests invested in stabilizing representations of the past. Indirectly *Heimat* disregards prevailing psychoanalytic formulations, such as those advanced by the Mitscherlichs, concerning the need for Germans to mourn the past and confront their guilt in order to assume ethical and political responsibility for past events. In fact, in its uses of history and melodrama, *Heimat* seems to rely on a different psychological paradigm, one that seeks to encourage a sense of self-esteem, a sense of identification with and identity through a reconstructed past.

Like responses to *Holocaust,* responses to *Heimat* reveal more about the status of current historical discourse than they do about the problems posed by *Heimat* itself and by any television series on Nazism and the Holocaust.[42] Particularly troubling to critics has been the "blatant tokenism with which the film handles the more problematic aspects of German history."[43] In particular, Reitz's recourse to the concept of *Heimat* (homeland) and its connections to Nazi cinema has been a source of contention. The concept of a German homeland is expressed through "the attachments and belongings of individuals to village, landscape, and dialect with the assertion of native German values against the universal claims deriving from the Enlightenment as expressed in the French Revolution and English economic liberalism."[44] The term "*Heimat*" takes on other connotations associated with resistance to urbanization and industrialization as well as to the power of the state. "*Heimat*" also recalls the feelings of postwar homelessness.

Affect associated with the use of this term and with Reitz's use of the *Heimatfilm* genre reveals that the film has touched a cultural nerve, one that extends to the heart of popular history and memory.

Speaking to the question of history, Gertrud Koch asserts that "the film resorts to fade-out strategies which are analogous to the defensive mechanisms of experience and as such elude critical reflection. . . . these are reconstructions of consciousness which reproduce the old gaps, pseudo-experiences and token acknowledgments of history which played a significant part in the post-war period."[45]

One of the major contentions arising from the debate around *Heimat* involves the texture and nature of historicizing. Klaus Kreimeier writes that "[t]he film is a product of the new sensibility toward the historicity of small spaces."[46] In other words, the film is attentive to the need to move away from the epic and monumental and to reach into the everyday with its inherent problems and contradictions. In Reitz's acknowledgment and defense of this method, he has said, "In the history books the lives of the mighty, the great wars, battles, great disasters are described. But the small everyday things which affect the majority of the people do not appear in the history books, and their testimonies and sources are not collected, preserved and handed down. The only thing we have is what we carry with us in our memory."[47] At first glance, Reitz's comments appear to be aligned with positions on popular memory and everyday reality articulated by Peukert and by postcolonial critics and hence invite an examination of the film from this vantage point.

*Heimat* invokes the cornucopia of everyday life in relation to the actions of the elders, Katharina and Matthias, the protagonist, Maria, and her sons Anton, Ernst, and Hermannchen. The commonsensical nature of everyday life is stressed. Daily life functions as "creative" memory in Reitz's terms. The film's invocation of the everyday is problematic. The crux of the problem is succinctly articulated by Gertrud Koch in her distinction of the "semantic between 'everyday fascism' and 'fascist everyday life.'"[48] Distinct differences emerge between these two modes of representing the past, differences that involve the questions: Who speaks for whom? Who is the guardian of memory? What distinguishes different investments in the past? In exploring the contradictory nature of an emphasis on daily life, Saul Friedlander affirms that memory is Janus-faced: It can lead to a more complex understanding of the nature of Nazi hegemony and of its residual elements, or it can serve to erase the memory of Nazism and its effects and "what gives the Nazi regime its specificity."[49]

*Heimat*, like common sense itself, valorizes folklore and immediate sensual experience, bringing together, by indirection, past and present. A subtle formalist reading of the television series is not required to detect the film's invitation to look at the past in unmediated terms—the reiterative photographs of the family and their friends in the village; the repetitive use of long, panning shots of the landscape; the images of the encroachments of industrialization; the nostalgic uses of folk music ("Ich hat ein Kamerad" and "Muss i denn," among others) in contrast to popular dance music and later to Paul's electronic composition; the use of clips from the 1938 film *Heimat*, starring Zarah Leander; the activity of movie-going in the vein of Giuseppe Tornatore's *Cinema paradiso* (1988); the communal meals; and the death of several generations. All these fleeting memories of an irrecoverable past contribute to the elegiac sense of a bygone world.

The family melodrama involves (1) Paul's abandonment of Appollonia, the "Gypsy," (2) Maria's abandonment by Paul, (3) her truncated affair with Wohleben, (4) Hermannchen's relationship to Klarchen, and (5) Anton and Ernst's numerous antagonistic encounters. The facets of the melodramatic narrative function to dramatize the constraints on daily life and the complexity of relations during times of war, occupation, and reconstruction. *Heimat* shares a kinship with John Boorman's *Hope and Glory* (1987), a film that eschews the more familiar dramas of World War II to focus on the everyday life of a British family, highlighting the notion that life goes on even during wartime, oblivious to political conflicts, and that focuses on the richness and vitality of immediate relationships and experiences. Anti-Semitism and the Holocaust appear to be remote—with the exception of the intrusive problem of Gypsies, Jews harassed by rowdies, the discomfort of having to establish an Aryan identity for the name Simon, a general bewilderment, and occasionally expressed hostility toward Jews but Reitz and affirmative critical responses to the film deem this understandable in the context of the more absorbing experiences in the flux of daily life.

*Heimat* "came out of . . . a new vision, a traumatic realisation that something was gone and that while it was there it hadn't been recognized."[50] The family melodramas within the chronicle framework, with their rhythmic sense of the ebb and flow of time within the natural environment, reinforce this backward and naturalized glimpse of a disappearing world. If Reitz had hoped to get his audiences to think critically about the film, something has gone wrong. By reproducing the common sense of everyday life, *Heimat,* like the photographs it displays, remains within the orbit of the familiar, the commonsensical, and the elegiac.

## Mourning, Melodrama, and Monumentalism: *Schindler's List*

Steven Spielberg's *Schindler's List* appeared a year after the opening of the Holocaust Museum in Washington, D.C. The film offers itself as a monument to Schindler and "his Jews," to their suffering and their survival. Some critics have compared the work to the Holocaust Museum, and some have tied both film and museum to the "cult of victimhood."[51] A blurb in an article in the *Smithsonian Magazine* reads: "A new museum in Washington opens to exhibit the lessons of history as a testament to the dead and a reminder to the living."[52] President Bill Clinton, in his remarks at the museum's opening, said:

> I believe that this museum will touch the life of everyone who enters and leave everyone forever changed; a place of deep sadness and a sanctuary of bright hope; an ally of education against ignorance; of humility against arrogance; an investment in a secure future against whatever insanity lurks ahead. If this museum can mobilize morality, then those who have perished will thereby gain a measure of immortality.[53]

In contrast to the president's elegiac words, one museum visitor's description of the experience was as follows:

> Violence and the grotesque are central to the American aesthetic and the Holocaust Museum provides both amply. It is impossible to take in the exhibition without becoming somewhat inured to the sheer graphic horror of the display. . . . The museum courts the viewer's fascination, encouraging familiarity with the incomprehensible and the unacceptable; one is repeatedly forced into the role of a voyeur of the prurient.[54]

Finding the identity cards of survivors—which each visitor is given upon entrance to the museum—in the trash can, this visitor concludes: "One way history is doomed to repetition at the Holocaust Museum is that day in and day out, year after year, the *Einsatzgruppen* murderers will play over and over."[55]

Memorials and monuments to the Holocaust continue to proliferate by way of museums and films. What is circulated in the name of memory becomes an exercise in ritual and commemoration, even if not in voyeurism, rather than dynamic historicizing. From *Holocaust* to *Schindler's List*, painstaking research, capital investment, and a reiterated emphasis on the importance of education and memory have seen to it that "[t]he Holocaust will be painfully reconstructed, in all its horrors and misery. The transport trains will roll, the ghetto will be populated and depopulated, even the chimneys of Auschwitz-Birkenau will belch forth anew in the full depiction of that particular hell on earth."[56]

James E. Young describes the contradictory trend toward documentation that assumes "that the more realistic a representation, the more adequate it becomes as testimonial evidence of outrageous events."[57] Particularly in relation to an understanding of "witnessing," Young reminds us that the term has a very specific meaning beyond merely recording a legal injunction to report an injustice.[58] The act of witnessing is related to the need to lament, to mourn, and to restore dignity to the victims and to the survivors. The creation of memorials— whether in stone or wood sculpture or in buildings—"now make memory and pedagogy their twin aims."[59] The memorials in Israel comprise not merely the memories of the Nazi past but of the pre-Nazi past and of the years following the Holocaust, especially those memorials concerning the creation and maintenance of the Jewish state. Thus the impetus toward creating monuments serves not one but many memorializing functions for the Jewish community. However, the issue of remembering and representing the Holocaust becomes more problematic, as writers have pointed out,[60] as the years pass or when those outside the Jewish community attempt to memorialize the Holocaust: The creation of monuments and museums is tied to the tendency to perpetuate not only the past but also knowledge of its irrecoverability.

Like museums and mausoleums, the films become part of a storehouse of images for the remains of the dead, calling forth rituals of commemoration, not necessarily expressions of the vital uses of memory and understanding. In Claude Lanzmann's terms: "The worst moral and artistic crime that can be committed in producing a work dedicated to the Holocaust is to consider the Holocaust as past. Either the Holocaust is legend or it is present; in no case is it a memory."[61]

What does *Schindler's List* contribute to this complex debate about the uses of the past?

That *Schindler's List* has been spoken of in the same context as the Holocaust Museum in Washington, D.C., is indicative of the film's elegiac and monumental character. According to Thomas Doherty: "No less than the opening of the Holocaust Museum on the Washington Mall, a site heretofore reserved for memorials to the American past, *Schindler's List* is a capstone event in a process that has been called the Americanization of the Holocaust.'"[62] Doherty, quoting Edward Lutvak, adds that "with the passage of time, the Holocaust has come to seem more and more the central event of World War II. More and more, too, Hollywood has come to seem the prism through which all history, genocidal and otherwise, is witnessed and felt."[63]

Critical responses to *Schindler's List* have not been characterized by the same level of polarization as was elicited by the television series *Holocaust* or *Heimat*.[64] The reception by critics and reviewers has been generally favorable, if cautious about the Spielberg film's subject matter. While there are cavilings with the drawing of certain characters and some negative criticism from right-wing and conservative critics in Germany, the response has focused either on the director and his "coming of age" in the film or on its formal qualities.[65] Critics like Richard Alleva seem to be more concerned with the status of the film in the international film canon than with the film's politics as expressed in its treatment of history.[66] John Gross commends the good work that this popular culture text can perform in the context of Holocaust "forgetfulness" and also in the context of the forgetfulness of the gulag, Cambodia, and Eritrea.[67] Why has this film not aroused the intense debate and criticism accorded to other film texts addressing the Holocaust? Is the wary response to it indicative of the ways in which the film has managed, in commonsensical fashion, to address both realists and revisionists? Has Spielberg managed to forestall objections because, like the Holocaust Museum and like the act of witnessing, the film has been able to produce an approximation of a testimonial? Or does the film appear on the movie horizon at a time when the politics of identity with their affect-laden scenarios are firmly entrenched? I single out this film for comment because it seems to exemplify the ways in which the common sense of folklore, that patchwork quilt of the past, works so effectively to forestall objections to its mode of representation. The film draws on a well-known language. Unlike

Fassbinder's antimelodrama melodrama, *Schindler's List* endows the events it represents with an affective intensity that validates the connection in popular historicizing between melodrama and representations of the past.

The film's investment in memorializing is made explicit from its first images, with a shot of a hand lighting a Shabbos candle, dissolving to a shot of a group of people in a room as a man intones the prayers, followed by a series of dissolves to candles as they burn down to nothing but wisps of smoke like the chimneys of Auschwitz, which are shown later belching smoke. The contrasting use of black-and-white and color, reminiscent of Alain Resnais's *Night and Fog* (1955), signals the shift between past and present (deviating from black-and-white only for Genia's red coat and for the Sabbath celebrated in the factory for the first time legally since internment). The conventional use of titles too indicates the passage of time, from the roundup of the Polish Jews in 1939 into the ghetto, through its destruction, to the stages of the Final Solution (1942–1945), to the end of the war, and to the present time in Israel.

The importance of the proper name is visually remarked throughout the film. As in the Holocaust Museum, the visualization of the names is central, as the initial sequences reveal. The Jews are rounded up as a Nazi bureaucrat calls out, "Name?" Slowly, elegiacally, the camera lingers on each character. They recite their names. In close-up, a typewriter prints the name for the audience to see, not once but several times. Visually a connection is made between the names and specific objects—clothing, jewelry, and money—as the sequence dissolves to Schindler's room while he dresses. The film will continue to reinforce the equation between characters and commodities. The dominant question, however, one that is reiterated in various terms throughout the film, is first asked, several times, in the cabaret sequence near the opening. The question is "Who is that man?"

In a style congruent with contemporary conceptions of melodrama, the film selects a flawed figure but one who, nonetheless, is finally capable of heroism, perhaps because of his flaws. Oskar is a Nazi, though not of the virulent type common to many film and television representations. He is attached to the Nazi party by conformity, opportunism, and indifference to ideology. The film does not minimize the facts that he profited from his traffic in Jewish workers, that he ran a labor camp (albeit benificently), that he was a sensualist, a man of

Schindler (Liam Neeson) as a contemporary Moses, in *Schindler's List*. Courtesy New York Museum of Modern Art, Film Stills Archive.

"hedonistic temperament." On the contrary, these are the qualities that ultimately mark him as exceptional: He has the requisite common sense to understand the bad "business" of Nazism. Moreover, it is his pragmatism that enables his conversion to altruism and self-sacrifice. And as the film progresses, Oskar increasingly comes to assume the role of a patriarch, a father figure to his Jewish children. The most magical scenes of salvation involve the episode in which the lethal Zyklon-B gas miraculously turns to water and the women are saved. However, the images in long shot of new inmates arriving and of the smoke rising in the chimneys are in dramatic contrast to the middle-distance and close-up shots reserved for the filming of Schindler's Jews. Moreover, in his large frame, athleticism, vitality, and magnanimity, Schindler evokes the familiar image of a gentile Moses prototype directing the Jews toward the Promised Land: out of bondage and slavery and into freedom. The narrative is transformed into a testimony of faith, exemplifying the ultimately benign designs of history. In this respect, the film joins other monumental films in their excessive attachment to a notion of deliverance through history, in their rehearsal of suffering, and in their reliance on identification with a savior. Schindler's distinctive role is underscored by the fact that events are mainly filtered through Schindler's gaze. The gaze of others, par-

ticularly Stern, are directed at Schindler, thus affording greater prominence and sanctity to Oskar's role.

Ralph Fienne's portrayal of Amon Goeth also displays an important difference from familiar images of the Nazi ideologue. Goeth, like
Schindler (but without any benevolence toward the workers), is cynical and inclined toward profit. He incarnates a bemused and dispas-
sionate cruelty rather than a zealous adherence to his work in relation
to the Jews, though he still adheres to the belief that Jews are different.
The crass materialism that he shares with other Nazi officers is evidence of cynicism rather than of pure fanaticism, most marked by his
expectation that Helen Hirsch, the object of his brutal treatment, will,
when called upon after the war, testify in his behalf. The similarities
between Schindler and Goeth serve to complicate the portrait of the
Nazi. Through these characters the film differentiates between levels
of villainy, opportunism, and even compassion. The parallels are reminiscent of Peukert's analysis of everyday Nazism, serving to differentiate degrees of adherence to the regime in contrast to the usual leveling
of differences in relation to age groups, status, and classes but also
serving in the film to elevate Schindler's heroism in the face of banality.

The most Spielbergesque aspect of the film, and the most emotion-
ally intense, is the stress on the images of the destruction of the children, especially in the focus on Genia of the red coat. Through the
film's contrasting use of black-and-white and color (her red coat), her
image is singled out from the others. Genia is an image of a life un-
realized, a memorial to the Nazi atrocities, a figure to be mourned, and
the turning point in Schindler's conversion. Genia becomes a synecdoche for the innocence of the children and their victimization at the
hands of the Nazis and an instance of the film's ultimate recourse to
melodramatic affect. Correspondingly, the figure of Stern is tailored to
suit the melodramatic scenario. Kingsley's role is the conventional
helper, the smaller but cleverer man, the brain to the protagonist's
physicality. His character conveys the familiar portrait of the wily Jew,
the carrier of Jewish wisdom and common sense, ostensibly without the negative qualities assigned to it in anti-Semitic renditions;
Stern is the appropriate "buddy" of the male-bonding film. He serves
the necessary function in the narrative of further ennobling the stature
of the heroic protagonist.

From beginning to end, the melodrama is cast in a monumental elegiac mode, literally ending with a scene of mourning at the grave site

"in the Catholic cemetery, which looks south over the valley of Hinom, called Gehenna in the New Testament."[68] The procession of mourners, survivors, and their families, accompanied by the actors who portrayed them or their relatives, file by Schindler's grave, each person stopping and placing a stone on Schindler's grave. The last to stand there is Liam Neeson, head bowed. Thus the film has been an elegy for the dead Schindler rather than a mourning ritual for the victims. Reading back through the film, the events leading to the Holocaust can be seen now to function as a "reminder" and a "testimonial." Like ritual mourners, the spectators must shed the required tears (which, according to reports, they do in copious amounts)—but for whom? for the victims of the Holocaust? for Schindler? for themselves? for the affect raised by a moving melodrama?

The melodrama is enhanced too by the film's operatic uses of music: a melange of popular, religious, and classical forms. The Yiddish folk songs, the chanting of ritual prayers, the singing of kaddish, the Elgar music played by Itzhak Perlman on violin and Sam Sanders on piano, accompany scenes with no dialogue. Particularly operatic are the episodes at Auschwitz and the farewell scenes between Schindler and his Jews. The music functions as the mute language of melodrama, heightening affect that cannot be articulated within the constraints of verbal language. The music serves memory, heightening unspeakable moments of suffering and giving them religious significance. It also has a ritualistic and elegiac dimension at the film's end when the mourners file past the grave. Titles designate their identity as survivors and relatives of survivors. The setting in Israel also identifies their connection to the state of Israel.

Through the use of titles and the references to actual persons and events, the film utilizes the docudrama format, thus protecting itself against the criticism usually leveled at feature films involving the Holocaust; namely, that they are fiction. As a biopic, the film invokes an actual figure, Oskar Schindler, and the names of the Jews he saved. In its narrative trajectory it follows, as the titles remind us, the actual events leading to the Final Solution. But it does not end there; it takes us into the present with the actual survivors and their families at Schindler's grave. Thus the film retains the semblance of a docudrama format. Nonetheless, the film's iconography of character, musical commentary, and contrasting uses of color and black-and-white reiterate and capitalize on familiar forms of melodrama that participate in conventional, commonsensical notions of heroism, judgment, and salvation.

In the film's monopoly of the Academy Awards, in the director's emotional acceptance speech at the awards ceremony, in the television news reports of and special programs on the film's release and after its winning of its Oscars, another dimension of the film's uses of history becomes apparent. The editorials and commentaries made explicit and implicit connections between the film and concerns about the survival of the state of Israel, about conflicts between Israelis and Arabs, and about anti-Semitic comments by some members of the African-American community. Moreover the film touches on local and global conflicts concerning questions of national identity as these relate to questions of gender, ethnicity, and sexuality. The film serves as a commonsensical reminder of contradictory, contentious, and unresolved issues concerning history and identity. Thus *Schindler's List* illustrates the persistence of a familiar and reiterative mode of representing history that can comfortably be assimilated into official historicizing and adopted in opposing fashion by any group and of any persuasion.

While the film raises to consciousness the importance of remembering what has been or is in danger of being forgotten, through its reliance on conventional gendered and generic conventions, it reinforces the truisms of official historicizing. By perpetuating the salvation scenario, the film does not interrogate received knowledge, its representations, or its omissions. Nor does the film focus on the subaltern for understanding the complex nature of victimization, the nature of subalternity, and the ways in which subalternity carries within it not the cause of its subjection but the tendency through monumentalism and antiquarianism to remain rooted in the past.

Reviews have repeatedly made the arguments that *Schindler's List* must be appreciated as a popular film and as an auteurist work. As commercial cinema, as biopic, as part of the Spielberg canon, and as memorial to the Holocaust, *Schindler's List* participates in discourses that have been identified with popular models of narration. The film is a text that relies on common sense to dramatize its relation to the history of the Holocaust—in its highlighting of the drama of survival, in its identifying that survival with a "just man," in its linking of survival to work, in its reenactment of the ritual of mourning, and in its recourse to an elegiac style that mimes mourning. The reception of the film confirms that it has succeeded in evoking an appropriately serious and respectful response in a language highly saturated with affect derived from drawing on the authentic experience of suffering. The world it creates is familiar, even if not reassuring.

Given the reevaluations of popular film forms, it is no longer possible to dismiss the film as yet another instance of the monolithic and demonic nature of the culture industry. We have been educated by media criticism—through television, radio, journals, and schools—to regard mass forms more seriously. Some critics have gone so far as to attribute powerful and important emotional effects to popular forms. Others have been able to identify popular texts as socially and culturally transgressive. Is *Schindler's List* a popular text? If by popular we mean that it has achieved huge box office receipts and won awards, the answer is yes. If affective involvement is a measure of the popular, then the film is popular. If what we mean by popular is the text's ability to muster commonsensical knowledge even while it is critical of that knowledge, to involve the spectators in an affective response even while the film is critical of the affect, then the film is not popular, though it does not follow that it is avant-garde. In its preoccupation with the past, *Schindler's List* exposes little uneasiness about that preoccupation.

A comparison between the film's and the novel's treatment of events sheds some light on alternative forms of historicizing in relation to Nazism and the Holocaust. Early on in what he terms a "novel," Thomas Keneally explains that he adopts "the texture and devices of a novel to tell a true story . . . because the novel's techniques seem best suited for a character of such ambiguity and magnitude as Oskar."[69] A comparison between Spielberg's and Keneally's Oskar illuminates the difference between a monumental and a critical treatment of history, between a conventionalized representation and an attempt to make evident the complexity of memory. The "novel" makes clear that Schindler is memorially constructed from the reminiscences and the personal narratives of survivors and from Emilie Schindler. The competing and sometimes negative recollections provide the ambiguity that the film undermines. In the novel, the agonizing choice of staying with a loved one and dying or choosing personal survival does not always involve Schindler's agency. In fact, the "novel" is the narrative of the people on the "list." Through the other characters, Keneally scans the history, not merely for monumentalizing Schindler's "strange virtue and . . . the places and associates to which it brought him"[70] but for scanning the nature of those associations.

The question of what transpired, never subject to foreclosure and summary explanation, is paramount. The novel unfolds with the gradually dawning awareness on the part of all that what happened was not a variation on a traditional pogrom but something quite different and still unfathomable. Keneally writes of this knowledge: "To write these things now is to state the commonplaces of history. But to find them out in 1942 . . . was to suffer a fundamental shock, a derangement in that area of the brain in which stable ideas about humankind and its possibilities are kept."[71] Schindler's image in the novel is put together like a puzzle with pieces missing: "At some point in any discussion of Schindler, the surviving friends of the Herr Direktor will blink and shake their heads and begin the almost mathematical business of finding the sum of his motives. For one of the commonest sentiments of Schindler Jews is still, 'I don't know why he did it.'"[72] The comments reinforce the precarious question of knowledge that is plumbed in the novel, involving the sources of information concerning Schindler. One is always aware that what is recorded is based on testimony and on "a haziness suitable to legend."[73] Keneally creates the narrative from the bits and pieces of information that he received from and about the Schindler Jews. Throughout the "novel" Keneally is self-conscious about his indebtedness to the testimonies of the survivors, testimonies that in retrospect border on folklore, but with the self-consciousness that the testimonies have become folklore. "One wonders," writes the narrator, "if some of Emilie's kindnesses . . . may not have been absorbed into the Oskar legend, the way deeds of minor heroes have been subsumed by the figure of Arthur or Robin Hood."[74]

The theme of knowledge most clearly differentiates the novel from the film. The reader is invited to share with the author the impossibility of arriving at a satisfactory unified explanation of the Holocaust. The survival of some and the death of so many remains an "absent meaning."[75] Keneally's concern with knowledge—with what the Germans, the world, and the victims knew—functions always with an awareness of his own voice as well as of those of the other commentators. The reader is also made aware of other voices, those of the survivors. The narratives are not uniform. The positions articulated and attributed to the various survivors even clash, and the question of what they knew and what they have learned is built into their narratives.

The nature and extent of this knowledge continues to be the source of much debate. Today the issue does not seem to involve a lack of information about the Nazi death camps, to judge by the multitude of media, literature, popular biographies, recollections of survivors, memorials, and academic studies. What is still deficient, judging by the ongoing debates about the meaning and impact of Nazism and the Holocaust, is a critical awareness of these events. Some critics attribute this lack to a mode of representation that has reduced past events to commodified and conventionalized images. By contrast, critical history as popular history does not rest comfortably in its complicity with discourses of nation, gender, sexuality and race. In fact, popular history may actually be unpopular history that challenges received knowledge. In the following section, I offer an instance of an unpopular popular text that addresses the history of Nazism in the present— *Veronika Voss*—a film that "creates a more richly nuanced 'picture' of the past and a wider range of possible contemporary interpretations."

## Re-Mediating History

The legacy of Rainer Werner Fassbinder has been the subject of a number of studies of the director and of his place in the context of what has come to be known as New German Cinema.[76] Anton Kaes aptly describes the concern with history in Fassbinder's work: "Fassbinder's approach is a critical one; he had little interest in 'the way it really was,' but rather wondered how the thoughts, feelings and actions of his contemporaries could be explained historically. Like Walter Benjamin, he wanted to deal with the constellation of past and present, with the moment of recognition in which the past and present mutually illuminate one another."[77]

Fassbinder's films were concerned with history, though many of his late 1960s and his 1970s films were not historical films in the conventional sense of being set in a remote time and self-consciously attempting to resurrect that past. In such films as *Katzelmacher* (1969), *The Merchant of Four Seasons* (1971), *The Bitter Tears of Petra von Kant* (1972), and *Ali, Fear Eats the Soul* (1973), the past is only alluded to through repetition in the present. The trilogy films—*The Marriage of Maria Braun* (1979), *Lola* (1981), and *Veronika Voss* (1982)—are more directly concerned with the Nazi period but, as always in Fassbinder's films, from the vantage point of the persistence of social structures and behavior in contemporary life.

*Veronika Voss* has received scant attention to its complex and critical treatment of history. In this film Fassbinder has orchestrated his concerns with history, melodrama, and common sense. According to Anton Kaes, following Jürgen Habermas's assessment of the 1970s, *Veronika Voss* exemplifies the "exhaustion of utopian energies." Kaes finds the film "cynical and resigned."[78] This assessment relies heavily on the film's ending, which, according to one reading, exposes the "corruption in private and public affairs,"[79] making the unfortunate assumption that an unhappy ending is a sure index to a film's point of view. By contrast, I find the film instructive for its orchestration of questions relating to historicizing, questions of representation, and specifically questions relating not only to the history of cinema but to media in general. The film's interrogative mode not only complicates the text but holds open the possibility that the failure it narrates is also instructive and challenging.

*Veronika Voss* is set in the context of 1950s German society, and yet its allegorical mode succeeds in conjoining the Nazi past with the 1950s and the 1950s with the 1980s and can be read as "an indictment of contemporary German society."[80] This reading reduces the film's complexity and does an injustice to the film's allegorical attempts to view the residual nature of the past in the present. The film's allusions to the Nazi past are compressed but inescapable: Veronika's own history as a star of the Nazi era (modeled on the career of Sybille Schmitz, a popular actress of the Nazi era), the sounds of the radio in the flashbacks involving Veronika (Rosel Zech) and her husband (Armin Müller-Stahl), the numbers from the Treblinka death camp tattooed on the arm of the elderly man, another victim of Dr. Katz (Annemarie Düringer), and the figure of Dr. Katz herself as a doctor of death, exploiting her patients for their wealth and eliminating them when they are no longer useful. The homology between that earlier history and contemporary German culture orchestrates issues involving economics, political power, discourses of health, and above all the role of media.

The complexity of the film entails the interweaving of star discourses, 1940s German cinema, 1950s Hollywood and German commercial cinema, and by example from this film, New German Cinema. The past represented in the film has to be read through the lens of the present. The film resists a linear presentation, constantly shifting between past and present, even blurring the line between the two. In its allusions to Nazism, the film does not gratify the audience with familiar images. Instead the audience is invited to contemplate the past through images that appear to be trivial and irrelevant to conventional political and historical analysis. The protagonist is not a public political figure but a star whose career has waned; her present fate is tied to her attempts to recapture her past successes. Robert Krohn (Hilmar Thate), the character who uncovers a sinister plot against Veronika, is a sports writer. The importance of these characters in the narrative is thus tied to popular music, as in the theme song of the film, "Memories Are Made of This."

The style of *Veronika Voss* combines film noir, German expressionism, classical Hollywood melodrama, and the crime detection genre. The elements rely on a play of *"Licht und Schatten"* (light and shadow), the essence of cinema, as Veronika dramatically explains to Robert. As an excursus on style, the acting in the film pits Hollywood stylization, as represented by Veronika, against the more casual styles of Robert and Henriette (Cornelia Froböss), his woman friend and accomplice and ultimately one of the film's several victims. Everywhere illusion overwhelms social realism. From the first moment of the film, the spectator is challenged by Veronika's watching herself in a film. The spectator does not know when the surrogate film ends and the *real* film begins. The boundaries between representation and "reality" are continuously blurred.

While the narrative assumes importance as a simulacrum of a crime detection film, the visual images, the intense close-ups of Veronika, and the focus on such objects as mirrors and mirroring fixtures call attention to spectacle, to lighting, reflections, and splintering, and to the connection of spectacle to the phenomenon of mass culture, and the film appears more interested in popular cinema as the locus of history and memory than in formal documentary or factual uses of the past. Veronika's role is modeled on star folklore in the way she dresses, in her calculated gestures, and in her utterance of clichés that appear to derive from melodrama. With her gestures, clothing, and low voice, Rosel Zech emerges as a camp version of Leni Riefenstahl or Marlene Dietrich, if not of a man in drag. Like certain stars, she seems to be neither man nor woman. Veronika's role, an aging actress who is always on stage, is reminiscent too of Gloria Swanson's in *Sunset Boulevard*

(1950), directed by the expatriate German director Billy Wilder—a fact that Fassbinder the cinéphile would have known.

Other boundaries are blurred by Veronika's character. A melodramatic figure, she plays victim to Dr. Katz's aggression but betrayer and aggressor to Robert and Henriette. Similarly she confounds the boundaries between past and present. She is an incarnation of memories of past stardom. Surviving uneasily into the present, she lives off the drugs provided her by Dr. Katz, who runs a clinic for nervous diseases. Along with other "survivors" of the Hitler era, Veronika pays the doctor from property derived from that earlier time, property expropriated from its earlier owners.

Whereas Veronika is a spirit of the Nazi past that survives in the present, Dr. Katz and her cohorts are the spirit of the present that survives through the reiteration of the past. Fassbinder constructs his allegory through such convergences. Though the former Nazis and their victims are drugged and finally destroyed, their legacy has passed into the hands of the new leaders, who are similar yet also different from their predecessors. In both narrative and spectacle, the film plays with the problem of repetition and difference. For this reason, placing heavy emphasis on the ending does an injustice to the play of difference that characterizes the focus of the entire film. The ending is itself a play of difference on conventional generic expectations.

Using the conventions of the crime-thriller genre and the excessiveness of melodramatic technique, *Veronika Voss*, like *Chinese Roulette* (1976), is involved in exposing the survival of Nazism in the present. As in film noir, the play with light and shadow underscores a number of motifs: the paranoid nature of the environment, the instability of the characters, their entrapment in conflicts over power and control, and their inability (and the audience's) to clearly discern moral valences. The cinematic effects also serve to advance the notion that memories are made of this: that film is responsible for constructing the world but that cinema is also a means of "detecting" the nature of this construction. Any history of the present becomes a history of representation, in its mystifying character as well as in its capacity to identify mystifications. Using popular genres and film styles, the film undertakes a critique of historical representation in cinema and of cinematic representation in history.

The film's historical investigation resides in the use of the clinic as the synecdoche for the nature and effects of the German economic

"Memories Are Made of This." Veronika (Rosel Zech), in *Veronika Voss*. Courtesy of New York Museum of Modern Art, Film Stills Archive, and by permission of Futura Films, Munich.

miracle of the 1950s. The doctor and her accomplices are the conduit that conjoins past and present history. The clinic evokes literal memories of Nazi practices while serving also as metaphor for present conditions. In the film's linking of past and present, the clinic conjures up memories of the elimination of "worthless" members of society. Dr. Katz profits from the misfortunes of her patients, who no longer have a function in the new technological order. The clinic's ties to the United States are personified in the silent African-American soldier who supplies the doctor with her drugs. The Nazi regime profited economically from the extermination of Jews, Gypsies, homosexuals, and the physically and mentally handicapped; the clinic profits from the exploitation and eradication of former Nazis, concentration camp inmates, and other disaffected and "troublesome" individuals.

The clinic brings to mind the technological elimination under National Socialism of psychiatric patients, who were "gassed or killed by injection with lethal drugs."[81] In speaking of that earlier period in German history, Ruth Hubbard emphasizes the idea that the task of ridding society of undesirables was "shouldered by the scientists and physicians who had earlier devised the sterilization and euthanasia programs."[82] Initially the Nuremberg Laws involved euthanasia for the "destruction of lives not worth living."[83] Later the Final Solution expanded this destruction to a mass scale. There is no need in *Veronika Voss* to produce flashbacks that make explicit the connection between Nazi "health" practices and the work of this clinic. The film offers the immediate drama of exploitation and state complicity as a phenomenon to be comprehended, not merely as a phenomenon from the past to be recorded and lamented.

In addressing similarities and differences between the Nazi past and the years of the economic miracle of the 1950s, *Veronika Voss* highlights the economic and institutional dimensions of the state apparatuses in collusion with civil institutions. The medical profession, health officials, and police, reinforced by the U.S. presence, are engaged in coercive practices. The clinic, with its excessive and blinding whiteness, also evokes the memory of the Nazi obsession with disease, corruption, and impurity. The only darkness is the presence of the African American, who is an uncomfortable and complicated reminder of racialism and subaltern complicity. Frau Dr. Katz presents a benign and professional appearance to investigators and patients. Gradually the dark side of the clinic is exposed in the doctor's cold treatment of the elderly couple, in the brutal killing of Henriette, and in the doctor's callous destruction of Veronika.

That Fassbinder makes the doctor's victims complicit raises disturbing questions about their relationship to their torturers. Were they metaphorically drugged? What was the nature of their dependence on the social institutions and on cinema? Though in the vein of melodrama, the patients are presented as complicit victims (as when Veronika refuses to expose the doctor to the police), and the film offers "clues" to address the questions. In psychological terms, the issue is raised of psychic dependence, which acts like a narcotic. Dr. Katz is able to exploit her patients because they share similar values concerning the importance of social usefulness and competence. Media representation plays the pivotal role in the film's exploration of dependence and addiction, closely tied to the melodramatic scenarios that by their repetitive nature dull the capacity to remember and to think.

An auteuristic reading can include Fassbinder in this scenario of victimization, given his own involvement with drugs, an element inextricable from the widely circulated Fassbinder folklore. In the film's recreation of the 1950s atmosphere, drugs come to signify how memories of the past are dulled. However, the desire to forget is replaced by a merely momentary obliteration through drugs. The film complicates the question of knowledge, not taking refuge in the reductive notion that "We didn't know" but instead suggesting that the memory of this knowledge is intolerable. In the case of Veronika, memory is overwhelming. She both invites memory and seeks to obliterate it. Hence the doctor is able to profit from the pain of others, from their inability to bear the intolerable burden of the past. Robert and Henriette are exceptional in their active effort to uncover the conspiracy of silence. Their failure to reveal the crimes does justice to the complexity of the historical problems that the film exposes. The ambiguity of the song "Memories Are Made of This" as well as the use of other 1950s lyrics, reinforces the sense that the past is inescapable. As the narrative reveals, death seems to be preferable to knowledge. This unsentimental position is not comforting, but it can hardly be described as cynical. It implicates the spectator in the conspiracy of silence and forgetting; it also reveals the futility not only of forgetting but of preserving the past through repetition.

In the last segment of the film, involving Veronika's "suicide," a number of motifs are interwoven, couched in a montage of images and episodes. Past and present collide as the sequences alternate between images of Veronika locked in the clinic and flashbacks from her farewell party. Veronika is shown disheveled, surrounded by drugs, receiving Dr. Katz's farewell Judas kiss; she is also shown in her former star persona, entertaining others, dressed in glittering lamé and singing "Memories Are Made of This." The song and the singer now capture the irony of singing about remembering while striving to forget. The final sequence shows Veronika alone in a small antiseptic room as sounds of the Easter mass and of popular American music from the armed forces network accompany her squalid, operatic demise.

*Veronika Voss* is a provocative essay on memory, challenging the spectator to rethink the past through its residual presence in cinema. In Anton Kaes's terms, Fassbinder's form of cinematic historicizing entails "weaving together many individual narrative threads into a text (in the sense of the Latin *textum*, something woven). The way in which the narrative threads are intertwined attaches a certain meaning to the historical event, which by itself has a multiplicity of potential meanings."[84] It is not only the narrative threads that are woven into the text but images and sounds, the reminders of the role of spectacle as it contributes to the work of assigning meaning. The emphasis on the polyphonic nature of the text becomes an oblique critique of monologic discourses, the language of official history.

Fassbinder's uses of melodrama validate the important role that affective investment plays in relation to memory, but as a phenomenon to be wary of and to be examined critically. Instead of reaffirming an unmediated sense of loss, guilt, and anticipated vindication, *Veronika Voss* seeks through allegory and its heteroglossia to intervene in the officially sanctioned and often reproduced representations of the past. The encyclopedic and multilayered text generates antagonisms, striking particularly at the heart of the familiar mourning paradigm that reiterates a commonsensical scenario involving questions of identity: its loss and restitution and the consolations of anticipated justice. Such a view entails a binary understanding of the relationship between victim and oppressor. Indeed, Fassbinder has been criticized for his disregard of his victims' sufferings, particularly the sufferings of his Jewish characters but also those of women and homosexuals in his films.[85] This criticism is symptomatic of the difficulty of and resistance to probing the nature of victimization, attacking its commonsensical representation in melodramatic scenarios, and challenging monumental, funerary, or nostalgic uses of the past that are characteristic of attempts to remember Nazism and its effects. Deleuze's comments on Syberberg's *Hitler: A Film from Germany* are equally applicable to *Veronika Voss* and are an appropriate point at which to close this discussion of cinematic uses of the past.

> The revolutionary courtship of the movement-image and an art of the masses become subject was broken off, giving way to the masses subjected as psychological automaton, and to their leader as great spiritual automaton. This is what compels Syberberg to say that the end-product of the movement-image was Leni Riefenstahl, and if Hitler is to be put on trial by cinema, it must be inside cinema, against Hitler the filmmaker, in order to "defeat him cinematographically, turning his weapons against him." . . . But at what price? A true psychomechanics will not be found unless it is based on *new associations,* by reconstituting the great mental automata whose place was taken by Hitler, by reviving the psychological automata that he enslaved.[86]

Like Fassbinder's films, Deleuze's comments undermine conventional expectations and forms of historicizing that are closely tied to what Nietzsche described as the excesses of monumental, antiquarian, and critical history with their melodramatic tendencies. In this last decade of the twentieth century, history and memory have become hotly contested commodities. Deleuze's analysis of cinema reinforces the facts that history has been and continues to be created in and circulated through media and that the imperative for change, for "new associations," entails a different mode of expression in and critical analysis of media. Earlier forms of popular history in their folkloric form are not only moribund but are obstacles to any understanding of contemporary forms of cultural production and their political and social effects. "What is in play is no longer the real and the imaginary," Deleuze writes, "but the true and the false. And just as the real and imaginary become indiscernible in certain very specific conditions of the image, the true and the false now become undecidable or inextricable: the possible proceeds from the impossible, and the past is not necessarily true."[87]

# Notes

## Introduction

1. Fredric Jameson, "Postmodernism, or the Cultural Logic of Late Capitalism," *New Left Review* 146 (1984): 53–92.

2. Stuart Hall, *The Hard Road to Renewal* (London: Verso, 1988).

3. *Ousmane Sembène: Dialogues with Critics and Writers*, ed. Samba Gadjigo, Ralph H. Faulkingham, Thomas Cassirer, and Reinhard Sander (Amherst: University of Massachusetts Press, 1993).

4. Antonio Gramsci, *Selections from the Prison Notebooks*, ed. Quintin Hoare and Geoffrey Nowell-Smith (New York: International Publishers, 1978), pp. 106–114.

5. Antonio Gramsci, *Selections from the Cultural Writings*, ed. David Forgacs (Cambridge, Mass.: Harvard University Press, 1985), p. 194.

6. Ibid., p. 189.

7. Gramsci, *Selections from the Prison Notebooks*, p. 423.

8. Gramsci, *Selections from the Cultural Writings*, p. 189.

9. Gramsci, *Selections from the Prison Notebooks*, p. 423.

10. Ibid., pp. 279–318.

11. Ibid., pp. 323–329.

12. Roland Barthes, *Mythologies* (New York: Hill and Wang, 1972), p. 11.

13. Gramsci, *Selections from the Prison Notebooks*, p. 9.

14. Stuart Hall et al. *Culture, Media, Language: Working Papers in Cultural Studies, 1972–79* (London: Hutchinson in association with The Birmingham Centre for Contemporary Cultural Studies, University of Birmingham, 1980).

15. Hall, *The Hard Road to Renewal*, p. 162.

16. Ibid., pp. 165–166.

17. Ibid., p. 167.

18. Gilles Deleuze, *Cinema 1: The Movement-Image* (Minneapolis: University of Minnesota Press, 1986), p. 190.

19. Fredric Jameson, *The Political Unconscious: Narrative as a Socially Symbolic Act* (Ithaca, N.Y.: Cornell University Press, 1981), p. 35.

20. Ibid., p. 102.

21. Ibid., pp. 19–20.

22. Ibid., pp. 29–30.

23. Fredric Jameson, *The Geopolitical Aesthetic: Cinema and Space in the World System* (London: BFI, 1992), p. 212.

24. Colin MacCabe, preface to Jameson, *The Geopolitical Aesthetic*, p. xv.

25. Edward W. Said, *Culture and Imperialism* (New York: Knopf, 1993), p. xxiii.

26. Ibid., p. xxv.

27. Frantz Fanon, *The Wretched of the Earth* (New York: Grove Press, 1979).

28. See Ranajit Guha and Gayatri Chakravorty Spivak, eds., *Selected Subaltern Studies* (New York: Routledge, 1988); see also Gayatri Chakravorty Spivak *In Other Worlds: Essays in Cultural Politics* (New York: Routledge, 1988) and *Outside in the Teaching Machine* (New York: Routledge, 1993).

29. Guha and Spivak, *Selected Subaltern Studies*, p. 9.

30. Ibid., p. 30.

31. See also Homi K. Bhabha, *Nation and Narration* (London: Routledge, 1990). See especially pp. 1–8, 291–323.

32. André Bazin, *What Is Cinema?*, vol. 2 (Berkeley and Los Angeles: University of California Press, 1972), p. 75.

33. As cited in Millicent Marcus, *Italian Cinema in the Light of Neorealism* (Princeton, N.J.: Princeton University Press, 1986), p. 18.

34. Accounting for dramatic changes in filmmaking and patterns of filmgoing in the 1960s Pierre Sorlin writes that "[t]he watershed of the 1960s was not merely a change of generation or a new trend in cinematic aesthetic. It happened at a time when the western film-market was turned upside down since Hollywood and the European cinemas were facing the same catastrophic decline in cinema-attendance." Curiously, Sorlin does not address the spectacle film or the various manifestations of the western that appeared. Such films are important for understanding the overdeterminations that account for the return of the historical film in the 1960s. Pierre Sorlin, *European Cinemas, European Societies, 1939–1990* (London: Routledge, 1991), p. 149.

35. Andrew Higson, "Re-Presenting the National Past: Nostalgia and Pastiche in the Heritage Film," in *Fires Were Started: British Cinema and Thatcherism*, ed. Lester Friedman (Minneapolis: University of Minnesota Press, 1993), pp. 109–130.

36. Marcia Landy and Stanley Shostak, "Postmodernism as Folklore in Contemporary Science Fiction," *Rethinking Marxism* (Summer 1993): 25–46; see also Marcia Landy, *Film, Politics, and Gramsci* (Minneapolis: University of Minnesota Press, 1994), pp. 185–211.

37. Geoffrey Nowell-Smith, "On History and the Cinema," *Screen* 31, no. 2 (Summer 1990): 160.

38. Pierre Sorlin, *The Film in History: Restaging the Past* (Totowa, N.J.: Barnes and Noble, 1980) and *European Cinemas, European Societies;* Marc Ferro, *Cinema and History*, trans. Naomi Greene (Detroit, Mich.: Wayne State University Press, 1988); Anthony Aldgate, *Cinema and History: British Newsreels and the Spanish Civil War* (London: Scolar Press, 1979); Jeffrey Richards, *The Age of the Dream Palace: Cinema and Society in Britain, 1930–1939* (London: Routledge, 1989); Michael Paul Rogin, *Ronald Reagan: The Movie and Other Episodes in Political Demonology* (Berkeley and Los Angeles: University of California Press, 1987); Robert Burgoyne, *Bertolucci's*

*1900: A Narrative and Historical Analysis* (Detroit, Mich.: Wayne State University Press, 1991); George Custen, *Bio/Pics: How Hollywood Constructed Public History* (New Brunswick, N.J.: Rutgers University Press, 1992); Robert Rosenstone, ed., *Revisioning History: Film and the Construction of a New Past* (Princeton, N.J.: Princeton University Press, 1995); Peter Baxter, *Just Watch! Sternberg, Paramount, and America* (London: BFI, 1993).

39. Bill Nichols, *Ideology and the Image: Social Representation in Film and in Other Media* (Bloomington: Indiana University Press, 1981), p. 5.

40. Richard Abel, *French Cinema: The First Wave, 1915–1929* (Princeton, N.J.: Princeton University Press, 1984), p. 445.

41. Sue Harper, "Historical Pleasures, Gainsborough Costume Melodramas," in *Home Is Where the Heart Is: Studies in Melodrama and the Woman's Film*, ed. Christine Gledhill (London: BFI, 1987), p. 181. See also Sue Harper's *Picturing the Past: The Rise and Fall of the British Costume Film* (London: BFI, 1994).

42. Harper, "Historical Pleasures, Gainsborough Costume Melodramas," p. 179.

43. Ibid., p. 178.

44. Patrice Petro, *Joyless Streets: Women and Melodramatic Representation in Weimar Germany* (Princeton, N.J.: Princeton University Press, 1989), p. xxiv. For a wide-ranging analysis of spectatorship and its relation to questions of historical representation, see Judith Mayne, *Cinema and Spectatorship* (London: Routledge, 1993).

45. Geoff Hurd, ed., *National Fictions: World War II in British Films and Television* (London: BFI, 1984), p. 7.

46. Anton Kaes, *From Hitler to Heimat: The Return of History as Film* (Cambridge, Mass.: Harvard University Press, 1989); Eric L. Santner, *Stranded Objects: Mourning, Memory, and Film in Postwar Germany* (Ithaca, N.Y.: Cornell University Press, 1990).

47. Jim Pines and Paul Willemen, eds., *Questions of Third Cinema* (London: BFI, 1989).

48. Friedrich Nietzsche, "On the Uses and Disadvantages of History for Life," in *Untimely Meditations*, trans. R. J. Hollingdale (Cambridge, Eng.: Cambridge University Press, 1991), p. 60.

49. Ibid., p. 63.

50. Ibid., p. 72.

51. Ibid., p. 71.

52. Ibid., p. 70.

53. Ibid., p. 75.

54. Ibid.

55. Ibid., p. 76.

56. Ibid.

57. Landy, *Film, Politics, and Gramsci.*

58. Maureen Turim, *Flashbacks in Film: Memory and History* (New York: Routledge, 1989), p. 2.

59. Ibid.

60. Ibid.

61. Christine Gledhill, "Introduction," *Stardom: Industry of Desire*, ed. Christine Gledhill (London: Routledge, 1991), p. xvi.

62. Richard Dyer, *Stars* (London: BFI, 1986).

63. Michaela Krutzen, *The Most Beautiful Woman on the Screen: The Fabrication of the Star Greta Garbo* (Frankfurt am Main: Peter Lang, 1992).

64. Christopher Frayling, *Spaghetti Westerns: Cowboys and Europeans from Karl May to Sergio Leone* (London: Routledge and Kegan Paul, 1981).

## Chapter 1: Folklore, Memory, and Postcoloniality in Ousmane Sembène's Films

1. Frantz Fanon, *The Wretched of the Earth* (New York: Grove Press, 1979), p. 225.

2. Ranajit Guha, "On Some Aspects of the Historiography of Colonial India," in *Selected Subaltern Studies,* ed. Ranajit Guha and Gayatri Chakravorty Spivak (New York: Oxford University Press, 1988), p. 40.

3. Amilcar Cabral, *Return to the Source,* ed. Africa Information Service (New York: Monthly Review Press, 1973), p. 41.

4. Hussein Abdilahi' Bulhan, "Black Psyches in Captivity and Crisis," *Race and Class: A Journal of Black and Third World Liberation,* 20, no. 3 (Winter 1979): 245.

5. Françoise Pfaff, lecture on *Guelwaar* presented at Carnegie Museum, Pittsburgh, Pennsylvania, March 3, 1994.

6. "Introduction," in *Ousmane Sembène: Dialogues with Critics and Writers,* ed. Samba Gadjigo, Ralph H. Faulkingham, Thomas Cassirer, and Reinhard Sander (Amherst: University of Massachusetts Press, 1993), p. 2.

7. See Lizabeth Malkmus and Roy Armes, *Arab and African Filmmaking* (London: Zed Books, 1991), pp. 53–62; Nourredine Ghali, "An Interview with Ousmane Sembène," in *Film and Film Production in the Third World,* ed. John J. Downing (Brooklyn, N.Y.: Automedia, 1987), p. 45; Claire Andrade-Watkins, "Film Production in Francophone Africa 1961 to 1967: Ousmane Sembène—An Exception," in *Ousmane Sembène,* ed. Gadjigo et al., pp. 31–36; Manthia Diawara, *African Cinema: Politics and Culture* (Bloomington: Indiana University Press, 1992).

8. Françoise Pfaff, "The Uniqueness of Ousmane Sembène's Cinema," in *Ousmane Sembène,* ed. Gadjigo et al., p. 14.

9. Ghali, "An Interview with Ousmane Sembène," p. 45.

10. Frederick Ivor Case, "Aesthetics, Ideology, and Social Commitment in the Prose Fiction of Ousmane Sembène," in *Ousmane Sembène,* ed. Gadjigo et al., p. 3.

11. Teshome Gabriel, "Toward a Critical Theory of Third World Films" and "Third Cinema as Guardian of Popular Memory," *in Questions of Third Cinema,* ed. Jim Pines and Paul Willemen (London, BFI, 1989), pp. 30–65.

12. Françoise Pfaff, *The Cinema of Ousmane Sembène: A Pioneer of African Film.* (Westport, Conn.: Greenwood Press, 1984), p. 36.

13. Mbye Cham, "Official History, Popular Memory: Reconfiguration of the African Past in the Film of Ousmane Sembène," in *Ousmane Sembène,* ed. Gadjigo et al., p. 24.

14. Ibid., p. 26.

15. Ousmane Sembène, "Remarks after the Showing of His Film 'Camp de Thiaroye,'" *Ousmane Sembène,* ed. Gadjigo et al., p. 85.

16. Homi K. Bhabha, "The Commitment to Theory," in *Questions of Third Cinema,* ed. Pines and Willemen, p. 128.

17. Gilles Deleuze, *Cinema 2: The Time-Image* (Minneapolis: University of Minnesota Press, 1989), p. 222.

18. Ibid., p. 222.

19. Spivak, "Introduction," *Selected Subaltern Studies,* ed. Guha and Spivak, p. 18.

20. Gayatri Chakravorty Spivak, "Responsibility," *boundary 2: an international journal of literature and culture* 27, no. 3 (Fall 1994): 20.

21. Ibid., p. 45.

22. Deleuze, *Cinema 2,* pp. 207–210.

23. Antonio Gramsci, *Selections from the Prison Notebooks,* ed. Quintin Hoare and Geoffrey Nowell-Smith (New York: International Publishers, 1978), pp. 419–423.

24. Etienne Balibar, *The Philosophy of Marx,* trans. Chris Turner (London: Verso, 1995), p. 59. For a brief discussion of the relation between the film's use of allegory and the concept of fetishism, see Ella Shohat and Robert Stam, *Unthinking Eurocentrism: Multiculturalism and the Media* (London: Routledge, 1994), pp. 275–276.

25. Etienne Balibar and Immanuel Wallerstein, *Race, Nation, Class: Ambiguous Identities* (London: Verso, 1991), p. 89.

26. Ibid., p. 86.

27. Guha, "On Some Aspects of the Historiography of Colonial India," p. 43.

28. Gayatri Chakravorty Spivak, "Subaltern Studies: Deconstructing Historiography," in *Selected Subaltern Studies,* ed. Guha and Spivak, p. 9.

29. Gramsci, *Selections from the Prison Notebooks,* pp. 56–106.

30. Walter Benjamin, *Illuminations* (New York: Schocken Books, 1976), p. 256.

31. Ibid.

32. Homi K. Bhabha, "DissemiNation: Time, Narrative, and the Margins of the Modern Nation," in *Nation and Narration,* ed. Homi K. Bhabha (London: Routledge, 1990); Balibar and Wallerstein, *Race, Nation, Class*; Gayatri Chakravorty Spivak, *In Other Worlds: Essays in Cultural Politics* (New York: Routledge, 1988); Gayatri Chakravorty Spivak, *The Post-Colonial Critic: Interviews, Strategies, Dialogues* (New York: Routledge, 1990); Guha and Spivak, *Selected Subaltern Studies.*

33. Pfaff, *The Cinema of Ousmane Sembène.*

34. Immanuel Wallerstein, *Historical Capitalism* (London: Verso, 1984), p. 85.

35. Peter Brooks, *The Melodramatic Imagination: Balzac, Henry James, Melodrama, and the Mode of Excess* (New York: Columbia University Press, 1985).

36. Pfaff, *The Cinema of Ousmane Sembène*, p. 146.

37. Homi K. Bhabha, "The Commitment to Theory," in *Questions of Third Cinema*, ed. Pines and Willeman, p. 120.

38. Spivak, *The Post-Colonial Critic*, p. 123.

39. Ibid.

40. Teshome Gabriel, "Toward a Critical Theory of Third World Films" and "Third Cinema as Guardian of Popular Memory," in *Questions of Third Cinema*, ed. Pines and Willeman, pp. 30–65.

41. Diawara, *African Cinema*, pp. 156–157.

42. Pierre Sorlin, *European Cinemas, European Societies, 1939–1990* (London: Routledge, 1991), p. 175; Diawara, *African Cinema*, pp. 156–157.

43. Sembène, "Remarks after the Showing of His Film 'Camp de Thiaroye,'" p. 85.

44. Maria Mies, Veronika Bennholdt-Thomsen, and Claudia von Werlhof, *Women: The Last Colony* (London: Zed Books, 1988), p. 5.

45. Nourredine Ghali, "An Interview with Ousmane Sembène," in *Film and Politics in the Third World*, ed. John D. H. Downing (Brooklyn, N.Y.: Automedia, 1986), p. 42.

46. According to Sembène: "For me, the problem over whether it's De-Gaulle or Pétain, is a problem of which horse's ass you are talking about." Ghali, "An Interview with Ousmane Sembène," p. 49.

47. Spivak, *Post-Colonial Critic*, p. 65.

48. Balibar and Wallerstein, *Race, Nation, Class*, p. 46.

49. Françoise Pfaff, "Guelwaar," *Cineaste* 20, no. 2 (Spring 1994): 49.

50. Ibid., p. 48.

51. Ibid.

52. W. E. B. Du Bois, *The World and Africa: An Inquiry into the Part Which Africa Has Played in World History* (New York: International Publishers, 1978), p. 308.

53. Julius K. Nyerere, *Ujamaa: Essays on Socialism* (London: Oxford University Press, 1966), pp. 23–24.

54. Paul A. Baran and Paul M. Sweezy, *Monopoly Capital: An Essay on the American Economic and Social Order* (Harmondsworth, Middlesex, Eng.: Penguin Books, 1977), p. 201.

## Chapter 2: "Which Way Is West?"

A different version of this chapter appeared in *boundary 2*, vol. 32, no.1 (1996): 35–61.

1. Friedrich Nietzsche, "On the Uses and Disadvantages of History for

Life," in *Untimely Meditations,* trans. R. J. Hollingdale (Cambridge, Eng.: Cambridge Unviersity Press, 1991), pp. 91, 94.

2. In seeking to develop the notion of excess in relation to historicizing, Leo Charney writes: "Every film's history configures not just its history of production but also the broader social contexts in which these forces move. These historical inscriptions indicate an excessive 'elsewhere' not contained by the film's narrative system, but they do not enter the film and just sit there, inert and segregated. Instead they become part of the textual system, a weaving together that invokes the very essence of context in its derivation from the Latin *contextere,* to weave together." "Historical Excess: Johnny Guitar's Containment," *Cinema Journal* 29, no. 4 (Summer 1990): 24.

3. Kristin Thompson, *Eisenstein's Ivan the Terrible* (Princeton, N.J.: Princeton University Press, 1981), p. 302.

4. Ibid., p. 293.

5. Antonio Gramsci, *Selections from the Prison Notebooks,* ed. Quintin Hoare and Geoffrey Nowell-Smith (New York: International Publishers, 1978), p. 418.

6. Ibid., p. 106.

7. Ibid., p. 286.

8. Ibid., p. 279.

9. Ibid., p. 295.

10. Ibid., p. 293.

11. Ibid., p. 307.

12. Ibid.

13. Ibid.

14. Ibid., p. 318.

15. Millicent Marcus, *Italian Cinema in the Light of Neorealism* (Princeton, N.J.: Princeton University Press, 1986) and *Filmmaking by the Book: Italian Cinema and Literary Adaptation* (Baltimore, Md.: Johns Hopkins University Press, 1993); Geoffrey Nowell-Smith, *Luchino Visconti* (London: Secker and Warburg in association with the British Film Institute, 1973).

16. André Bazin, *What Is Cinema?* vol.2 (Berkeley and Los Angeles: University of California Press, 1972), pp. 47–60.

17. Marcus, *Italian Cinema in the Light of Neorealism,* p. 19.

18. For a discussion of genre films under fascism, see James Hay, *Popular Film Culture in Fascist Italy: The Passing of the Rex* (Bloomington: Indiana University Press, 1987); see also Marcia Landy, *Fascism in Film: The Italian Commercial Cinema, 1930–1943* (Princeton, N.J.: Princeton University Press, 1991); Peter Bondanella, *Italian Cinema: From Neorealism to the Present* (Bloomington: Indiana University Press, 1993).

19. Paul Ginsborg, *A History of Contemporary Italy: Society and Politics, 1943–1988* (London: Penguin Books, 1990), p. 239.

20. Bondanella, *Italian Cinema,* p. 142.

21. Ernesto G. Laura, *Comedy Italian Style* (Rome: A. N. I. C. A., National Association of Motion Pictures and Affiliated Industries, n.d.), p. 104.

22. Pierre Sorlin, *European Cinemas, European Societies, 1939–1990* (London: Routledge, 1991), p. 168.

23. Ibid., p. 169.

24. Bondanella, *Italian Cinema*, p. 253.

25. Christopher Frayling, *Spaghetti Westerns: Cowboys and Europeans from Karl May to Sergio Leone* (London: Routledge and Kegan Paul, 1981). See also, for the treatment of Mexico in the spaghetti westerns in contrast to its treatment in Hollywood films, Edward Buscombe, "The Magnificent Seven," in *Mediating Two Worlds: Cinematic Encounters in the Americas* (London: BFI, 1993), pp. 15–25.

26. Frayling, *Spaghetti Westerns*, p. 157.

27. Friedrich Nietzsche, *The Gay Science*, trans. Walter Kaufmann (New York: Vintage Books, 1974), pp. 258–259.

28. Frayling, *Spaghetti Westerns*, p. 29.

29. Jerre Mangione and Ben Morreale, *La Storia: Five Centuries of the Italian and American Experience* (New York: Harper Perennial, 1992), pp. 31–67.

30. Frayling, *Spaghetti Westerns*, p. 65.

31. Pamela Falkenburg, *Rewriting the Classic Hollywood Cinema: Textual Analysis, Ironic Distance, and the Western in the Critique of Corporate Capitalism* (Ann Arbor, Mich.: University Microfilms International, 1986), p. 412.

32. Quoted in Frayling, *Spaghetti Westerns*, p. 64. For a historically nuanced discussion of spectatorship see Judith Mayne, *Cinema and Spectatorship* (London: Routledge, 1993).

33. Antonio Gramsci, *Selections from the Prison Notebooks*, ed. Quintin Hoare and Geoffrey Nowell-Smith (New York: International Publishers, 1978), p. 345.

34. Cited in Francesco Savio, *Cinecittà anni trenta*, vol. 2 (Rome: Bulzoni, 1979), p. 440.

35. Cited in ibid., p. 521.

36. Brian Taves has made an initial foray into the dynamics of the adventure film in *The Romance of Adventure: The Genre of Historical Adventure Movies* (Jackson: University Press of Mississippi, 1993).

37. See John G. Cawelti, *Adventure, Mystery, and Romance: Formula Studies as Art and Popular Culture* (Chicago: University of Chicago Press, 1976), pp. 192–260; John H. Lenihan, *Showdown: Confronting Modern America in the Western Film* (Urbana: University of Illinois Press, 1980); Jack Nachbar, "Introduction," in *Focus on the Western* (Englewood Cliffs, N.J.: Prentice-Hall, 1974), pp. 1–9; Jennie Calder, *There Must Be a Lone Ranger* (London: Hamish Hamilton, 1974); Rita Parks, *The Western Hero in Film and Television: Mass Media Mythology* (Ann Arbor, Mich.: UMI Press, 1982); George N. Fenin and William K. Everson, *The Western: From Silents to Cinema* (New York: Bonanza Books, 1962); Jim Hitt, *The American Western from Fiction (1823–1976) into Film (1909–1986)* (Jefferson, N.C.: McFarland and Company, 1990).

38. Jim Kitses, *Horizons West: Anthony Mann, Budd Boetticher, Sam Peckinpah. Studies of Authorship within the Western* (Bloomington: Indiana University Press, 1969); Will Wright, *Six Guns and Society: A Structural Study of the Western* (Berkeley and Los Angeles: University of California Press, 1975); Thomas Schatz, *Hollywood Genres, Formulas, Filmmaking, and the Studio System* (New York: Random House, 1981); Lane Roth, *Film, Semiotics, Metz, and Leone's Trilogy* (New York: Garland Publishing, 1983); see also Bazin, *What Is Cinema?* vol. 2.

39. Fenin and Everson, *The Western*, pp. 10–12.

40. Kitses, *Horizons West*, p. 8.

41. Paul Smith, *Clint Eastwood: A Cultural Production* (Minneapolis: University of Minnesota Press, 1993), pp. 19–26.

42. Schatz, *Hollywood Genres*, pp. 45–80; Cawelti, *Adventure, Mystery, and Romance*, pp. 221, 225.

43. Cawelti, *Adventure, Mystery, and Romance*, p. 251.

44. Ibid.

45. For a discussion of gender in the western, see Virginia Wright Wexman, *Creating the Couple: Love, Marriage, and Hollywood Performance* (Princeton, N.J.: Princeton University Press, 1993).

46. Wright, *Six Guns and Society*, pp. 97-99.

47. David Thomson, *A Biographical Dictionary of Film* (New York: Morrow Press, 1981), p. 344.

48. Mark Kermode, "Endnotes," *Sight and Sound* (October 1994): 63.

49. Antonio Gramsci, *Selections from the Cultural Writings*, ed. David Forgacs (Cambridge, Mass.: Harvard University Press, 1985), p. 380.

50. Robert C. Cumbow, *Once upon a Time in the Films of Sergio Leone* (Metuchen, N.J.: Scarecrow Press, 1987), p. 129.

51. Gramsci, *Selections from the Cultural Writings*, p. 194.

52. Laurence Staig and Tony Williams, *Italian Western: The Opera of Violence* (London: Lorrimer Publishers, 1975), pp. 27–28.

53. For a discussion of the affective nature of "faciality," see Gilles Deleuze, *Cinema 1* (Minneapolis: University of Minnesota Press, 1986), pp. 87–102.

54. Angela Dalle Vacche, *The Body in the Mirror: Shapes of History in Italian Cinema* (Princeton, N.J.: Princeton University Press, 1992), p. 6.

55. For a detailed discussion of the history of the commedia, see Allardyce Nicoll, *Masks, Mimes, and Miracles: Studies in the Popular Theatre* (New York: Cooper Square Publishers, 1963); for a discussion of the adaptations of the commedia to various cultural forms of representation from Shakespeare to modernity, see David George and Christopher J. Gossip, eds., *Studies in the Commedia dell'arte* (Cardiff: University of Wales Press, 1993); and for a specific discussion of the kinds of *lazzi*, see Mel Gordon, *Lazzi: The Comic Routines of the Commedia dell'arte* (New York: Performing Arts Journal, 1983). See also Flaminio Scola, *Scenarios of the Commedia dell'arte: Flaminio Scala's Il teatro delle favole rappresentative*, trans. Henry F. Salerno (New York: New York University Press, 1967); and Martin Green and John Swan, *The Triumph*

*of Pierrot: The Commedia dell'arte and the Modern Imagination* (New York: Macmillan Publishing Company, 1986).

56. Gordon, *Lazzi*, p. 5.
57. Ibid., p. 9.
58. Nicoll, *Masks, Mimes, and Miracles*, p. 276.
59. According to Cumbow, this film was not originally to be directed by Leone. He writes: "Only after a planned collaboration with Peter Bogdanovich proved unworkable did Leone step in to direct his fifth film," *Once upon a Time in the Films of Sergio Leone*, p. 96.
60. Nicoll, *Mimes, Masks, and Miracles*, p. 258.
61. Ibid., p. 283.
62. Frayling, *Spaghetti Westerns*, pp. 60–62.
63. Cumbow, *Once upon a Time in the Films of Sergio Leone*, p. 98.
64. Gramsci, *Selections from the Prison Notebooks*, p. 324.

## Chapter 3: The Operatic as History

1. Barrymore Laurence Scherer, "The Flickering Light," *Opera News*, December 11, 1993, pp. 42–43, 60.
2. Jeremy Tambling, *Opera, Ideology, and Film* (London: St. Martin's, 1987), pp. 41–67.
3. David J. Levin, "Introduction," *Opera through Other Eyes*, ed. David J. Levin (Palo Alto, Calif.: Stanford University Press, 1993), p. 13.
4. Jean Starobinski, "Opera and Enchantresses," in *Opera through Other Eyes*, ed. Levin, p. 20.
5. Theodor Adorno, "Bourgeois Opera," in *Opera through Other Eyes*, ed. Levin, p. 37.
6. Christine Gledhill, ed., *Home Is Where the Heart Is: Studies in Melodrama and the Woman's Film* (London: BFI, 1987), p. 48.
7. See Felice Todde, "Gramsci e la musica," *Nuova rivista musicale italiana i trimestrale ali cultura e informazione musicale* 3 (July/September 1995): 491–500.
8. David Littlejohn, *The Ultimate Art: Essays about and around Opera* (Berkeley and Los Angeles: University of California Press, 1992), p. 77.
9. Peter Conrad, *Romantic Opera and Literary Form* (Berkeley and Los Angeles: University of California Press, 1977), p. 5.
10. Nicholas Vardac, *From Stage to Screen: Theatrical Method from Garrick to Griffith* (New York: Benjamin Blom, 1968), p. 94.
11. Ibid., p. 118.
12. Mary Ann Doane, *The Desire to Desire: The Woman's Film of the 1940s* (Bloomington: University of Indiana Press, 1987), p. 98.
13. Starobinski, "Opera and Enchantresses," p. 21.
14. See Edward Said, *Culture and Imperialism* (New York: Knopf, 1993), pp. 111–132.
15. Susan Sontag, "Fascinating Fascism," in *Movies and Methods*, vol. 1,

ed. Bill Nichols (Berkeley and Los Angeles: University of California Press, 1976), pp. 31–44.

16. Friedrich Nietzsche, "On the Uses and Disadvantages of History for Life," in *Untimely Meditations*, trans. R. J. Hollingdale (Cambridge, Eng.: Cambridge University Press, 1991), p. 70.

17. Ibid., p. 75.

18. Ibid., pp. 67–77.

19. Catherine Clément, *Opera, or the Undoing of Women* (Minneapolis: University of Minnesota Press, 1988).

20. Said, *Culture and Imperialism*, p. 114.

21. Ibid., 131–132.

22. Littlejohn, *The Ultimate Art*, p. 167.

23. Wayne Koestenbaum, *The Queen's Throat: Opera, Homosexuality, and the Mystery of Desire* (New York: Poseidon Press, 1993), p. 142.

24. Ibid., p. 104.

25. Paul Robinson, *Opera and Ideas: From Mozart to Strauss* (New York: Harper and Row, 1985), pp. 174–179.

26. Ibid., p. 177.

27. Tambling, *Opera, Ideology, and Film*, p. 80.

28. Catherine Turocy, "Beau Geste: Dance Was at the Root of Baroque Opera," *Opera News* 59, no. 1 (July 1994): 32–34.

29. Conrad, *Romantic Opera and Literary Form*, pp. 144–179.

30. Peter Brooks, *The Melodramatic Imagination: Balzac, Henry James, Melodrama, and the Mode of Excess* (New York: Columbia University Press, 1985), pp. 56–82.

31. Claudia Gorbman, *Unheard Melodies: Narrative Film Music* (London: BFI, 1987), pp. 1–7. See also Hanns Eisler, *Composing for the Films* (Freeport, N.Y.: Books for Libraries Press, 1971).

32. Pierre Sorlin, *European Cinemas, European Societies 1939–1990*, (London: Routledge, 1991), p. 174.

33. Francesco Savio, *Cinecittà anni trenta*, vol. 1 (Rome: Bulzoni, 1979), p. 125.

34. Ibid., p. 128

35. Antonio Gramsci, *Selections from the Prison Notebooks*, ed. Quintin Hoare and Geoffrey Nowell-Smith (New York: International Publishers, 1978), p. 307.

36. Robinson, *Opera and Ideas*, p. 158.

37. Ibid., p. 157.

38. Ibid., p. 196.

39. Sorlin, *European Cinemas, European Societies*, p. 174.

40. Robinson, *Opera and Ideas*, p. 167.

41. Gaia Servadio, *Luchino Visconti: A Biography* (New York: Franklin Watts, 1983), p. 133.

42. Angela Dalle Vacche, "Nouvelle Histoire, Italian Style," *Annali d'Italianistica* 6 (1988): 101.

43. Ibid., p. 101.

44. Gramsci, *Selections from the Prison Notebooks,* pp. 323–325.

45. Koestenbaum, *The Queen's Throat,* p. 117.

46. David Gilmour, *The Life of Giuseppe di Lampedusa* (New York: Pantheon Books, 1988), pp. 101–103. Gilmour recounts Lampedusa's disdain for the melodramatic qualities of nineteenth-century opera.

47. Millicent Marcus, *Filmmaking by the Book: Italian Cinema and Literary Adaptation* (Baltimore, Md.: Johns Hopkins University Press, 1993), p. 57.

48. "O lovely scenes, again I see you / Where in serenity I spent / The calm and happy days / Of my earliest youth! / Beloved places, I have found you / But those days I'll never find." Libretto for *La sonnambula* from performance at La Scala, 1957. EMI, 1957.

49. Marcus, *Filmmaking by the Book,* p. 59.

50. Claretta Tonetti, *Luchino Visconti* (Boston: Twayne Publishers, 1983), p. 102.

51. "[T]he custom of all the gentleman of the house was to betake themselves straightway after supper to my lady Duchess; where, among other pleasant pastimes and music and dancing that continually were practised, sometimes neat questions were proposed." Baldassare Castiglione, *The Courtier,* in *Prose and Poetry of the Continental Renaissance in Translation,* selected and edited by Harold Hooper Blanchard (New York: David McKay, 1955), p. 327.

52. Sir John Davies, "Orchestra," in *Silver Poets of the Sixteenth Century,* ed. Gerald Bullett (London: Dent, 1966), p. 333.

53. Marcus, *Filmmaking by the Book,* p. 54.

54. Ibid.

55. Servadio, *Luchino Visconti,* p. 179.

56. Roy M. Prendergast, *Film Music: A Neglected Art. A Critical Study of Music in Films* (New York: Norton, 1992), p. 40.

57. Pio Baldelli, *Luchino Visconti* (Milan: Gabriele Mazzotta, 1973), p. 225.

58. Marcus, *Filmmaking by the Book,* p. 52.

59. Gramsci, *Selections from the Prison Notebooks,* p. 260.

60. Ibid., pp. 257–261.

61. Geoffrey Nowell-Smith, *Luchino Visconti* (London: Secker and Warburg, 1973), pp. 101, 112, Marcus, *Filmmaking by the Book,* p. 52; see also David Gilmour, *The Last Leopard: A Life of Giuseppe di Lampedusa* (New York: Pantheon Books, 1991), p. 210.

62. Gramsci, *Selections from the Prison Notebooks,* p. 210.

63. Baldelli, *Luchino Visconti,* p. 235.

64. Marcus, *Filmmaking by the Book,* p. 58.

65. Gilles Deleuze, *Cinema 2: The Time-Image* (Minneapolis: University of Minnesota Press, 1989), p. 83.

66. Ibid.

67. Deleuze, *Cinema 2,* p. 94.

68. Ibid.

69. Ibid., p. 95.

70. Ibid., p. 96.

71. Joseph Kerman, *Opera as Drama* (Berkeley and Los Angeles: University of California Press, 1988), p. 172.

72. Gramsci, *Selections from the Prison Notebooks*, p. 71.

73. Said, *Culture and Imperialism*, p. 131.

74. Marcus, *Filmmaking by the Book*, p. 49.

75. Nowell-Smith, *Luchino Visconti*, pp. 51–54. On the operatic in *The Damned*, see Servadio, *Luchino Visconti*, p. 195.

76. Peter Bondanella, *Italian Cinema: From Neorealism to the Present*, (Bloomington: Indiana University Press, 1993), p. 100.

77. Robert Kolker, *The Altering Eye: Contemporary International Cinema* (Oxford: Oxford University Press, 1983), p. 80.

## Chapter 4: Sheets of the Past

1. Kenneth Anger, *Hollywood Babylon*, vol. 1 (New York: Dell, 1975), pp. 3, 12.

2. Gore Vidal, *Screening History* (Cambridge, Mass.: Harvard University Press, 1992), p. 32.

3. George Custen, *Bio/Pics: How Hollywood Constructed Public History* (New Brunswick, N.J.: Rutgers University Press, 1992), pp. 5–6.

4. Jacques Derrida, *The Ear of the Other: Otobiography, Transference, Translation* (Lincoln: University of Nebraska Press, 1985), p. 5.

5. Christopher Norris, *Derrida* (Cambridge, Mass.: Harvard University Press, 1987), p. 132.

6. Kristin Thompson, *Ivan the Terrible: A Neoformalist Analysis* (Princeton, N.J.: Princeton University Press, 1981), p. 293.

7. Ibid., p. 296.

8. Custen, *Bio/Pics*, pp. 5–6.

9. Steven Bach, *Marlene Dietrich: Life and Legend* (New York: William Morrow, 1992), p. 178.

10. Peter Baxter, *Just Watch! Sternberg, Paramount, and America* (London: BFI, 1993), pp. 177–178.

11. Antonio Gramsci, *Selections from the Cultural Writings*, ed. David Forgacs (Cambridge, Mass.: Harvard University Press, 1985), p. 120.

12. Donald Spoto, *Falling in Love Again: Marlene Dietrich* (Boston: Little, Brown and Company, 1985), p. 73.

13. See Peter Baxter, "Introduction," in *Sternberg*, ed. Peter Baxter (London: BFI, 1980), p. 7; see also Bach, *Marlene Dietrich*, pp. 119–120; Richard Dyer, *Stars* (London: BFI, 1986), pp. 179–180.

14. Andrew Britton, "Stars and Genre," in *Stardom: Industry of Desire*, ed. Christine Gledhill (London: Routledge, 1991), pp. 198–207.

15. For earlier explorations of the star phenomenon, see Alexander Walker, *The Celluloid Sacrifice: Aspects of Sex in the Movies* (New York: Hawthorn Books, 1967) and his *Stardom: The Hollywood Phenomenon* (New York:

Stein and Day, 1970); Mollie Haskell, *From Reverence to Rape: The Treatment of Women in the Movies* (Harmondsworth, Middlesex, Eng.: Penguin, 1974); Rebecca Bell-Metereau, *Hollywood Androgyny* (New York: Columbia University Press, 1985); Gledhill, *Stardom;* and Richard Dyer, *Stars* (London: BFI, 1986).

16. Laura Mulvey, *Visual and Other Pleasures* (Bloomington: Indiana University Press, 1989), pp. 14–26, 29–37; Gaylyn Studlar, *In the Realm of Pleasure: Von Sternberg, Dietrich, and the Masochistic Aesthetic* (Urbana: University of Illinois Press, 1988). See also E. Ann Kaplan, *Woman and Film: Both Sides of the Camera* (New York: Methuen, 1983).

17. Pierre Sorlin, *European Cinemas, European Societies, 1939–1990* (London: Routledge, 1991), p. 12.

18. Richard Johnson, "What Is Cultural Studies Anyway?" pp. 39–75; see also his Frameworks of Culture and Power," *Critical Studies* 3, no. 1 (1991): 17–61.

19. Gramsci, *Selections from the Cultural Writings*, p. 189.

20. Ibid.

21. Christine Gledhill, ed., *Home Is Where the Heart Is: Studies in Melodrama and the Woman's Film* (London: BFI, 1987); also Peter Brooks, *The Melodramatic Imagination: Balzac, Henry James, and the Mode of Excess* (New York: Columbia University Press, 1985).

22. Gledhill, *Stardom*, p. 212.

23. Maria Riva, *Marlene Dietrich* (New York: Knopf, 1993), pp. 134–136.

24. Gertrud Koch, "Dietrich's Destiny," *Sight and Sound* 2, no. 5 (September 1992): 24.

25. Bell-Metereau, *Hollywood Androgyny*, p. 104.

26. Mercedes de Acosta, *Here Lies the Heart* (New York: Reynal and Company, 1960), p. 229.

27. Ibid.

28. Leslie Frewin, *Dietrich* (New York: Stein and Day, 1967), p. 77.

29. Baxter, *Just Watch!*, p. 57.

30. Thomas Schatz, *The Genius of the System: Hollywood Filmmaking in the Studio Era* (New York: Pantheon Books, 1988), pp. 69–81.

31. Kristin Thompson, "Early Alternatives to the Hollywood Mode of Production: Implications for Europe's Avant-Gardes," *Film History* 5, no. 4 (December 1993): 386–405

32. Vidal, *Screening History*, p. 39

33. Custen, *Bio/Pics*, pp. 248–256.

34. Josef von Sternberg, *Fun in a Chinese Laundry: An Autobiography* (New York: Collier Books, 1965), pp. 164–165.

35. Bach, *Marlene Dietrich*, p. 183.

36. Frederic Sands and Sven Broman, *The Divine Garbo* (New York: Grosset and Dunlap, 1979), p. 118.

37. Richard Griffith, ed., *The Talkies: Articles and Illustrations from Photoplay Magazine, 1928–1940* (New York: Dover Publications, 1971).

38. Cited in Homer Dickens, *The Films of Marlene Dietrich* (New York: Citadel Press, 1968), p. 115.

39. Alexander Walker, *Dietrich* (New York: Harper and Row, 1984), p. 116.

40. Thierry de Navacelle, *Sublime Marlene* (London: St. Martin's Press, 1972), p. 65.

41. Andrea Weiss, "A Queer Feeling When I Look at You," in *Stardom: Industry of Desire*, ed. Gledhill, p. 291.

42. Acosta, *Here Lies the Heart*; see also Salka Viertel, *The Kindness of Strangers* (New York: Holt, Rinehart, and Winston, 1969).

43. Sternberg, *Fun in a Chinese Laundry*, p. 265.

44. Bach, *Marlene Dietrich*, p. 179.

45. Walker, *Dietrich*, pp. 80, 84; see also Charles Higham, ed., *Hollywood Cameramen: Sources of Light* (Bloomington: Indiana University Press, 1970), pp. 41–52.

46. For a discussion of photographing Dietrich, see Lee Garmes's discussion in *Hollywood Cameramen*, ed. Higham, p. 42.

47. Louis Audibert, "The Flash of the Look," in *Sternberg*, ed. Peter Baxter (London: BFI, 1980), p. 100.

48. Barry Salt, "Sternberg's Heart Beats in Black and White," in *Sternberg*, ed. Baxter, pp. 110–111.

49. Gilles Deleuze, *Cinema 1: The Movement-Image* (Minneapolis: University of Minnesota Press, 1986), pp. 89–93.

50. Jeffrey Richards, *The Age of the Dream Palace: Cinema and Society in Britain, 1930–1939* (London: Routledge, 1989), p. 262. See also Marcia Landy, *British Genres: Cinema and Society, 1930–1960* (Princeton, N.J.: Princeton University Press, 1991), pp. 63–64.

51. Deleuze, *Cinema 1*, p. 106.

52. Ibid., p. 99.

53. Ibid., p. 97.

54. Gramsci, *Selections from the Cultural Writings*, p. 190.

55. Carole Zucker, *The Idea of the Image: Josef von Sternberg's Dietrich Films* (Rutherford, N.J.: Fairleigh Dickinson University Press, 1988), p. 67.

56. Spoto, *Falling in Love Again*, p. 113.

57. Zucker, *The Idea of the Image*, p. 67.

58. Audibert, "The Flash of the Look," p. 100.

59. Studlar, *In the Realm of Pleasure*, p. 149.

60. Maria Riva, *Marlene Dietrich*, p. 288.

61. Zucker, *The Idea of the Image*, p. 77.

62. Higham, *Marlene*, p. 139.

63. Studlar, *In the Realm of Pleasure*, p. 154.

64. Deleuze, *Cinema 1*, p. 95.

65. Ibid., p. 113.

66. Peter Baxter, *Just Watch!*, p. 189.

67. Gilles Deleuze, *Coldness and Cruelty* (New York: Zone Books, 1991).

68. Gramsci, *Selections from the Cultural Writings*, p. 190.

69. Ibid., p. 189.

## Chapter 5: "You Remember Diana Dors, Don't You?"

1. Candy Darling, *Candy Darling* (Madras: Hanuman Books, 1992).

2. Gayatri Chakravorty Spivak, *In Other Worlds: Essays in Cultural Politics* (New York: Routledge, 1988), p. 166.

3. Karl Marx, *Capital*, vol. 1 (London: Dent, 1974), pp. 43–44.

4. Ibid., p. 47.

5. Ibid., p. 71.

6. Antonio Gramsci, *Selections from the Prison Notebooks*, ed. Quintin Hoare and Geoffrey Nowell-Smith (New York: International Publishers, 1978), p. 137.

7. Ibid., p. 413.

8. Christine Gledhill, "Signs of Melodrama," in *Stardom: Industry of Desire*, ed. Christine Gledhill (London: Routledge, 1991), p. 225.

9. Darling, *Candy Darling*, pp. 93–94.

10. Laurence Marks and Tony Van Den Bergh, *Ruth Ellis: A Case of Diminished Responsibility?* (London: Penguin Books, 1990), p. 134.

11. Diana Dors, *Dors by Diana: An Intimate Self-Portrait* (London: MacDonald Futura, 1981), p. 12.

12. Ibid., p. 21.

13. Ibid., p. 36.

14. Ibid., p. 32.

15. Ibid., p. 10.

16. Ibid., p. 22.

17. Mary Ann Doane, *The Desire to Desire: The Woman's Film of the 1940s* (Bloomington: Indiana University Press, 1987), p. 41.

18. Diana Dors, *For Adults Only* (London: W. H. Allen, 1978), p. 251.

19. Ibid., p. 180.

20. Ibid., p. 18.

21. Christine Gerahty, "Diana Dors," in *All Our Yesterdays: 90 Years of British Cinema*, ed. Charles Barr (London: BFI, 1986), p. 341.

22. Ibid., pp. 341–342.

23. Ibid., p. 342.

24. David Lusted, "The Glut of the Personality," in *Stardom*, ed. Gledhill, p. 257.

25. Ibid., p. 258.

26. John Hill, *Sex, Class, and Realism: British Cinema, 1956–1963* (London: BFI, 1986), pp. 19–20.

27. Paul Swann, *The Hollywood Feature Film in Postwar Britain* (New York: St. Martin's Press, 1987), pp. 13–30.

28. Richard Dyer, *The Matter of Images: Essays on Representation* (London: Routledge, 1993), p. 100.

29. Ibid.

30. Dors, *Dors by Diana*, p. 21.

31. Dors, *For Adults Only*, p. 18.

32. Leslie Halliwell, *Halliwell's Film Guide*, 7th Ed. (New York: Harper and Row, 1989), p. 1140.

33. Mike Prokosch, "Imitation of Life," in *Douglas Sirk*, ed. Laura Mulvey and Jon Halliday (Edinburgh Film Festival in association with the National Film Theatre and John Player and Sons, 1972), p. 98.

34. Jackie Byars, *All That Hollywood Allows: Reading Gender in 1950s Melodrama* (Chapel Hill: University of North Carolina Press, 1991), pp. 121–131.

35. Dors, *For Adults Only*, p. 12.

36. Marks and Van Den Bergh, *Ruth Ellis*, p. 162.

37. Ibid., p. 159.

38. For example, see also Jonathan Goodman and Patrick Pringle, *The Trial of Ruth Ellis* (Newton Abbot, Eng.: David and Charles, 1974). There is also a reference to an Australian television documentary on Ellis in Marks and Van Den Bergh, *Ruth Ellis*, p. 198. See also Jacqueline Rose, "Margaret Thatcher and Ruth Ellis," *New Formations* 6 (1988): 3–29.

39. James Park, *British Cinema: The Lights That Failed* (London: Batsford, 1990), p. 159.

40. Ibid., p. 160.

41. Ibid., p. 175.

42. Ibid.

43. Ibid.

44. Mike Davis, *The City of Quartz: Excavating the Future in Los Angeles* (London: Verso, 1991), p. 44. Davis identifies a "major revival of noir . . . in the 1960s and 1970s."

45. Dana Polan, *In a Lonely Place* (London: BFI, 1993).

46. David N. Rodowick, "Madness, Authority, and Ideology: The Domestic Melodramas of the 1950s," in *Home Is Where the Heart Is: Studies in Melodrama and the Woman's Film*, ed. Christine Gledhill (London: BFI, 1987), p. 272.

47. Vincent Canby, "Are 'New' Women's Movies Guilty of Sexism in Reverse?," *New York Times* (November 10, 1985), p. 162.

48. Andrew Higson, "Re-Presenting the National Past: Nostalgia and Pastiche in the Heritage Film," in *Fires Were Started: British Cinema and Thatcherism*, ed. Lester Friedman (Minneapolis: University of Minnesota Press, 1993), p. 128.

49. Japa, "*Dance with a Stranger*," *Variety* 318, no. 7 (March 13, 1985).

50. Paul Giles, "History with Holes: Channel Four Television Films of the 1980s," in *Fires Were Started*, ed. Friedman, p. 81.

51. Marks and Van Den Bergh, *Ruth Ellis*, p. 15.

52. Richard Combs, "The Social Slide," *Times Literary Supplement* (March 8, 1985), p. 260.

53. Rose, "Margaret Thatcher and Ruth Ellis," p. 9.

54. Marks and Van Den Bergh, *Ruth Ellis*, p. 175.

55. Ramona Curry, "Mae West as Censored Commodity: The Case of *Klondike Annie*," *Cinema Journal* no. 1 (Fall 1991): p. 78.

56. Ibid.

57. Ibid.

58. On the subject of the "feminine character," Theodor Adorno has written that it "is a negative imprint of domination. Whatever is in the context of bourgeois delusion called nature, is merely the scar of social mutilation. . . . what passes for nature in civilization is by its very substance furthest from nature," *Minima Moralia* (London: Verso, 1974), pp. 95–96.

## Chapter 6: Historical Capital

1. Jacques Derrida, "Spectres of Marx," *New Left Review* 205 (May/June 1994): 35.

2. Saul Friedlander, *Memory, History, and the Extermination of the Jews of Europe* (Bloomington: Indiana University Press, 1993), p. 47.

3. Florence Jacobowitz, "Rethinking History through Narrative Art," *Cineaste* 34 (June 1994): 6.

4. Ibid., pp. 9–10.

5. Andreas Huyssen, "The Politics of Identification: 'Holocaust' and West German Drama," *New German Critique* 19 (Winter 1980): 130.

6. Eric L. Santner, *Stranded Objects: Mourning, Memory, and Film in Postwar Germany* (Ithaca, N.Y.: Cornell University Press, 1990).

7. Marcia Landy, "Language and Mourning in 'Lycidas,'" *American Imago*, 30, no. 3 (Fall 1973): 294.

8. Alexander Mitscherlich and Margarete Mitscherlich, *The Inability to Mourn: Principles of Collective Behavior* (New York: Grove Press, 1975), p. 25.

9. Friedrich Nietzsche, "On the Uses and Disadvantages of History for Life," in *Untimely Meditation*, trans. R. J. Hollingdale (Cambridge, Eng.: Cambridge Univerisity Press, 1991), p. 101.

10. Mitscherlich and Mitscherlich, *The Inability to Mourn*, p. 25.

11. Ibid., p. 297.

12. Gilles Deleuze and Félix Guattari, *Anti-Oedipus: Capitalism and Schizophrenia* (New York: Viking Books, 1972), p. 101.

13. Saul Friedlander, *Reflections of Nazism: An Essay on Kitsch and Death* (New York: Harper and Row, 1982) pp. 26–30.

14. Ibid.

15. Stuart Marshall, "The Contemporary Political Use of Gay History: The Third Reich," in *How Do I Look?: Queer Film and Video*, ed. Bad Object Choices (Seattle: Bay Press, 1991).

16. Primo Levi, *Survival in Auschwitz: The Nazi Assault on Humanity* (New York: Collier Books, 1961), p. 36.

17. Friedlander, *Memory, History, and the Extermination of the Jews of Europe*, pp. 5–6.

18. Susan Sontag, "Fascinating Fascism," in *Movies and Methods*, vol. 1,

ed. Bill Nichols (Berkeley and Los Angeles: University of California Press, 1976), p. 43.

19. Detlev J. K. Peukert, *Inside Nazi Germany: Conformity, Opposition, and Racism in Everyday Life* (London: Penguin Books, 1993), p. 180.

20. Christian Delage, in his *La Vision nazie de l'histoire: Le Cinema documentaire du Troisième Reich* (Lausanne: L'Age d'homme, 1989), writes: "[L]'antisémitisme nazi trouve un terrain d'expression filmique en se déployant sur trois axes: la révélation d'une typologie des traits physiques spécifiques aux hommes et aux femmes juives; la dénonciation d'un mode de vie et de coutumes religieuses montrés comme barbares; enfin la comparison des juifs à des parasites. Le montage et le commentaire auront par ailleurs le fonction d'opposer constamment les images négatifs des ghettos à celles des ouvriers, des paysans et des artisans allemands incarnant, avec l'armée et le SS, les fondements positifs de la société préparant la venue du nouvel Etat raciste du *Reich du milles ans.*" [Nazi anti-Semitism finds filmic terrain of expression in its deployment of three axes: the revelation of physical traits for Jewish men and women; the denunciation of a way of life and religious clothing shown to be barbaric; finally the comparison of Jews to parasites. The editing and the narration moreover serve the function of continuously opposing negative images of the ghettos to those of German workers, peasants, and German artisans, incarnating, with the army and the SS, the positive foundation of a society preparing for the coming of the new racist state of the Thousand Year Empire.] p. 63 (my translation).

21. For a discussion of the circumstances surrounding production, see Erwin O. Leiser, *Nazi Cinema* (New York: Collier Books, 1974), pp. 82–89; David Stewart Hull, *Film in the Third Reich: A Study of the German Cinema, 1933–1945* (Berkeley and Los Angeles: University of California Press, 1969), pp. 162–172.

22. Peukert, *Inside Nazi Germany*, p. 209.

23. Klaus Theweleit, *Male Fantasies*, vol. 1, *Women, Floods, Bodies, History* (Minneapolis: University of Minnesota Press, 1987), p. 104.

24. For a discussion of the rhetorical dimensions of many of these biopics, see Julian Petley, *Capital and Culture: German Cinema, 1933–1945* (London: BFI, 1979), pp. 106–158.

25. George Mosse, *Nazism: A Historical and Comparative Analysis of National Socialism* (New Brunswick, N.J.: Transaction Books, 1978), p. 54.

26. Klaus Theweleit, *Male Fantasies*, vol. 2, *Male Bodies: Psychoanalyzing the White Terror* (Minneapolis: University of Minnesota Press, 1989), pp. 80–81.

27. Ibid., p. 88.

28. Peukert, *Inside Nazi Germany*, p. 244.

29. Josef Goebbels, *The Goebbels Diaries*, ed. Hugh Trevor-Roper (London: Secker and Warburg, 1978), p. xix.

30. Ibid.

31. Quoted in Carlo Ginzburg, *Clues, Myths, and the Historical Method* (Baltimore, Md.: Johns Hopkins University Press, 1986), p. 125.

32. Ibid., p. 129.

33. Mosse, *Nazism*, p. 87.

34. Ginzburg, *Clues, Myths, and the Historical Method*, p. 135.

35. Andrea S. Markovits and Rebecca S. Hayden, "'Holocaust' before and after the Event: Reactions in West Germany and Austria," *New German Critique* 19 (Winter 1980): 53–80.

36. Siegfried Zielinski, "History as Entertainment and Provocation: The TV Series 'Holocaust' in West Germany," *New German Critique* 19 (Winter 1980): 89.

37. Markovits and Hayden, "'Holocaust' before and after the Event," p. 57.

38. Ibid., pp. 60–62.

39. Huyssen, "The Politics of Identification," pp. 134-135.

40. Christine Gledhill, ed., *Home Is Where the Heart Is: Studies in Melodrama and the Woman's Film* (London: BFI, 1987).

41. Thomas Elsaesser, "Our Germany," *American Film* 10, no. 7 (May 1985): 31–32.

42. "Dossier on *Heimat* with Contributions by Karen Witte, J. Hoberman, Thomas Elsaesser, Gertrud Koch, Friedrich P. Kahlenberg, Klaus Kreimeier, and Heidi Schlüpmann," *New German Critique* 36 (Fall 1985): 66.

43. Ibid., p. 9.

44. Martin Chalmers, "*Heimat*: Approaches to Word and Film," *Framework* 26/27, no. 85 (1985) pp. 91–92.

45. "Dossier on *Heimat*," p. 17.

46. Ibid.

47. Quoted in Franz A. Birgel, "You Can Go Home Again," *Film Quarterly* 34, no. 4 (Summer 1986): 7.

48. "Dossier on *Heimat*," p. 17.

49. Friedlander, *Memory, History, and the Extermination of the Jews of Europe*, p. 83.

50. Carole Angier, "Edgar Reitz," *Sight and Sound* 60, no. 1 (Winter 1990/1991): 38.

51. Simon Louvish, "Witness," *Sight and Sound* 4, no. 3 (March 1994): 12–16.

52. Michael Kernan, "A National Memorial Bears Witness to the Holocaust," *Smithsonian* 24, no. 1 (April 1993): 51.

53. Bill Clinton, April 22, 1993, "U.S. Museum Dedicated," *U.S. Department of State Dispatch* 4, no. 19 (May 19, 1993): 322.

54. Philip Gourevitch, "Behold Now Behemoth," *Harper's* 287, no. 1718 (July 1993): 61.

55. Ibid., p. 62.

56. Louvish, "Witness," p. 12.

57. James E. Young, *Writing and Rewriting the Holocaust: Narrative and the Consequence of Interpretation* (Bloomington: Indiana University Press, 1988), p. 17.

58. Ibid., p. 18.

59. Ibid., p. 183.

60. Annette Insdorf, *Indelible Shadows: Film and the Holocaust* (New York: Random House, 1983).

61. Claude Lanzmann, "From the Holocaust to 'Holocaust,'" *Dissent* 28, no. 2 (1981): 188–194.

62. Thomas Doherty, "Schindler's List," *Cineaste* 20, no. 3 (1994): 51.

63. Ibid.

64. Scott Denham, "Schindler Returns to Open Arms: The Reception of *Schindler's List* in Germany." Lecture delivered at the German Studies Association Conference (October 1, 1994): 1–14.

65. Stephen Schiff, "Seriously Spielberg," *The New Yorker* 70, no. 5 (March 21, 1944): 94–109.

66. Richard Alleva, "Saintly Sybarite," *Commonweal* 12, no. 3 (February 11, 1994): 17.

67. John Gross, "Hollywood and the Holocaust," *New York Review of Books* 41, no. 3 (February 3, 1994): 16.

68. Thomas Keneally, *Schindler's List* (New York: Simon and Schuster, 1993), p. 397.

69. Ibid., p. 10.

70. Ibid., p. 14.

71. Ibid., p. 217.

72. Ibid., p. 281.

73. Ibid., p. 290.

74. Ibid., p. 333.

75. Friedlander, *Memory, History, and the Extermination of the Jews of Europe*, pp. 133–134.

76. Jane Shattuc, *Television, Tabloids, and Tears: Fassbinder and Popular Culture* (Minneapolis: University of Minnesota Press, 1994); Ronald Hayman, *Fassbinder: Filmmaker* (New York: Simon and Schuster, 1984); Thomas Elsaesser, *New German Cinema: A History* (New Brunswick, N.J.: Rutgers University Press, 1989); Anton Kaes, *From Hitler to Heimat: The Return of History as Film* (Cambridge, Mass.: Harvard University Press, 1989), Eric Rentschler, *West German Film in the Course of Time* (Bedford Hills, N.Y.: Redgrave Publishing Company, 1984); Timothy Corrigan, *New German Film: The Displaced Image* (Austin: University of Texas Press, 1983); Robert C. Reimer, *Nazi Retro Film: How German Narrative Cinema Remembers the Past* (New York: Twayne Publishers, 1992).

77. Kaes, *From Hitler to Heimat*, p. 79.

78. Ibid., p. 102.

79. Hayman, *Fassbinder*, p. 113.

80. Ibid.

81. Ruth Hubbard, *The Politics of Women's Biology* (New Brunswick, N.J.: Rutgers University Press, 1990), p. 190.

82. Ibid.

83. Ibid., p. 186.

84. Kaes, *From Hitler to Heimat*, p. 84.

85. Ibid., p. 95.

86. Gilles Deleuze, *Cinema 2: The Time-Image* (Minneapolis: University of Minnesota Press, 1989), p. 264.

87. Ibid., pp. 274–275.

# Index

**Marcia Landy** received her Ph.D. from the University of Rochester. She is professor of English and film studies at the University of Pittsburgh and teaches courses on world film history, women and film, film genres, and critical and cultural theory. Her publications include *Fascism in Film: The Italian Commercial Cinema, 1930–1943*; *British Genres: Cinema and Society, 1930-1960*; *Imitations of Life: A Reader on Film and Television Melodrama*; *Film, Politics, and Gramsci*; and most recently *Queen Christina* (with Amy Villarejo), (BFI, 1996). She has published numerous articles in such journals as *Screen*, *boundary 2*, *Film Criticism*, *Annali d'Italianistica*, and *Critical Studies*.